Globalisation and Europeanisation in Education

Stephen Ronald Stoer 1943-2005
This book is dedicated to the memory of Steve Stoer,
a key member of GENIE from its inception, and a model
and much-loved scholar, colleague and friend.

Globalisation and Europeanisation in Education

Edited by
Roger Dale & Susan Robertson

SYMPOSIUM
BOOKS

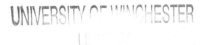

Symposium Books
PO Box 204 Didcot Oxford OX11 9ZQ United Kingdom
the book publishing division of wwwords Ltd
www.symposium-books.co.uk

Published in the United Kingdom, 2009

ISBN 978-1-873927-90-8

© Symposium Books, 2009

Typeset by wwwords Ltd
Printed and bound in the United Kingdom by Cambridge University Press

Contents

Introduction

This book is one outcome of the work of the European Union (EU) Erasmus Thematic Network, GENIE – Globalisation and Europeanisation Network in Education. GENIE was formed in 2002 and ran formally until 2005, with 42 members, from 33 universities, in 27 countries. The overall coordinator of GENIE was Susan Robertson, assisted by Roger Dale, both of whom are located in the Centre for Globalisation, Education and Societies in the Graduate School of Education at the University of Bristol.

The substantive work of GENIE took place over each of the academic years, by means of virtual forms of communication, an annual meeting, and regular steering group meetings. These annual meetings were brilliantly convened by Dr Helen Phitiaka in Nicosia, Cyprus (2003), Professor M'hammed Sabour in Joensuu, Finland (2004) and Professor Palle Rasmussen in Aalborg, Denmark (2005) respectively, whilst the GENIE Steering Group not only provided an anchor for the project, but has become a basis for further ongoing work. Professor Annie Vinokur, of the Université de Paris X, Nanterre, was GENIE's chosen evaluator. Annie provided critical, sympathetic and valuable feedback on the unfolding of its agenda and programme of work.

Pedagogical workshops and a Summer Institute, both involving doctoral students working in GENIE member institutions, were convened in Barcelona, Spain (January 2005) and Aalborg, Denmark (July 2005). These students were funded by their own institutions, augmenting the funding from the European Commission. GENIE's work was based around six themes: Polycentric Globalisation; Social Europe; Languages; Governance; Knowledge Economy; and Identities and Citizenship, some of whose products are collected in this book. These themes were the outcome of deliberations over the course of year one, where the key substantive themes for GENIE's work were identified.

Finally, we want to make special mention of our colleague and friend, Steve Stoer, from the University of Oporto. Steve was central to the work of GENIE. He was a member of the GENIE Steering Group and a module coordinator. Not only was Steve always a brilliant, funny and insightful colleague, but when he passed away on New Year's Eve 2005, GENIE members immediately became aware of not only what they had lost, but also, more acutely, of what they had gained from having been privileged to know and work with Steve.

GENIE as a Pedagogical Project

The formation of GENIE was a response to the increasing scope of Europeanisation and the increasing pace and penetration of globalisation and their various impacts on national education systems. The intention was to bring together, for the first time, a network of academics and related organisations across Europe around the theme of teaching globalisation and Europeanisation. The purpose of the network was to document, review and share resources, experiences and expertise of those involved in teaching various aspects of globalisation and education and its articulation with the European dimension. Opportunities to meet and work together, through the annual meetings, doctoral classes and Summer Institute, for instance, were particularly formative. For GENIE, Europeanisation and globalisation were not just the topic of the work, but also its medium – collaborative production by European scholars – and, in a very real sense, its outcome; we were very much aware that we were 'doing' and 'making' Europe' at the same time as, and by means of, studying it. The aim was not to bring about a convergence of content to be taught, so much as to facilitate the production of new means of understanding the nature of the issues generated by the various intersections of globalisation and Europeanisation in education, that would offer new analytic purchase at local and national, as well as at global and regional, scales. The focus was on EU Education Policy, rather than education policies in the EU, and directed as much to the effects on 'Europe' of those processes as to its impacts on the domestic structures and institutions of Member States (or, indeed, non-Member States; several members of the network came from countries not at that time full members, but eligible to partake in educational initiatives).

It is significant and far from coincidental that GENIE was set up in the wake of the March 2000 Lisbon Council, which can be seen to represent the core of the EU's response to the challenges of globalisation. The agenda set at Lisbon called for Europe to become the most economically competitive and dynamic region in the world, and at the same time achieve greater social cohesion. Crucially, it specified an important role for education in achieving this, with concrete objectives for national education systems across Europe, which, it was insisted, could only be met at the European rather than the national level. Lisbon thus reflects both the changing relationship between Europeanisation and globalisation, and a changing conception of the role and governance of education, with the elaboration of the possibility of a Pan-European educational response. This dual agenda framed the specific challenge to which the network sought to respond and provided a focus for deepening our understanding of these processes.

Globalisation as Context and Pretext

The first part of this dual agenda was based on a recognition that especially since the collapse of the Berlin Wall in 1989, processes of globalisation and regionalisation had, quite rightly, caught the attention of social theorists and politicians, and become a major area of focus for work within the academy, with governments and experts struggling to come to terms with these shifts, which were clearly part of a bigger 'structural change' in economies and societies. At the same time, Europeanisation was becoming an increasingly complex and sophisticated process and while its features and effects were also being more effectively analysed, its interactions with globalisation and its relationships with national education systems were rather less well understood.

While discussions of globalisation and regionalisation figure prominently in debates within the social sciences as well as in public discussion, there has been very little systematic work on the relationship between them, and, more importantly from our point of view, their relationship to education and the European dimension. This is especially unfortunate since education systems are implicated in globalisation and Europeanisation in three key ways. First, education systems are confronted with new challenges as a result of the growing importance of knowledge, learning, new communication technologies and social inclusion both within Europe and in the global knowledge economy. Second, they are themselves greatly influenced by Europeanisation and globalisation. Third, processes of Europeanisation and globalisation are important curriculum topics. However, the nature of the body of knowledge in the field is a major challenge to those engaged in teaching these topics.

It is clear that academics face new and important challenges in making sense of these changes and how to appraise, incorporate and critique the information, knowledge and understandings these generate. These challenges are the greater since there are differing and opposed views on definitions of globalisation and regionalisation and their causal dynamics; on the relationships between these processes and Europeanisation; on what are the most important substantive issues within these fields; and on their methodological implications. At the same time, the knowledge that might make up the resource base for teaching is scattered; its status has not been systematically reviewed; it is likely to come in quite different forms, or to be in languages that are not easily accessible. It may be located in new types of institutions and sites as a result of global and regional shifts, it often requires new sorts of skills (especially based on information and communication technologies, or ICT) to facilitate access, and it is very likely to be rapidly replaced.

A further feature of the new global knowledge economy and knowledge society is that it is increasingly dependent upon the collective and diverse intelligence of networks. While there have always been informal networks within the academy, these have often been focused around a traditional discipline (e.g. sociology, economics). They have tended to take the form of loose liaisons rather than being systematically organised (and here the EU's explicit encouragement of transnational academic networks is of especial interest), and their activities have been focused around individual efforts rather than a programme of work. In particular, understanding globalisation and Europeanisation and their relationships as complex processes is highly dependent upon new ways of arranging knowledge (that is multidisciplinary, thematic), new ways of exchanging knowledge (networks) using rapid methods of knowledge acquisition and transfer (for example, ICT) that take into account learners who might have been excluded from traditional models of higher education and more flexible ways in which this knowledge can be acquired.

A direct and practical consequence of globalisation and Europeanisation within higher education sectors has been for universities to become more international in their reach and student body, and for regional organisations like the EU to encourage increased mobility amongst students to further European social and economic integration. These elements raise questions about the resources we use to teach with (multidisciplinary, non-parochial, critical) and how processes of globalisation and Europeanisation are not only differently experienced in different settings but also recontextualised in particular ways as a result of specific historically developed institutional patterns of organisation. Students in higher education institutions engaged in learning about globalisation and Europeanisation will only be challenged when teachers create learning experiences that encourage them to critically read and assemble complex and different knowledges, to draw conclusions in the face of rapid and constant change, and to use those insights to generate new knowledge.

These developments question the status of knowledge about globalisation and regionalisation, and are themselves a product of globalisation and regionalisation – they lead to the rapid creation and displacement of knowledge, to new networks for knowledge dispersion, and to knowledge intensification. For those teaching in higher education institutions these developments require new levels of understanding about how to incorporate and develop these themes within their teaching.

Part One. Governance and the Knowledge Economy

One general point should be made before going on to brief descriptions of the chapters making up Part One. Quite intentionally, all the chapters operate at quite high levels of abstraction and assume some prior understanding of European education. In particular, they are not intended as commentaries on the existing literature so much as attempts to locate both that literature and the problems that it addresses in their wider contexts. This is because one objective of Part One is to provide a means of analysing and locating existing work in the field, rather than taking it as either topic or resource.

The main foci of Part One are governance and knowledge. The first of these is a 'new' or reintroduced concept, while the second is a very well-worked concept but one that takes on new forms and meanings in the context of discussions of the relationships between globalisation, Europeanisation and education. In a sense, a re-examination of both governance and knowledge is made necessary by the inadequacy of existing concepts and assumptions in explaining the consequences of processes like globalisation and Europeanisation in terms of both what is to be explained and how it might be explained.

This inadequacy has been evident most notably in the case of 'methodological nationalism', where the assumption that nation states are containers of 'society', and the equation of sovereignty and territory, has been clearly exposed by processes such as globalisation and Europeanisation. As far as 'governance' is concerned, in Chapter 1 Dale points to the parallel difficulties of 'methodological statism', which, as well as typically assuming a national state, also attributes a particular form of governing to that state. The question of governance was intensely debated in the GENIE network, especially by a small group consisting of Roger Dale, Marek Kwiek, Sverker Lindblad, Christian Maroy and Rimantas Zelvys, all of whom had contributed significantly to the literature on governance of education, with two of them, Lindblad and Maroy, the coordinators of major European projects on the topic, respectively EGSIE and REGULEDUC.[1] The lexical complexities here are manifold, but 'governance' was taken not as a model of administrative probity, as in the World Bank's use of the term, 'good governance', or as itself referring to a form of coordination, similar to state and market, but as the 'coordination of coordination' of the funding, provision and regulation of education, taken to be operating at more than the national scale.

Widespread and profound changes in the uses of 'knowledge' have also characterised the era of globalisation, and penetrated the vocabulary and imaginaries of European education, most clearly through the concept of the knowledge economy, which appears to be accepted unproblematically as a description of what is occurring in and to the European economy, and hence of central concern to European education. This is perhaps most evident in its linking to the project of lifelong learning, which is now the umbrella term under which all education activity within the European Commission is grouped. Problematising the concept of knowledge, asking how it is used, where, by whom and with what consequences, was central to debates about the globalisation and Europeanisation of education in the network, as is evident in the contributions to both parts of this volume.

In Chapter 1 of Part One, Roger Dale sets out the methodological and theoretical bases of the arguments that inform both this Chapter and Chapter 6, which may be seen as a pair. The methodological approach draws on Robert Cox's distinction between problem solving and critical theory, which, it is argued, is both crucial in itself and enables the basis of the position taken here to be distinguished from much writing on European Education Policy, which, it is suggested, starts from an essentially 'problem-solving' position.

The critical position adopted in these chapters requires both seeking to locate the sources of the problems to be addressed, rather than taking them as preformed, and to reflect on our own processes of theorising. The first of these is tackled through a discussion of the relationship at the core of this book, that between globalisation and Europeanisation, and the second by means of a debate over the meaning and importance of the concept of governance. The main part of the chapter is given over to an extended treatment of the differences between European Education Space (EES) and European Education Policy (EEP). The former is seen as an opportunity structure framed *formally* by the Treaty, *substantively* by the Lisbon Agenda, and *historically* by pre-2000 European education initiatives. European Education Policy is framed by the Open Method of Coordination, the work of Directorates General, mainly but not exclusively Education, and existing conceptions of the nature and capacity of education. This distinction is elaborated in a discussion of the relationship between the Lisbon Agenda, its condensation of issues, constellations of problems and catalytic role for EU education. The chapter ends with an account of implications of the 'hegemonic project' of Europe, and the discourses, processes and mechanisms through which it is constructed for education governance at both national and regional levels.

In 'Education, Knowledge and the Network Society', Chapter 2, Stephen Stoer & António Magalhães trace out the status and form taken by the 'traditional' dichotomy between education as the formation or development of the individual and as means of socialising new generations into the demands of capitalism. However, they suggest that the changing nature and status of knowledge in contemporary capitalism, which sees it playing a central place in production, means that this tension has been translated into one between education for competences and education for individual development. They resist this reading, arguing that the development of individuals cannot be reduced to either pole, suggesting, for instance, that the Europeanisation of education takes on forms of 'local' recognition as well as being shaped by the labour market, that it is concerned with the 'education of responsible citizens' as well as with preparing them for work. Their attention is centred on the 'development of individual capacities' as these are shaped by the simultaneous 'top-down' and 'bottom up' pressures that are experienced by national education systems, as they find themselves implicated in novel forms and scales of education agendas. They argue that in terms of top-down pressures what is experienced is the transformation of knowledge itself into money, while bottom-up pressures involve movements of knowledge from the national education level to the local community, interpreted as the 'educative city', where a 'transparent' communicational pedagogy prevails. However, they want to resist the dichotomies (such as knowledge as education/formation versus knowledge as competences) implied by such conceptualisations, essentially on the grounds that knowledge is simultaneously local and global, that knowledge produced locally does not exist independently of globalised capitalism and hence clearly has a global dimension. And they conclude that: 'The epistemological fragility of knowledge does not dilute its formative character and, simultaneously, informationalism, in itself, does not empty knowledge of its potential for political and social intervention'.

The first of two contributions from Susan Robertson, Chapter 3, 'Europe, Competitiveness and Higher Education: an evolving project', directly addresses the relationship between globalisation and Europeanisation and elaborates very clearly one major example of how that link is forged through education, and what that may mean for our understanding of it. Her focus is European higher education as it has been constructed through the Bologna Process. As she shows, this was the culmination of EU activism in the area that had been set in place in the early 1970s, but it has taken on a very different status since the signing of the Bologna Agreement in 1999, and particularly since the development of increasingly close links between Bologna and the Lisbon Process (for an account of the changing meanings of Bologna over this period, see Dale, 2007). Robertson begins by spelling out the very important distinction between globalisation and internationalisation in higher education, and as her argument develops we can see that it also brings considerable clarity to the relationship between globalisation and Europeanisation. Rather than this being conceived, as it often has been, in a hierarchical way – globalisation-regionalisation-national level – she shows that (as argued also in Dale's opening chapter) Europe has not just a competitiveness project but also a geopolitical project. And in the case of higher education, we can see an element of this geopolitical project, with the global consequences of the spread of the Bologna Process invoking concerned reaction and responses from, for instance, the USA and Australia. This explicit project of making European higher education 'more attractive in a world education market', as the Commissioner for Education put it, she sees as part of a globalising project that is simultaneously a regionalising project that enables a European higher education system, and a 'different' conception of 'Europe' to come into existence.

In Chapter 4 Palle Rasmussen addresses the issue of lifelong learning (LLL), which has been of particular interest to students of European Education Policy since it was announced as the umbrella under which all EU education activities would be grouped in 2006. In essence, Rasmussen acknowledges the strength of and reasons for the fairly hostile and critical response to recent conceptions, but is nevertheless keen not to throw the baby out with the bath water. His aim is to restate the case for a human need for lifelong learning and at the same time to show how this has been stifled by educational policies that instrumentalise LLL and ignore those crucial needs of learners. He regards the current prominence of LLL as indicating a paradigmatic change, one of whose characteristics has been a shift of responsibility from individuals to institutions and markets, with consequent dangers of increasing social divisions. He illustrates his argument with the example of changes in the nature and provision of LLL in Denmark, a pioneer of the concept and practice, from its nineteenth-century origins in adult education through folk high schools to the current phase where LLL (rather than adult education) is characterised by an increasing focus on achieving vocational qualification with programmes corresponding to the main levels in full-time education, which he discusses as a form of Habermasian 'colonisation of the life-world'. He sees the main role of the EU in LLL as not so much developing policies – or practices – but in promoting and legitimising an important part of the formation of the future European citizen. However, in this process, 'the picture of the learning citizen is distorted [and] [t]he meaning of "learning" changes from context to context and slips between the fingers like sand'.

Susan Robertson sets herself the task in Chapter 5 of 'Unravelling the Politics of Public Private Partnerships in Education in Europe'. The purpose is to reveal and appraise one novel response to the shift from government to governance of education, especially at the European level. While we have become used to the idea of such a shift, we have tended not to look too far beyond the headline catchers like the Open Method of Coordination (OMC). Robertson focuses here on an increasingly prominent mechanism of governance in the field of education, the Public Private Partnership or PPP, which she sees as not merely a pragmatic initiative, but a deeply ideological one. This initiative is intended to depress the role of the state in the provision of public services, as it opens up space for transnational firms, and provides them with a mechanism of articulation with national policies and agendas. She outlines the origins of PPPs, pointing to their links with the Stability Pact, whose limitations on public spending created significant opportunities for private funding of the provision of public infrastructure. Education is by no means exempt from this, as Robertson's examples show. Her main focus is ICTs in schools, which are seen as a central plank of the European knowledge economy, as making great demands on funding, and as a matter for Europe rather than individual Member States. She looks in particular at the role of the European Commission's eLearning Summit – which, despite its name, is dominated by major computer manufacturers who make many familiar points about the shortcomings of education systems, but who, unlike other areas, go on to make funding the desirable initiatives through PPPs a central feature of their report. Overall, she suggests that large ICT companies are now significant participants, unhindered by the politics of subsidiarity and Member States' interests, in the creation of a European Education Space, as well as beneficiaries of it.

Roger Dale's Chapter 6, on Lisbon, the OMC and beyond, falls into three parts. The first part elaborates the specificity of the EES and EEP by focusing on the differences between them and national education systems. This is done by means of an interrogation of each of the components of national, education, system to demonstrate both that they do not do the same things in the same way, and that, consequently, different tools are necessary to analyse them. Dale argues that analysis of each of the three components is inhibited by the adoption of a set of methodological 'isms'; fixed, taken-for-granted, unexamined, absolute and ahistorical assumptions, such as methodological nationalism, that assumes the nation state as the container of 'society'; methodological statism, that assumes that the kinds of institutions through which polities were administered in earlier times change in degree but not principle; and methodological educationism, that assumes that what is taken as 'education' is (a) taken to be characterised by a common scope, knowledges and practices; and (b) necessarily coherent and without internal contradictions. On this basis it is argued that the EES and EEP are quite distinct from national education systems. The second, and largest, section of the chapter focuses on the OMC. This is taken not so much as a means of simply implementing the Lisbon Agenda, but as having a more complex relationship with the EES and EEP. The ways that these are framed mean that the OMC is likely to: be concerned with policy paradigms rather than policy reforms and programme ontologies rather than programmes; depoliticised but not apolitical; and directed at Member States' education systems rather than education policies. Finally, Dale speculates that one possible outcome of the structures and processes described may be the emergence of distinct and parallel new 'education' sectors at EU and Member State levels, with different mandates, capacities and forms of governance.

Part Two. Citizenship, Identity and Language

Crucial features of the European project being advanced in reaction and relation to globalisation are 'citizenship', 'identity' and 'language'. These three elements, simultaneously the objects and outcomes of struggles both within and at the borders of the European space, are intimately tied to a particular 'northern' and European paradigm of globalisation. This raises the often-overlooked point that globalisation is a political project, a process (that has temporal and spatial dimensions), and a condition (an ontological claim), and that its advance, take-up and effects are different in different parts of the world. Having said this, Europe is intimately tied to the 'south' through old and new colonial ties which it continues to exploit through what might be called 'benevolent' forms of imperialism (Hartmann, 2007).

Building Europe as a territory and legitimate political project is a complex process entailing notions of citizenship and identity. Citizenship entails rights and responsibilities as a consequence of territorial and sovereignty claims. But the bases on which these claims are made are being transformed as a result of identity and other 'recognition' claims within and across Europe. What makes the European project particularly interesting, and yet also more complex, is that it must articulate with other competing claims to identity (including elites' identities) and citizenship at different scales of rule. Identity claims are also mediated by language claims, yet language itself operates instrumentally (as in English increasingly being a pragmatic language to advance communication across the European space) and strategically (as in the middle classes using English as a strategy for advancing their own class mobility project). At the same time, English may also be perceived as aligned with the advance of neoliberal policies within the European Union, and therefore as an instrument of imperialism. This makes for a heady mix of claims, strategies, identities and linguistic communities, all of which – as the authors below show – mediate globalisation and Europeanisation.

In Chapter 7, '"In the Name of Globalisation": southern and northern paradigms of educational development', Xavier Bonal & Xavier Rambla site their analysis before and after the Washington Consensus in order to observe the development of new paradigms in education and development. Arguing that globalisation has altered educational agendas worldwide, and that some similarities in the global agenda can be identified, the authors suggest that the ways in which those agendas are produced, distributed and carried out at different scales of decision making may explain different implementation processes as well as different impacts on educational development and inequalities. This chapter explores how southern and northern paradigms of educational development have shifted for the last decades, by identifying the explanatory and normative frameworks of different political agendas. By doing this they show that globalisation is used with different meanings and has different implications in shaping southern and northern education policy agendas. The analysis of the 'southern case' takes a general form while European Education Policy is taken as a specific case of a 'northern' paradigm of education and development. Bonal & Rambla conclude by pointing out how different power relations impinge on the different mechanisms that set southern and northern agendas.

In Chapter 8, 'Education, Equality and the European Social Model', Palle Rasmussen, Kathleen Lynch, Jacky Brine, Pepka Boyadjieva, Michael Peters & Heinz Sünker argue that the concept of 'Social Europe' is an ambiguous and contested one. Keeping in mind Bonal & Rambla's arguments above around 'northern' versus 'southern' development paradigms, Rasmussen et al show that a dominant northern discourse, 'Social Europe', is not a single and univocal discourse but more complicated and containing at least three different meanings. These they identify as: 1. an area of European Union policies – for example, employment, quality of work, gender equality, social cohesion, social inclusion and the quality of social policy; 2. a broader sense of 'Social Europe' (and more recently the 'European Social Model') to designate qualities of social life and welfare that characterise Europe in contrast to other parts of the world, not least the United States; and 3. a discourse mobilised by certain actors, not least socialist parties and trade unions, to indicate the qualities they strive to realise in the European Union. These actors emphasise social equality and solidarity as part of their vision for Europe, and as alternatives to neoliberalism. The chapter then turns to what the implications are of the discourse of Social Europe for education.

In Chapter 9, 'Languages, Education and Europeanisation', Janet Enever provides a broad introduction to the topic of languages in contemporary Europe. She contextualises current trends, debates and implications for education within a broader picture of a pattern of shift and change in language choice across many domains of use over time. Enever argues that such changes are a response to shifts in the balance of power within and between nations in recognition of the economic and political benefits for speakers of particular languages, rather than an expansion of the language purely for the intrinsic worth it might offer its speakers. By problematising the role of contemporary state and regional legislation in support of minority and plurilingual language agendas, Enever is then able to examine the real impact on both schooled and unschooled learning of languages.

Chapter 10, by M'hammed Sabour, is titled 'Globalisation and Europeanisation: unicentricity and polycentricity and the role of intellectuals'. Sabour builds upon Pierre Bourdieu's (1992) conception of Europe, which is seen as a space where various national interests and particularities struggle for distinction, recognition, domination, equality, prominence and/or leadership. Framed in this way, Sabour sheds new light on both the problematic of European integration, and the relationship between globalisation and Europeanisation, in discussing Europeanisation as involving an 'endogenous' as well as an 'exogenous' process. Exogenous Europeanisation, the spread of European economy, politics and culture across the world, was both one of the creating forces of, and, simultaneously, the outcome of, globalisation. Endogenous Europeanisation, on the other hand, involves the construction of a unicentric, techno-bureaucratic and politically unified Europe under the auspices of its economically strongest and politically most influential members. In addition to a short account of the dominant discourse on globalisation, Sabour offers an analysis of the position and role of differently located and positioned intellectuals in this discourse, as guardians and watchdogs of polycentric Europeanisation and globalisation pitted against the homogenising and hegemonising project that he sees emerging from Brussels' unicentric and technocratic Europeanisation.

Chapter 11, 'What is Language Europe?', by Kirk Sullivan & Janet Enever, returns to the theme of language in Europe which Enever opened up in an earlier chapter. They explore two recent trends in language choices across education in Europe, interpreting them in the light of global, regional and local pressures that currently drive them forward. In selecting evidence of language curricula from the contrastive contexts of higher education and the early primary years, Sullivan & Enever propose that these strands may represent a supranational layering for creating a new flexible, mobile elite with fluency in at least one regional or global language in addition to their local/national language, rather than an initial framework for achieving the oft-stated goal of creating a whole population with this potential ability. They identify this new elite as a technocratic elite, equipped with the cultural capital of 'technical' skills (that is, language/intercultural skills) necessary to facilitate business deals in a global economic and political world today. Sullivan & Enever also consider the educational realities of inclusion and exclusion for membership of this elite, highlighting an increasing urban/rural divide in some regions of Europe, as well as contrasting real and perceived differences in resourcing and expertise at both primary and tertiary levels of education.

Chapter 12, 'Performance, Citizenship and the Knowledge Society: a new mandate for European Education Policy', by António Magalhães & Stephen Stoer, approaches the question of the scope of European Education Policy from a somewhat different direction, though maintaining an insistence on the need to move the analysis beyond the relatively narrow economic competitiveness agenda. This remains the case despite the first half of their chapter focusing on the shortcomings and deficits identified in the more 'liberal' pedagogies of the Fordist era, and the response and alternative to them that is contained in the emphasis on the importance of competences (which, very interestingly, they trace back to Edith Cresson's 1995 White Paper on the knowledge society) and what they refer to as performance. They contrast the 'performance' approach, where there is a preoccupation with a pedagogy of teaching based on the transmission of knowledge, and a 'pedagogical' approach to pedagogy, characterised by a pedagogy of learning where the pupils' sociocultural and educational characteristics are central; and these two approaches are represented respectively in meritocratic and democratic conceptions of schooling. However, Magalhães & Stoer see it as crucial to get beyond a simple dichotomy, and construct instead a continuum across the two positions, which, in a labour market context structured by flexible capitalism, and where the school has ceased to be seen as the only source of education and competences, can change education's role in the relationship between social origins and destinations. And they go on in the second half of the chapter to suggest that the new mandate for European education coincides with a range of cultural changes. These are reflected both in lifestyle changes and new forms of (post-national) citizenship, both of which signal changes away from the social contract of modernity. They discuss in particular 'rebellions of difference', which include epistemological as well as political and cultural assumptions, and look to the emergence of forms of 'demanded' or 'claimed' citizenship that contrast with its 'attributed' nature in the modern nation state.

Taken together, we hope that these chapters will open up new lines of debate around globalisation, Europeanisation and education, as well as providing an important resource to policymakers, academics and students interested in this historical, and fascinating, project.

Note

[1] The EGSIE project (Educational Governance and Social Integration and Exclusion in Education) ran from 1998 to 2001. It was funded by the European Commission and coordinated by Sverker Lindblad. The best source for the work of the project is the Special Issue of the *European Educational Research Journal*, Volume 1, Number 4, published in 2002 (http://www.wwwords.eu/EERJ). REGULEDUC (Changes in Regulation Modes and Social Production of Inequalities in Educational Systems: a European comparison) was also funded by the European Commission. It ran from 2001-04 and was directed by Christian Maroy (see Dupriez & Maroy, 2003; Maroy, 2006). Maroy's contribution was especially important, pointing out as he did that the term 'governance' did not have a direct equivalent in French, while the French term *régulation* translated equally inadequately into English.

References

Castells, Manuel (1999) *The Network Society*. Oxford: Blackwell.

Dale, Roger (2007) Changing Meanings of 'the Europe of Knowledge' and 'Modernising the University', from Bologna to the 'New Lisbon', *European Education*, 39(4), 27-42. http://dx.doi.org/10.2753/EUE1056-4934390402

Dupriez, Vincent & Maroy, Christian (2003) Regulation in School Systems: a theoretical analysis of the structural framework of the school system in French-speaking Belgium, *Journal of Education Policy*, 18(4), 375-392. http://dx.doi.org/10.1080/0268093032000106839

Maroy, Christian (2006) Ecole, Régulation et Marché: une comparaison de six espaces scolaires locaux en Europe. Paris: Presses Universitaires de France.

PART ONE

Governance and the Knowledge Economy

CHAPTER 1

Contexts, Constraints and Resources in the Development of European Education Space and European Education Policy[1]

ROGER DALE

SUMMARY This chapter suggests that globalisation and Europeanisation are to a degree co-constituting, with what is seen as globalisation emerging in part from the contests and competition between the members of the triad, a competition that also shapes them, their priorities and policies. The chapter also emphasises that the European project is not exclusively to be seen as an economic project, but that it has geopolitical elements, too. Another result of the changes in the global political economy and the particular constitution of the EU is that it has developed a peculiar form of governance. The central argument of the chapter is that these two sets of conditions act to frame the nature and possibilities of European education policy, with the European Education *Space* framed formally by the treaty, substantively by the Lisbon agenda, and historically by pre-200 EU education initiatives. The chapter argues that though European Education *Space* and European Education *Policy* overlap and interact, they may be seen as analytically distinct., with the former marking the areas that the latter may seek to fill. It closes with a discussion of the place of European education, which it insists cannot be taken as a scaled-up version of national policies.

The fundamental argument of this chapter, as explained in the Introduction to the volume, is to set out briefly the historical, economic, political and educational contexts from and through which something that might be referred to as a European Education Space (EES) and a European Education Policy (EEP) emerged, and the kinds of institutional and discursive legacies, resources and constraints that these contexts provided, which enabled – but in no sense either required or guaranteed – the development of the EES and the EEP. Having discussed the sources of 'Europe' and 'governance', I will go on in the main part of the chapter to outline the emergence of what it will be argued are the distinct spheres of European Education *Space* and European Education *Policy*. Through this process, I will develop the approach to educational governance that will be adopted, and briefly sketch some significant wider contextual features without which it is difficult to comprehend the nature and purposes of the EES and EEP. The chapter ends with a brief discussion of the 'place' of the EES and EEP in the relationships between globalisation and Europeanisation.

A Methodological Note

The basic methodological starting point of this chapter (and also of Chapter 6) is that while we have a range of excellent and insightful studies of the enigma known as European Education Policy, they tend collectively to be insufficiently 'critical' in the sense in which Robert Cox uses that term. He distinguishes what he calls 'problem-solving' theory from 'critical' theory, where:

> The general aim of problem solving is to make [social and power] relationships and institutions [into which they are organised] work smoothly by dealing effectively with particular sources of trouble. ... The strength of the problem-solving approach lies in its ability to fix limits or parameters to a problem area and to reduce the statement of a particular problem to a limited number of variables which are amenable to relatively close and precise examination. (Cox, 1996, p. 88)

By contrast:

> Critical theory, unlike problem-solving theory, does not take institutions and social power relations for granted but calls them into question by concerning itself with their origins and how and whether they might be in the process of changing. It is directed toward an appraisal of the very framework for action ... which problem-solving theory accepts as its parameters. (Cox, 1996, pp. 88-89)

It will be the argument here that most of the work on EES and EEP has fallen into the problem-solving category, especially when its focus is confined to investigating the 'effects of' European Education Policy on national education policies. This formulation contains most of the elements that get in the way of a more effective understanding of EES and EEP.
They assume:

- a level of correspondence/equivalence between regional and national education policies;
- a homogenisation of the roles, scope and place of education policy;
- a hierarchical relationship between Europe and national levels;
- methodological nationalist and statist assumptions;
- more specifically, that the Lisbon Agenda and the Open Method of Coordination (OMC) both have relatively fixed meanings and that they jointly constitute and comprise the agenda of European Education Policy.

The point about this list is that it is made up of precisely the kinds of categories and phenomena that critical theory insists have to be problematised, and that is the fundamental basis for such analyses.

Globalisation and Europeanisation

Conceptions of the relationship between globalisation and Europeanisation tend to be disciplinary specific. From the point of view of International Relations, perhaps the dominant interested discipline, one way that the complexity of this relationship has been conceived is through what Rosamond (2002a) refers to as 'Castells' paradox' –that 'European integration is, at the same time, a reaction to the process of globalisation, and its most advanced expression' (Castells, 2000, p. 348). This is a very useful position from which to begin our analysis of the relationship between globalisation, Europeanisation and education, since in essence our response to the paradox is that it is both, and that recognising why that may be the case is an effective way of tracing out the nature and consequences of the relationship. The basic argument is that Europe, in the sense of the Euopean Union (EU), is involved in the construction of globalisation *and* that globalisation frames economic, political, cultural (etc.) possibilities for Europe.

In terms of the first of these, Castells' argument that Europe is the highest expression of globalisation assumes that the relationship between them is not a hierarchical one. This is a key part of the argument here, for the global-Europe-national hierarchy appears to be assumed in much work on education – possibly following its use in International Relations, which Rosamond (2002a) discusses. From our point of view, globalisation is best seen as a level of abstraction rather than as some kind of entity equivalent to 'Europe' that similarly 'contains', and seeks to order, economic, political, cultural (etc.) activities. More appropriate conceptions, then, are global economy, or institutions of global governance. Conceiving of the relationship in this way removes the possibility of a hierarchical relationship between two levels, because in a sense they are not two levels, but different instances of the same level. Rosamond suggest that there are two ways in which Europe can be seen as a realisation of globalisation (2005, p. 24). The first is as a form of liberal market order. This emerges most clearly through the example of 'competitiveness' as the master discourse emerging from the Lisbon Agenda.[2] As it is translated into practice, what competitiveness means is competition with the United States and Japan above all, which is seen as essential because Europe's relatively poor comparative level of competitiveness is perceived to be the major threat to its future success. The crucial point here is that the very competition between the triad regions (at its simplest, America, Europe and Asia) contributes to, indeed constructs, 'globalisation', and in turn draws on and is shaped by it. However, globalisation is not reducible to inter-triad competition and does not exhaust it, because on the one hand, inter-triad competition is not and could not be a 'fight to the death', and on the other, there are economic, political and ecological limits to competition, while the consequences of the 'global governance' set up in part to regulate that competition are not confined to the triad, but reverberate across the world – one of the possible definitions of globalisation. This argument has the great theoretical virtue of undermining the hierarchical conception of the relationship between scales.

The second way in which Rosamond suggests that Europe may be seen as a realisation of globalisation is as a 'hybrid form of multi-level polity', which sees it as 'an agent for the unraveling of (Westphalian) European space, the spread of certain policy orthodoxies across the continent and the emergence of hybrid forms of governance that depart from the models most associated with twentieth-century European political economy' (2005, p. 24). Here, for us, the crucial point is that Lisbon specifies 'Europe', and not Member States, as the level at which competitiveness is to be achieved. It indicates an incipient shift from 'national government' to 'European governance' in the Lisbon Agenda.

Rather more attention has been paid to the other element of Castells' paradox, European integration as a reaction to globalisation, and certainly it has featured more prominently in discussions of the consequences for education policy. The 'obvious' way of approaching it might seem to be to look for the 'effects' of the 'global' on the regional, the nature of the indirect/instrumental relationship between globalisation and EU, and from there to consider what that might mean for EU education policy. This is essentially the position Susan Robertson and I took in the paper we wrote on the effects of regional organisations on education policy (Dale & Robertson, 2002). The argument was that the EU and other regional organisations (the North American Free Trade Agreement and the Asia-Pacific Economic Cooperation) were set up as a defence against globalisation, and the purpose was to ascertain the consequences of this for education policy. This led us quickly to focus on Lisbon, which seemed to be a perfect case for this kind of analysis. However, it rested on implicitly hierarchical, tiered, assumptions about the relationships between the 'scales' of global, regional and national, where the regional acted as a kind of 'collective security', that required the 'national' to cede some of its powers/discretion to the collective/regional, in order to secure its fundamental interests more effectively; this saw the

European level somehow 'mediating' between the global and the national. This account is quite plausible, even convincing, as far as it goes, especially as it was modified in the case of the regional organisations to the argument set out in the last paragraph, that far from operating at a different scale from globalisation, it was the competition between the 'triad' regional organisations that comprised the main force and driver of 'globalisation'.

However, certainly in the case of Europe, because of its qualitatively different basis, history and range of objectives from other regional and international organisations, promoting economic competitiveness, acting as what we might call a 'collective competition state', is not sufficient to account for its relationship with education policy. Even in terms of Lisbon, it is not sufficient to focus only on fostering competitiveness. The other components of Lisbon may be less prominent and less promoted, but they are nevertheless extremely important in terms of the wider view of Europe. This is especially evident in the case of the 'European Social Model', which underpins the 'social' items on the Lisbon agenda, and is seen as the main means of differentiating Europe from the United States. Thus, Lisbon is claimed to represent a version of a more humane and equitable form of and response to global capitalism, where the EU itself has become a model of globalisation, or a 'laboratory of globalisation' (Lamy, quoted in Rosamond, 2002a, p. 9).

One crucial difference between Europe and other regional organisations, that also makes it *sui generis* as a political-economic cultural entity, is that it is a result of 'the founding of a polity by the deliberate interaction of the members of that new polity ... [so that] European political integration can fruitfully be seen as an attempt at world-making' (Wagner, 2007, p. 254). We do not need to follow Wagner in going on to argue that Europe represents an alternative form of modernity to the dominant US form, which he refers to as 'Imperial Modernism', to recognise both that there is at least a glimpse or embryo of an alternative 'European' project that is not reducible to economic competition, and that there is a distinct 'Europe-centred' project whose aim is to 'thicken' the discourses and institutions of Europe, irrespective of economic competition. And it is a central argument here that it is very important to recognise that education's expected contributions to that project, both as a medium of competence establishment and building, and as a means of substantiating the idea of Europe, were crucial parts of that project, without which neither the project nor education can be adequately appreciated.

Thickening the idea of Europe itself is also advanced through the relationship with globalisation. As Rosamond (2002a) puts it, 'globalisation', as a concept, slots into the processes of deliberation and persuasion that characterise institutional interaction in the EU. In this regard it is worth noting that 'globalisation' has been used as an exogenous referent by actors seeking to argue for the further Europeanisation of governance capacity and deeper European economic integration.

> Much of this is bound up with the discursive elaboration of a
> 'European economy' or of 'European firms', which seek a
> European-level regulatory framework to assure 'competitiveness'
> globally. ... Of particular significance is the way in which
> 'globalisation' has been inserted into the discursive practices of
> 'norm entrepreneurs' who contribute to the social construction of
> 'Europe' as a valid and viable economic space populated by
> discernible European actors. This in turn fits neatly with the
> continued advocacy of supranational governance solutions.
> (Rosamond, 2002a, p. 10)

A further relevant aspect of Europe as region is to be found in the area of geopolitics, where it has clear ambitions that are not wholly without consequences for education. One way in which this emerges is in the shadow of discourses of security rather than of economy. Here, education has not been heavily involved or referred to, though there are suggestions – for example, in the European Neighbourhood Policy (see Pace, 2007) – that education, and especially higher education, may be expected to make a significant contribution. While I have deliberately made very little reference to higher education in these chapters, it appears to play a potentially major part in the geopolitical strand of the EU project. This is seen most clearly through activities around the Bologna Process, in particular the development of the European Higher Education Area, the Tuning Project (especially through programmes such as Tuning America Latina, for instance) and the Erasmus Mundus programme. Robertson's examples in Chapter 3 provide excellent evidence of this expansion. Each of these potentially makes a contribution to the project of Europe as a 'player' on world stages in which education would be centrally involved, potentially enabling, respectively, access to human resources, ability to control market rules and an ability to shape the pattern of the higher education curriculum.

It is clear, then, that 'Europe' is unusual if not unique among regional and other international organisations in having more than economic ambitions, and seeing its project spreading wider and deeper than short-term collective economic benefit.

Governance and the State

A key feature that distinguishes governance from government is that it requires us to problematise, rather than take for granted, the nature of and the relationships between the spaces, subjects and coordination of governing – in this case, the governing of education and how it is attempted and achieved at the level of the EU.

At its most basic, the problematic of governance may be seen as establishing the coordination of activities and agents that make the work of organisations of all kinds possible. It is fundamentally an issue of who does what, over what area – and then how, why and with what consequences for whom? It thus covers a wide range of questions, around institutional structures, methods of political decision making and forms of policy instruments, for instance.

In a sense, the key context for the emergence of both 'Europe' and 'governance', and consequently of an EES and EEP, is the spread and intensity of the project of neoliberal globalisation, whose central assumption is the need for the removal of all barriers to free trade, but whose central governing device is to achieve this through harnessing the apparatuses of the state to its own purposes in place of the decommodifying and 'market-taming' role the state had played under social democracy. Rather than merely reforming government through minimising regulation, it seeks to construct new ways of reducing transaction costs without resorting to laissez-faire. Stephen Gill has characterised this 'new constitutionalism' as

> to separate economic policies from broad political accountability
> in order to make governments more responsive to the discipline of
> market forces and correspondingly less responsive to popular-
> democratic forces and processes ... Central objectives in this
> discourse are security of property rights and investor freedoms,
> and market discipline on the state and on labour to secure
> credibility in the eyes of private investors, e.g. those in both the
> global currency and capital markets. (Gill, 1998, p. 5)

So, in terms of the emergence of an idea of 'governance', the most relevant and effective way of beginning to ground the issue is to focus initially on states. The state has been simultaneously the means by which the conditions of existence of capitalism are most fully assured and a key *institution* of modernity. However, following Santos (2004), the state that was to implement regulation is itself incorporated into the project of neoliberalism, as regulation is ceded to the market, and emancipation is reduced to market freedom.

Thus, the social-democratic model of the state that was earlier seen as the protector of the principles of modernity and nationhood, and the best possible shell for capitalism (see Jessop, 1978), is now seen as a barrier to free trade, and no longer the institutional base that capitalism needs to embed and monitor the rules of global economic governance. That form of the state is seen as increasingly unable to manage the tensions intrinsic to its role as the key institution of both modernity and capitalism. It had been able to manage these tensions largely through its capacity to regulate to protect forms of emancipation that did not rely on the market, to 'decommodify' particular institutions and practices, an approach that reached its high water mark in the *trente glorieuses*, the exceptional 30 years that followed (at least in the west) the Second World War. However, as Santos puts it, following the iconic fall of the Berlin Wall: 'The state ceased to be the controlling agency over the articulations among the three pillars of modern regulation (State, market and community) to become the servant of the market and redesign the community to become the same' (2004, p. 154).

This has come about through a number of changes, many of which can be traced to the changing relationships (in both directions) between globalisation and Europeanisation. They include:

(a) the decline of the national state as the basis of the economy (without a national economy it is more difficult to build a national welfare state, for instance) with the reversal of the relationship between the economic and the social, from one where the former served the latter to its opposite; and consequently

(b) the declining influence of borders, especially as constraints on the movement of capital, as well as the growth of international organisations that carry out many of what were formerly regarded as 'national' prerogatives and responsibilities;

(c) the recognition (in the form of the New Public Management, see, for example, Kettl, 1997; Pollitt & Bouckaert, 2004) that many of what had come to be seen as 'obviously' state activities, could, and should, be funded and provided by other, often private, bodies, with benefits to both state expenditure and quality of service;

(d) the dominant role of the state becoming the promotion of national economic prosperity, on the assumption that the wealth so created would trickle down so that all would eventually benefit from it;

(e) the associated shift of state activity towards economic activity; and the accompanying emphasis on 'productive social policy'; and

(f) a shift from state to individual responsibility for security and risk, especially in the area of employment.

We should also note the social-democratic form of the state came to be seen as setting a normative as well as an analytic benchmark, in that it has been seen as the highest realisation of the possibilities of the state acting to ensure that the benefits of capitalism were redistributed – and indeed Zurn & Leibfried (2005) refer to it as the 'Golden Age' of the state. Central – and, we might argue, unique – to this conception was that all four dimensions of the state distinguished by Zurn & Leibfried (resources, law, legitimacy and welfare) converged in national constellations, and national institutions. What Zurn & Leibfried make clear, however, is that 'the changes over the past 40 years are not merely creases in the fabric of the nation state, but rather an unravelling of the finely woven national constellation of its Golden Age' (2005, p. 1). As Edgar Grande (2006) puts it:

> with the new forms of complex governance, the state *form* ... loses
> its monopoly position in the production of collective solutions to
> collective problems. Collectively binding decisions are no longer
> taken by the state alone, or among sovereign states, but rather
> with the involvement of various types of societal actors, sometimes
> even without governments. (2006, p. 92, emphasis in original)

Such an accommodation requires not just the 'reform' of existing states but transforming them by constructing new spaces and sectors of *governance*. This fundamentally reflects a shift from the assumption that 'the state does it all' (and must do so, certainly in the area of education) to the recognition that those activities can be defined and divided differently, among different potential agents, and crucially for present purposes, between different scales, with the regional having a role to play, that is increasingly based on its economic competitiveness.

The culmination of these changes came in the Lisbon Agenda, where a set of implications and responsibilities for education were elaborated, with the proviso that they could only be met at the level of the Union, not that of individual Member States. The content of the 'Concrete Future Objectives' for education systems enunciated at Lisbon may not have been especially dramatic or novel in itself, but the fact that it was accepted by Member States represented the beginning of a new stage in Europe's involvement in education and training, the framing of which we will now discuss. More than this, the changes listed above created a highly critical stance toward existing provision in many areas, which were seen as being out of date and not up to the task of modernising Europe in the ways required by Lisbon, and education was no exception to this.

European Education Space and European Education Policy

However, that apparently simple statement conceals enormous complexities. Something of the nature of the problems it generates is caught in the terminology used to describe/locate educational activities and possibilities at a European level, which presents a fascinating range of alternatives. Hingel, for instance, refers in the course of one paragraph to a European *Space* of Education, a European *Model* of Education, deriving from common principles, and a European *House* of Education, with its foundations in the annual meeting of Member State Ministers of Education (2001, p. 4), while later (p. 9) he refers to a European *Area* of Education. The range of terms is not only fascinating, however, but also very instructive. It is clear that Hingel uses the different terms to refer to different and non-substitutable elements or characteristics of an emergent – and elusive – 'European education', and that the terms chosen reflect its novelty – though perhaps most importantly they represent its 'existence' as experienced by a senior member of the Directorate General for Education. When we come to consider issues around the scope and nature of 'European education', what most importantly and most significantly distinguishes it is that it must be assumed to be different somehow from Member States' 'national' education. But that then raises the further question, 'different in what it does and/or in how it does it ?' The development of 'European education' over the period since Hingel was writing has produced both a clearer empirical emergence of what it involves, and a more precise theoretical appreciation of its nature, and these have led us to distinguish between the *presence* of 'European education', and the *activities* of 'European education'. This is reflected here and in Chapter 6 in the argument that it is very useful to separate the two terms that have been most commonly used to conceptualise the issues we are considering here, European Education *Space*, and European Education *Policy*.

These terms have typically been used as if they were interchangeable, as if it were a matter of relative indifference which of them was used to name what was seen as essentially the same phenomenon. However, a key argument underlying the two chapters will be that the terms do indeed denote different analytic areas which, though they overlap and interact in multiple ways, are not reducible to each other, and that focusing on one neither means that the other can be ignored, nor that access to the other is *ipso facto* guaranteed.

These arguments will be elaborated and exemplified in the chapters, but it will be useful to develop them a little further here. First (and as will be elaborated in Chapter 6), these spaces and policies are not to be regarded as equivalent to, or upscaled versions of, national education spaces and policies; they are qualitatively, and not just quantitatively, different. They rest on the claim that the European Education *Space* can be seen as an opportunity structure framed *formally* by Treaty responsibilities, *substantively* by the Lisbon Agenda and the European Social Model, and *historically* by the 'pre-Lisbon' education activities of the European Commission. European Education *Policy*, by contrast, is framed by not just the Open Method of Coordination, and the relevant Directorates General – Education, pre-eminently, but also Employment, Social Inclusion and Research – but by existing Member State policies and preferences – and, in addition, what has been rather overlooked in the debates around these issues, existing conceptions of the nature and capacity of 'education' which, it will be suggested, have an existence that is relatively independent of, and pervade, in different ways, all Member State education policies.

European Education Space

As the first marker of the European Education Space (EES), there is little disagreement that the formal Treaty designation of education as a national responsibility is accepted as fundamentally defining the terrain. In a sense, then, the EES is defined by negatives, what is not possible.

Moreover, 'Europe' does not have anything approaching the equivalent of national ministries of education, with their range of services and bureaucratic and professional support. And it clearly dos not speak with a single voice, or inflection (see for instance Jones's [2008] account of the contests between the European Council and the European Commission over the wording of a highly strategic document). On the other hand, ' Europe', and the Commission in particular, is not as wholly excluded from education policy making as might be assumed from the Treaty articles (for a rather different but nevertheless converging view of this suggestion, see Hingel, 2001). Flexible interpretations of Article 149.1, for instance, which indicates that 'the Treaty states that "The Community shall contribute to the development of quality education by encouraging cooperation between Member States and, if necessary, by supporting and supplementing their actions, while fully respecting the responsibility of Member States for the content of teaching and the organisation of education systems and their linguistic and cultural diversity"' (European Union, 2006), opened the door to considerable 'agenda amplification', particularly through the 'tofu'-like nature (with no taste of its own, it takes on the taste of whatever flavour it is attached to) of the concept of 'quality' (see Dale [2007] for an exemplification of this, in the shape of '16 Quality Indicators of European Education' already being developed in the late 1990s). And if we take that into account, beyond this, the actions of the Community in the field of education should aim at:

- developing the European dimension in education;
- encouraging the mobility of students and teachers;
- promoting co-operation between educational establishments;
- exchange of information and experiences;
- encouraging the development of distance education.

(European Union, 2004, Article 149.2)

we can clearly see that educational activity on the part of 'Europe', and the Commission in particular, was clearly not entirely without possibilities – though it is also crucial not to forget that any European actions within education have to be approved by Member States.

This means that, though it may be to a degree skirted or reinterpreted quite creatively, in the ways just mentioned, in the end the formal possibilities for developing a European Education Policy, in the terms in which that is normally conceived, are strictly limited. The EU has no discretion over the areas that dominate national education politics and policies in most Member States. Questions about the distribution of educational opportunities, allocation of school places, distribution of available funding between different levels of the education system, and so on, are no concern of the EU. However, that would only be a problem for the EU if it wished to intervene in such issues, which carry intense 'political' loading in all Member States. We have become used to associating 'education policy' with precisely such issues, that are everywhere contested, but on very nationally specific grounds, with nationally specific understandings of the stakes involved.

There is one further element of the 'education system' of Europe that shows how misleading it is to assume that because it does not adhere to the assumed pattern of stateness, then it cannot act within education. This is what might be called the obverse of the famous 'democratic deficit'. This may create problems for legitimation but it does to a degree 'liberate'

European policy from the need to follow electoral cycles and have an eye to electoral pressures. Indeed, one consequence of Article 149 might be seen as a fundamental 'apoliticisation' of education policy, that, as we will see, could be exploited and developed through the construction of 'de-nationalised' expertise.

However, we should note that:

(a) there are a number of possible loopholes, or opportunities for policy entrepreneurship or agenda amplification, contained in the exclusion of vocational education from the subsidiarity rule, and from the possibility of the Union intervening to assist Member States in improving the quality of their education, the latter of which we will take up later;

(b) policy also develops in the interstices of subsidiarity, and emerges contingently, rather than in any determined way;

(c) most importantly, the role assigned to education in the Lisbon Process itself effectively bends and stretches, if it does not break, the formal (Treaty) designation of education, not least in the statement that the Lisbon goals in education can only be met at the level of the Community, not at national level.

The Lisbon Agenda and Education

The Lisbon Agenda, and its immediate and broader implications, are, of course, as has been widely recognised, extensive and very diverse, possibly to the point of mutual contradiction (see Dale, 2003), and, indeed, the problems generated by that diversity of goals and their possible implications for education have become the staple of studies of European Education Policy. However, we might see two significant problems with this effective equation of 'Lisbon' with the EES – and EEP.

First, it seems often to be overlooked, or taken for granted, that what crucially distinguishes the EES as framed by Lisbon from national education spaces is that it is concerned with Education *only in so far as it may be seen as related to those purposes and implications*. That is to say, the EES is characterised by its relatively abbreviated and concentrated scope and purpose. Many of the issues that press most directly on national ministries of education – issues like access, equity, efficiency, effectiveness – are relatively peripheral to the EES, on grounds of both substance – their relevance to Lisbon – and form – education as a Member State responsibility. The problem is that while the latter is frequently recognised and its implications discussed, the former seems often to be subsumed under a general assumption that European Education Policy is in most relevant dimensions similar to national education policies. Policies are assumed to be made in the same way, *mutatis mutandis*, by similar bodies, for similar purposes, and cover similar kinds of areas. The consequence of these assumptions is that the national can be scaled up to the regional with no loss of meaning; European Education Policy is formally directly comparable to, and accessible as a model of, existing national education policy. Crucially, this informs the level of analysis at least as much as that of description; that is to say, the national provides the template, or benchmark against which European Education Policy is matched and judged, in terms of its 'authenticity' and its fitness for purpose, and the comparative perspective through which it is analysed. This issue will be considered at greater length in Chapter 6.

The second problem is a tendency to focus on the immediate issues, such as the Lisbon Declaration and the nature of the Open Method of Coordination, or Communications published by the Education Directorate General. Such studies have produced a large quantity of interesting and important material, some of it containing very insightful and revealing analyses. The outcome of this is that Lisbon and, to a lesser extent, the OMC have taken on an iconic status in the analysis of EU education activities.

This is by no means inappropriate; they are immensely important, interesting and fruitful areas of inquiry. The problem is that they tend to be accepted on to the analytic terrain 'on their own terms', as it were, already formed and known. However, it is widely and clearly acknowledged that the Lisbon Declaration was not the only way that the EU's policy dilemma could have been conceived and represented – indeed, there is a considerable literature on this (e.g. Esping-Anderson, 2002; Rodrigues, 2004). So, though it may possibly be formally acknowledged as one particular *condensation* and representation of the problems and solutions that faced the EU, its iconic status means that that particular condensation and representation remains fairly unchallenged, almost 'naturalised', at least in its diagnosis. That is, it is recognised that 'Lisbon' is a political slogan but it is nevertheless accepted relatively unproblematically as the basis for analysis, and interestingly, this seems to have remained the case, certainly in discussions of education, following the major shifts in emphasis and direction (though with the rubric unchanged) brought about by the Mid Term Review. Effectively, 'Lisbon' is taken unproblematically as not only representing but exhausting the issues facing the European economy. It becomes reified and frozen, and strangely unreflexive; competitiveness and 'social cohesion', and the relationships between them, are taken as the 'same' in 2008 as in 2000, despite the years of intense effort to change them.

There is also a strong tendency to abstract Lisbon from the wider political economic issues facing Europe and the rest of the world. These are fully recognised in the shape of the dominant 'competitiveness' agenda, but this itself does not exhaust problems at a global level. This is, of course, how the agenda is represented 'officially' in Communications on Education, which all take 'the Lisbon goals' as continuing, and assumedly unchanged, benchmarks which shape the *constellation* of issues for policy, as represented, most notably, in the Detailed Work Programme. As the chapters in these volumes indicate, several alternative constellations of issues and representations of the nature of Lisbon for Education are possible.

Finally, Lisbon often seems to be taken as the sole, and not just the dominant, *catalyst* for the emergence of European Education Policy in the forms in which we encounter it. This leads to another form of this tendency – to which I certainly have fallen prey – which is almost to assume that there was no European Education Policy before Lisbon, or, if there was, it was so different that it could be ignored with no penalty. Indeed, not only is there such a history, but it is clear that it continues to influence conceptions of the scope and boundaries of the EES.

European Education Policy

In terms of the EEP, the main tendency in the literature on education has been to focus on the 'effects' of a putative 'European Education Policy' on Member States' domestic education policies. The assumption often seems to be that the main purpose/goal/objective of European Education Policy is to replace or at least (more commonly) to modify national education policies, in whole or in part, in the sense of having effects on them that would not otherwise have come about (in other words, very much like the highly popular academic tendency to see, and/or look for, evidence of Europe's influence through its effects on domestic policies – which may include the emergence of hybrids, etc). This is not to say either that there are no such effects, or that they are not important, or that it is not important to look for them; it is, though, to say that confining ourselves to such searches unnecessarily, and misleadingly, limits our capacity to understand the nature of European Education Policy. As was argued in our discussion of approaches to the EES, it essentially adopts a 'problem-solving' conception of the issues rather than a critical one. It limits the range of both outputs, outcomes and consequences, and the number of variables to be taken into account in explaining them. Interestingly, there appears to be much more interest in searching for the domestic effects of European Education Policy than in assessing the degree to which it attains the objectives set for it, reflecting a tendency to look for effects on Members States' education policies rather than on 'Europe'. Such an approach also leads directly to two further assumptions, to be examined further in Chapter 6, that European Education Policy exists only in so far as it can be shown to have achieved these things, and that implicit in all the above is a zero-sum assumption about the relationship between Europe and Member States' education policies.

The alternative argument to be developed here about the nature of European Education Policy is both formal and substantive. Formally, on the one hand its scope is framed by the EES. On the other hand, its content is framed by the distinct and different place and form taken by 'policy' in European educational governance. Substantively, in order to adequately come to terms with the mandate, capacity and governance of European education, it is necessary to problematise the agendas that education is summoned to address at the European level. These agendas are taken to include, as well as the Lisbon Agenda, the European Social Model, and Europe as an entity.

Beyond this, what is also needed is an analysis of where both the agenda and the issues to be addressed, *and* the resources for response, come from, because they have a crucial and independent effect on the framing of both. Further key issues here are what is conceived of as mandate, capacity and governance of European education, where those conceptions come from, how they differ from national conceptions, how they are combined, and what constraints, opportunities, resources and so on, they offer. These issues are discussed more fully in Chapter 6.

In more formal terms, the European agendas for education are seen as part of the particular 'hegemonic project' that fundamentally underlies the Community enterprise, and that includes the three agendas noted above for education. A hegemonic project is taken as a political project advanced by coalitions between different groups and interests, where the main basis of making the coalitions coherent is sets of representations of: (a) the nature of problems facing the (particular) world, and (b) how they might be overcome. Education plays a key role in hegemonic projects, and the overall hegemonic project may be seen as the basis of its prioritisation and approach to its basic role of addressing the core problems of education (which are set out briefly below). And this also means that there are changes not only in the problems to be addressed by education, but also in the *ways* that they are to be addressed, and the *nature* of education's contribution to them; further, not just the contents of education programmes, but the theories of how they are to contribute to the required changes, and the means through which they are to bring about, or contribute to, the change specified in the hegemonic project, themselves change. These further, rather less obvious, aspects of the differences between national and European education policy are further elaborated in the final section of this chapter, and in Chapter 6.

Taking this range of differences between European and national education policy, and their consequences for the governance of education at the two levels, into account, clearly requires some revision of the theories of governance developed to account for national systems. Essentially, it means shedding, or at least bracketing, the methodologically nationalist and statist assumptions (see Dale & Robertson, 2007) that have characterised the study of educational governance. One way of doing this is to start from a version of Przeworski & Teune's (1970) principle of replacing the 'names of things' with 'variables'. What that means here is that we look for the fundamental purposes and activities associated with the governance of education rather than with the particular means we have become accustomed to associate with achieving them. If we move a step further, and define education governance as *the means of bringing about the relationship between the multiple goals of education and the ways that education can bring about change*, then we can recognise more clearly the nature, sources and consequences of the less visible and tangible differences between European and national education governance. In this context, 'the ways that education can bring about change' are fundamentally framed and limited by the nature of the EES. We shall take up this point in much more detail in Chapter 6, where we shall introduce the distinction between 'education programmes' and what will be referred to as their 'programme ontology', the ways that education can bring about change, and suggest that the Open Method of Coordination is best understood as such a programme ontology.

In terms of the substance of EEP, it is suggested that the hegemonic project of Europe is made up of three very broad and basic elements: economic competitiveness, developing a European Social Model, and enhancing 'Europe's' claims to be a distinct and significant political/economic/cultural entity. And to repeat the point made earlier in this chapter, this means that Europe's education agenda is rather more restricted than that of its component Member States, though it is also necessary to recall the point that the relationship between the two levels is neither zero-sum, or top-down, but involves both levels, and influences working in both directions.

It is very widely recognised that EEP is fundamentally a response to the Lisbon goals and especially the competitiveness agenda, particularly as it has been further prioritised following the Mid Term Review [3] of the Lisbon process, with a heavy emphasis on the need for Europe to move towards becoming a knowledge economy. Indeed, this has been the explicit purpose of education policy since 2000, the basis of the Concrete Future Objectives for education and for the Detailed Work Plans through which education systems would achieve the contribution to the achievement of the Lisbon goals set out in Education and Training 2010 (see Council of European Union, 2004). However, as we see in Chapter 6, the possibilities framed by the EES channel the policy responses to the Lisbon Agenda.

Education and the European Social Model

The second, substantive parameter both limits and directs legitimate European intervention in education. We have already emphasised the centrality of the 'master discourse' of Lisbon, competitiveness, as far as education policy and efforts are concerned. However, we should recall that Lisbon also saw a key role for education in contributing to the European Social Model and European Social Policy, where the central features are 'investment in people', 'building an active welfare state' effectively, and 'productive social policy'. The first of these means that 'Europe's education and training systems need to adapt both to the demands of the knowledge society and to the need of an improved level and quality of employment' (Council of the European Union, 2000).

A key point to be noted here is that the Lisbon summit 'does not acknowledge education as a "teleological" policy area, an area in itself. [It] is part of social policy, labour market and overall economic policy' (Gornitzka, 2005, p. 17). There is also evidence that the high profile of education is due as much to pressures from the wider social policy area, and especially the employment area, as it is to pressure from education ministers, for instance. Gábor Halász (2003), for instance, suggests that:

> Most of the motives that lead to the need for policy harmonisation in education can be found outside the sector ... [and] the strongest force that leads to policy harmonisation in education is, even if this sector resists this, that it is not possible to draw sharp borderlines between different sectors. (p. 3)

He goes on to list a number of social and employment policy-related interventions that involve educational inputs, and concludes that:

> [By the time of the 2000 National Action Plans for Employment] it became clear for education ministers that if they remained aloof from the rapidly developing policy-coordination process and if the education sector did not develop its own procedure for this, coordination of policies in their sectors will [*sic*] be done by others. (Halász, 2003, p. 4)

Halász concludes that:

> Since the middle of the nineties the non-education sector players have been successful both in extending the scope of employment policy to issues that traditionally have belonged to the jurisdiction of the education sector and in pushing these issues up to community level. As a consequence, not only the community level sectoral players... but also those at the national level ... could have the feeling that an increasing number of education policy issues are dealt with in the framework of the common employment policy. (Halász, 2003, p. 7)

One of the main implications of this discussion lies in the question of how far 'European education' may be becoming a distinct sector in its own right, distinct from, and parallel to, national education sectors, and this is taken up in Chapter 6.

Education and Europe as an Entity

We have emphasised several times above how education supports Europe as an entity by its very existence, or by the implicit acceptance of its existence. At one level GENIE itself is taken as an example of this; at another Wagner's conception of Europe as a 'world-making' project. It is notable in the policy of emphasising 'Europe' as the subject of action sentences – most notably in the Lisbon Declaration itself – thereby reinforcing both its presence and its competence. And as Ase Gornitzka puts it, writing about the OMC and education, ultimately, the key point was that the need for a common education policy was accepted by Member States (2006, p. 14).

The Place of Education in EU Policy

Having discussed the EES and the EEP I want to conclude this chapter with a brief excursus on what I will call the 'place' of education in European policy, which will also act as a link to Chapter 6. By the 'place' of education, I mean the *nature* of its contribution and to how it fits into the projects with which it is associated. *How* is it assumed that education will contribute to those ends? A very simple example may be helpful here. In post-war social democracy it was assumed that education could contribute most effectively by expanding equality of opportunity by bureaucratic administration of access and availability; this often took the form of comprehensive schools, for instance. By contrast, in the 1980s and 1990s, the idea was that education could best contribute to the wider social project of expanding wealth through markets, by making education and schools behave themselves in market-like ways. This relationship is rarely studied, but it is crucial to a full understanding of the nature of education and how it is defined and administered. That is especially the case when we are dealing with an entity that appears in many respects sufficiently similar to national education systems to justify using them as a model for analysis, but which is, as has been argued here, sufficiently different to make such comparisons misleading.

I have tried in this chapter to demonstrate the *sui generis* character of European education as a space and a policy, and Figure 1 is intended to provide a way of conceiving of the place of education at a European level.

Hegemonic project	Place of education	Mechanism	Implications for/ drivers of education governance
Constructing Europe, economically, politically, culturally	OMC as programme ontology	Common EU policy paradigm and taxonomies	?Parallel? European and national 'education' sectors

Figure 1. The place of education in European policy.

As Figure 1 shows, it is not possible to consider the place of education in isolation from the purposes which it is to serve, on the one hand, nor helpful to do so without indicating some of the consequences of that place. The first column, then, describes the hegemonic project of the EU, as it has been briefly set out in this chapter. It is the second column where we find the 'place' of education. Here it is argued that the place of education has to be framed in ways that respect both the hegemonic project and the framing of the EES and the EEP; and the fact that the OMC is intimately linked with both the hegemonic project and the EES and EEP means that it fills the place of education. The OMC is conceived as much more than a means of implementation of a programme; it is the link rather than the means of implementing the link. And this, and the accounts of how this is related to the mechanisms and drivers, will be taken up in Chapter 6.

Notes

[1] I am extremely grateful to Christian Maroy, Marek Kwiek, Sverker Lindblad and Rimantas Zelvys for the contributions they made to the development of the 'Governance' strand of work in the GENIE project, and can only apologise to them for not representing their contributions more adequately in this chapter and Chapter 6.

[2] The argument in the rest of this paragraph is based on Dale (2003b), a paper presented at the first GENIE conference.

[3] A 'main political orientation' following the 2005 Mid Term Review of the Lisbon Process is that 'new priorities [be] defined for national education policies, i.e. turning schools into open learning centres, providing support to each and every population group, using the Internet and multimedia' (Rodrigues, 2004, p. 5).

References

Castells, Manuel (2000) *End of Millennium*. Oxford: Blackwell.

Cox, R. (1996) *Approaches to World Order*. Cambridge: Cambridge University Press.

Council of the European Union (2000) Lisbon European Council 23 and 24 March 2000. Presidency Conclusions.[ON-LINE] [Brussels]: Council of the European Union, [08.06.2007]. Nr: 100/1/00. http://www.consilium.europa.eu/ueDocs/cms_Data/docs/pressData/en/ec/00100-r1.en0.htm.

Council of the European Communities (2004) *Education & Training 2010:the success of the Lisbon strategy hinges on urgent reforms*. Joint interim report of the Council and the Commission on the implementation of the detailed work programme on the follow-up of the objectives of education and training systems in Europe. COM (2003) 685 final Brussels, 3 March.

Dale, Roger (2003b) Globalisation, Europeanisation and the 'Competitiveness' Agenda: implications for education policy in Europe, paper presented to GENIE conference, July, Nicosia, Cyprus.

Dale, Roger (2007) Construire l'Europe en Bâtissant un Espace Européen de l'Education, *Education et Sociétés*, 18, 42-54.

Dale, Roger & Robertson, Susan L. (2002) The Varying Effects of Regional Organizations as Subjects of Globalization of Education, *Comparative Education Review*, 46(1), 10-36. http://dx.doi.org/10.1086/324052

Dale, Roger & Robertson, Susan L. (2007) Beyond Methodological 'Isms' in Comparative Education in an Era of Globalisation, in A. Kazamias & R. Cowen (Eds) *International Handbook of Comparative Education*, pp. 1099-1113. Springer.

Esping-Andersen, Gosta (2002) *Why We Need a New Welfare State*. Oxford: Oxford University Press.

European Union (2006) European Union: Consolidated Versions of the Treaty on European Union and of the Treaty Establishing the European Community, *Official Journal of the European Union*, 29 December.

Gill, S. (1998) European Governance and *New Constitutionalism*: economic and monetary union and alternatives to disciplinary neoliberalism in Europe, *New Political Economy*, 3(1), 5-26. http://dx.doi.org/10.1080/13563469808406330

Gornitzka, Ase (2005) Coordinating policies for a 'Europe of Knowledge'. Emerging Practices of the 'Open Method of Coordination' in Education and Research. Arena Working Paper No. 16, March. Centre for European Studies, University of Oslo.

Gornitzka, Ase (2006) The Open Method of Coordination as Practice – a watershed in European Education Policy? Arena Working Paper No. 16, December. Centre for European Studies, University of Oslo.

Grande, Edgar (2006) Cosmopolitan Political Science, *British Journal of Sociology*, 57(1), 87-111. http://dx.doi.org/10.1111/j.1468-4446.2006.00095.x

Halász, Gábor (2003) European Co-ordination of National Education Policies from the Perspective of the New Member Countries in Roger Standaert (Ed.) *Becoming the Best: educational ambitions for Europe*. Enschede: CIDREE Yearbook 3.

Hingel, Anders (2001) Education Policies and European Governance. European Commission Directorate General for Education and Culture/Policy Unit A1, Brussels.

Jessop, Bob (1978) Capitalism and Democracy: the best possible shell? in G. Littlejohn, B. Smart, J. Wakeford & N. Yuval-Davies (Eds) *Power and the State*. London: Croom Helm.

Jones, Peter (2008) 'Requisite Irony' and the 'Knowledge Based Economy', in N. Fairclough, B. Jessop & R. Wodak (Eds) *Education and the Knowledge Based Economy in Europe*. Rotterdam: Netherlands: Sense Publications.

Kettl, Donald F. (1997) Global Revolution in Public Management: driving themes, missing links, *Journal of Policy Analysis and Management*, 16(3), 446-462. http://dx.doi.org/10.1002/(SICI)1520-6688(199722)16:3%3C446::AID-PAM5%3E3.0.CO;2-H

Pace, Michelle (2007) Norm Shifting from EMP to ENP: the EU as a norm entrepreneur in the south? *Cambridge Review of International Affairs*, 20(4), 659-675. http://dx.doi.org/10.1080/09557570701680704

Pollitt, Christopher & Bouckaert, Geert (2004) *Public Management Reform: a comparative analysis*, 2nd edn. Oxford: Oxford University Press.

Przeworski, Adam & Teune, Henry (1970) *The Logic of Comparative Social Inquiry*. New York: Wiley-Interscience.

Rodrigues, Maria-Joao (2004) *An Overview of the Lisbon Strategy – the European agenda for competitiveness, employment and social cohesion*, paper presented at

Konferenz des Kompetenzteams Wirtschaft: So profitiert Österreich. Vienna: Renner Institute.

Rosamond, Ben (2002a) Globalisation and the European Union 1. National Europe Centre Paper No. 12. Paper presented to conference on The European Union in International Affairs, National Europe Centre, Australian National University, Canberra, 3-4 July.

Rosamond, Ben (2005) Globalization, the Ambivalence of European Integration and the Possibilities for Post-disciplinary EU Studies, *Innovation*, 18(1), 23-43. http://dx.doi.org/10.1080/1351161042000334772

Santos, Boaventura de Sousa (2004) *Towards a New Legal Common Sense*. London: Butterworth.

Wagner, Peter (2007) Imperial Modernism and European World-making, in Nathalie Karagiannis & Peter Wagner (Eds) *Varieties of World Making: beyond globalization*. Liverpool: Liverpool University Press.

Zurn, Michael & Leibfried, Stephan (2005) Reconfiguring the National Constellation, *European Review*, 13, 1-36. http://dx.doi.org/10.1017/S1062798705000177

CHAPTER 2

Education, Knowledge and the Network Society

STEPHEN R. STOER & ANTÓNIO M. MAGALHÃES

SUMMARY The 'development of individual capacities', in addition to the education of 'responsible citizens' and the 'preparation for work', constitutes one of the most important objectives to be achieved by education systems and, in this sense, makes up one of the main planks of that which Dale terms 'mandates for the education system', i.e., projects for education based on 'conceptions of what it is desirable and legitimate for the education system to bring about'. In a previous work, the authors tried to map out, on the basis of the objectives 'preparation for work' and 'education of responsible citizens', the outlines of a new mandate for European education policy that appears to be in the making in accord with recent socio-economic, political and educational developments. In this chapter, the authors centre their attention on the 'development of individual capacities' in an attempt to map out the effects of the simultaneous pressure, top-down and bottom-up, that has been increasingly brought to bear on the nation-state and on the education system. With regard to the first, it is argued that what is at stake is the transformation of knowledge itself into *money* (i.e., pure performance); while with regard to the second, there appears to be taking place a movement of knowledge from the school (national level) to the local community in which this latter is interpreted as the 'educative city' (where a 'transparent' communicational pedagogy holds sway). This work aims at challenging the dichotomy constructed by way of an analysis of the implications, for both pedagogy and the development of individual capacities, of the development and consolidation of a network state and society.

Modernity, Knowledge and Emancipation

The Modern Age celebrated knowledge, above all scientific knowledge, as the touchstone of the emancipation of individuals and nations. To know the world – natural or social – was equivalent to unveiling its laws, such that the world – natural and social – could be appropriated and dominated by humanity, which, thus, became the central subject of history.

This enlightenment dimension of knowledge projected itself in different ways onto education and onto the role that knowledge should assume in the education of children and youth. In another work, we have referred to the modern matrix of school systems (Magalhães & Stoer, 2003); in this one we try to emphasise the central role attributed to knowledge in individual development.

In fact, in the same way that knowledge, as the intellectual appropriation of the forces and of the laws that rule over nature and society, is seen as enabling human societies to enjoy increasing domination over natural and social processes, making it possible even for history to be led (as is particularly evident, for example, in some Marxist perspectives on political action), the individual, also, through his or her own development may conceive the world and action upon it as free from forces that are normally considered either magical or occult, in short, impossible to control. Rational knowledge is thus able to supply individuals with a potential for consciousness, for action on the world and for citizenship that enables them to be the lords of their own destiny. This kind of optimism was particularly evident in Hegel, who assumed that individual liberty would find its maximum realisation in the figure of the citizen, that is, in the individual bound by the state given that it was in the state that 'liberty acquired its objectiveness and lived its own coming into being' (Hegel, 1965, p. 11). In the last analysis, modernity hoped that the individual would be emancipated on the basis of the same knowledge that (it was hoped) would emancipate humanity organised in nation states. Knowledge was, effectively, assumed to be in this dominion the privileged means by way of which individuals would again find themselves, would find release from unknown fears and superstitions through the taking on of citizenship. Thus a functional form of knowledge was conceptualised with the capacity to lead the individual from alienation to citizenry.

It is in this sense that modernity conceived of the school – more precisely, the school system – as one of the central instruments of its own realisation. If seen from this angle, the foundation of education systems in different European countries gains notable consistency and coherence; the production of citizens by way of the education of citizens. School systems were elected as the privileged form of the construction and consolidation of nation states (see, for example, Nóvoa, 1998; Candeias, 2002).

Knowledge surges, in this context, as both a mediator between ignorance and knowledge and as the organiser of the relationship between nature and humanity. School socialisation arises as the way in which the natural nature of human beings transforms itself into a social nature. It is at this point that pedagogy – as the prime mover of this relationship – and the modern social contract converge. The 'Rousseaunian turn' in pedagogy (Magalhães & Stoer, 1998) takes on, from this point of view, an interesting dimension: in postulating that the centre of the teaching–learning process is not a body of knowledge, but, rather, he or she who learns, that is, the learning subject with his/her respective characteristics. The importance of the pedagogic mediation of the relationship between the natural and the social is emphasised.

Capitalism, School Socialisation and the Education of Workers

On the other hand, when modernity combines with capitalism, the mandate for the education system becomes more complex and school socialisation takes on the somewhat ambiguous function of enlightening and emancipating individuals and of transforming the citizen into a disciplined worker. In attempting to trace the historical evolution of the relations between education and employment, Alaluf (1993) states that, at a certain moment, it was the school's task to create 'good workers', meaning that its task was to combat vagrancy, to develop discipline, punctuality and the 'honesty' of workers, for what counted was not only creating good *workers*, but above all *good* workers.

Thus, knowledge, assumed to be by the sociocultural paradigm of modernity a basis for the emancipation of individuals, arises simultaneously as a powerful form of social regulation. Effectively, knowledge of the laws of nature and of society became a means of domination of this same nature and society. A link was created between knowledge and power that was historically unprecedented. On the one hand, capitalism developed its own apparatus of social regulation while, on the other, it incorporated knowledge into its own processes by rationalising them. In other words, a process of rationalisation was incorporated into the productive process and social organisation.

With regard to the mode of production, knowledge was integrated as a productive factor (as science and technology) and at the level of the organisation of work (for example, as Taylorism). With regard to social organisation, knowledge was also integrated in two ways: firstly as a factor of legitimation that normally arises as particularly evident in the narratives of the nation state, or in national saga; secondly as an organising element of social life, for example as crystallised in the bureaucratic organisations of the state and of civil life in general. The Weberian metaphor of the 'iron cage' comes to mind here as particularly appropriate.

Thus, capitalism overlapped its logic of obtaining the maximisation of surplus value with the cognitive and instrumental rationality of the sociocultural paradigm of modernity, producing that which Santos (1991) has termed the hyper-rationalisation of the pillar of emancipation, that, in conjunction with the pillar of regulation, narratively propped up the paradigm of modernity. Santos argues that the concentrations and reductions that modernity produced have resulted in the hyper-scientisation (knowledge as the domination of nature and society) of the pillar of emancipation, a fact that 'has upset the balance of the relations of reciprocal bonding between this pillar and the pillar of regulation' (1991, p. 24). In addition, there has occurred the structural emptying of the principle of community by the principle of the market and in the colonisation, by this same principle, of the principle of the state.

This combination of modern rationality with the logic of capitalism and with state organisation has had wide consequences for the mandates concerned with school socialisation, not only visible in the above-mentioned education of 'good workers', but also in the very conception of the role of knowledge in individual development. Enlightenment knowledge has reconfigured itself in three important phases, as an instrument that confers competencies in the name of individuals, above all in the act of the repositioning of individuals on the labour market. It is that which, in another work (Magalhães & Stoer, 2003), we designated as the process of the transformation of knowledge into *throughput* (knowledge functions as if it were money, passing through individuals without altering them, see Bernstein, 1996). The first phase is that which we referred to above and which, according to Alaluf (1993), corresponds to the demand for the school system to produce 'disciplined' and 'honest' workers. The second is the phase in which the adaptation of schooling to the specific job progressively assumed central importance, in a Keynesian mode of regulation in which educational progress adjusted itself to new developments in production. The third, as a result of unemployment, above all the unemployment of holders of diplomas, and given the incapacity of decision makers to foresee the need for certain professional profiles, is based once again

> on giving value to criteria of individual conformity. It is not the content of schooling that is of interest to the employer, but the capacity of individuals to survive in a situation of ferocious competition. It is necessary to develop 'procedural competencies' based more on 'learning styles' than on content.
> (Alaluf, 1993, pp. 14-15)

From the Keynesian Labour Market to the Network: the relationship between knowledge and education

It is through this process of the transformation of knowledge into *throughput* that, in our perspective, one can initiate the archaeology of the discourse on competencies. As knowledge gains centrality as a factor of production and transforms itself into a commodity (Lyotard, 1989), the competencies to which knowledge allows access are reconfigured in a way that distances this same knowledge from its modern matrix (knowledge as education of the individual, as input). The model of cognitive competence as a means of emancipation appears to be replaced by an archetype of competency adapted to the demands of the labour market, now transformed into the central arena where the personal and social development of individuals takes place. If 'to be someone' in the modern matrix is synonymous with having knowledge of the processes and the contexts in which individuals find themselves involved, perhaps in the new emerging situation the famous Cartesian slogan can be glossed in the following way: 'I have a place in the labour market, therefore I exist!' School competencies reflect in a more or less direct way this reconfiguration of knowledge. Indeed, in another work, we referred to this reconfiguration of educational competencies, in the wake of Harvey (1989), as an eventual determination by the economy *in the first instance* (Magalhães & Stoer, 2003).

This reconfiguration of competencies towards the individualisation of individuals in new social contexts has been denounced, above all by Rousseaunian-inspired pedagogues, as the influence of flexible capitalism in education processes and by neoliberal ideology in education. For our part, we would like to make more subtle this analysis by reiterating our argument (Magalhães & Stoer, 2002) that there is no pedagogy without performance and no performance without pedagogy. In other words, on the one hand, it is not possible to continue today to think of educational competencies as strictly related to individual development, as if the articulation of individuals to the labour market were not a major concern. On the other hand, in attempting to choose between what Barnett (1997) has termed the *critical self* and the *corporate self*, the opposition between the two shows itself to be rather artificial, as if it were possible to develop either of these selves in a social and pedagogical vacuum.

The concept of competency cannot be, in fact, reduced to its function of articulating education with the demands of the labour market. To do so is to fall into the simplistic opposition between pedagogy and performance and, in terms of the conception of individual development, to oppose in an idealist way (Stoer, 1994) the process of individuation (a process where, according to Beck [1992], the reflexive individual becomes master of his/her own choices) to the process of individualisation. A more careful analysis of the concept allows one, on the one hand, to emphasise the autonomy of the education field, which it would be crass to ignore, and, on the other, permits one to sustain the thesis of Harvey (1989) of 'determination in the first instance' of culture and education by flexible capitalism. Taking into account Bernstein's assumption that a determination of this type would threaten the autonomy of the pedagogic recontextualising field (see Bernstein, 1990, pp. 198, 202), we are suggesting that this latter is not totally diluted in the indetermination of the possibilities that characterise current contexts. The educators who see in performance only the materialisation of determination in the first instance are struggling for a distancing of educational practices and discourses from the postures that articulate the demands of the labour market, thus making deeper in this way the gap between pedagogy and performance (see Magalhães & Stoer, 2002). Does it make sense to discuss the concept of competency with the aim of separating out 'good' competencies from 'bad' ones? What competencies serve individuals independently from their being positioned on the labour market? Is it not the concept of the role of knowledge in the education of the individual that is at stake and not the concept of competency? In other words, if the concept of competency is a mediating concept, it cannot be manipulated by only one of the fields between which it mediates. In the same way, it cannot be appropriated by only one of the two sides, that is, either by pedagogy alone (which would imply an intentional non-articulation with the economic) or by the labour market alone (which would imply a functional articulation between the two fields).

In an official document, the Portuguese Ministry of Education, in 2001, attempted to define the concept of competencies:

> The term 'competency' can take on different meanings, such that it is important to make clear in which sense it is being used in the present document. One has adopted here a wide notion of competency, that integrates knowledges, capacities and attitudes and that can be understood as knowledge *in action*, or *in use*. In this way, one is not adding on a group of knowledges to a certain number of capacities and attitudes, but, rather, promoting the integrated development of capacities and attitudes that makes possible the use of knowledges in diverse situations that are more or less familiar to the pupil. (Ministry of Education, 2001, p. 9)

Thus, the document defines the concept of competency much as one defines 'functional literacy', presupposing that what is at stake is the acquisition of a group of knowledges and basic processes that should not be reduced to the 'memorised knowledge of basic terms, facts and procedures that shows no sign of comprehension, interpretation and problem solving' (Ministry of Education, 2001, p. 9). An effort is also made to make the concept autonomous and to emphasise the specificity of the education field, underlining the fact that competency 'is not linked to training for, at a given moment, producing answers or executing previously determined tasks' (p. 9). The organisation of the teaching–learning process on the basis of this concept suggests that the acquisition of competencies

> is related to the process of activating resources (knowledges, capacities, strategies) in diverse types of situation, namely in problematic situations. For this reason, one cannot speak of competency without associating it to the development of some degree of *autonomy* in relation to the use of knowledge. (Ministry of Education, 2001, p. 9)

Thus, the articulation of competencies as a central part of the teaching–learning process aims, in the words of a policymaker from the Department of Basic Education, at aiding the

construction of a new culture of the curriculum and more
autonomous and flexible practices of curriculum management ... .
On the one hand, at stake is a process that contests the strong
tradition of the production of programmatic orientations based on
specific topics and dispersed among the disciplines and years of
schooling. On the other, the nature of the work makes it always
unfinished and susceptible to improvements of diverse kinds.
(Abrantes, 2001, p. 3)

This definition of the concept of competency arises as an opportunity to
delimit a central concept of current education policy. The concept, such as it
is defined in the document, we would argue, in spite of attempts to the
contrary, remains ambiguous and thus is often interpreted, particularly by
Rousseaunian-inspired pedagogues, as collapsing into a precipitous logic of
articulation with the labour market, a labour market that is itself increasingly
volatile and unpredictable, that is, in transition. Apparently, what is at stake
is the concern with the learning subject and the abstract alternative of
knowing who is managing competencies: the individual or the labour market.
The conception of the education/formation of the subject, present in this
work, appears to translate itself into the dilemma of knowing whether it is the
individual who manages competencies or the social and educational systems
that manage themselves by way of competencies, thus producing the process
of individualisation that is referred to by Bauman (2001), that is, the
inescapable condemnation of subjects to being individuals.

Such a process of individualisation is not only made up of the emptying
of knowledge, reduced to *throughput* as we referred to above, it is also a reflex
derived from the present predominance of the market in the regulation of
social life. To promote 'essential competencies' in this context, in a form that
might be capable of challenging individualisation and knowledge as
throughput, would involve taking on board at least some of the implications of
what it means to live in a 'network society' and, perhaps even more
importantly, would imply confronting the market as a social space that has
the tendency to promote a logic based on the homogenisation of differences
(of gender, ethnicity, age, way of living, social class, etc.), reducing the
knowledge that is possible to construct on differences to their own status as
consumers. Within the scope of this logic, knowledge loses both its form and
its content and, thus, no longer contains its potential for promoting a
reflexive teaching–learning process. In our recent paper on the outlines of a
new mandate for European Education Policy (Magalhães & Stoer, 2003), we
tried to map out, precisely, some of the implications for education of the
transition the labour market is going through. We also presented a relational
model for understanding difference with regard to education and citizenship
based on the heterogenisation of difference.

In this same sense of an education articulated essentially to the market,
in general, and to the labour market, in particular, appears to be the
European Commission document, coordinated by Edith Cresson, *Teaching*

and Learning: on route to the learning society, which was published back in 1996. In this document, the starting point is the idea of 'three basic impulses' that are transforming in a profound and long-lasting way the context of economic activity and the functioning of western societies.

> These three impulses are the advent of the information society, of scientific and technical civilisation and the globalisation of the economy. All three contribute to the development of a learning society. Although they may represent risks, they can also be seen as opportunities that are important to take advantage of.
>
> The construction of this society will depend upon the capacity Europe has to provide two big responses to the implications of these impulses: the first is centred on general culture; the second has to do with the development of vocation for employment and for being active. (Cresson, 1996, p. 21)

Everything appears to take place, then, as if the knowledge inherent in the teaching–learning process were an extension of the demands of economic globalisation, on the one hand, and functional to the new emerging needs of the scientific and technological reconfiguration of the processes of production and distribution. Indeed, the document states this almost explicitly:

> The ultimate aim of education is to develop the autonomy of each person and of his/her professional capacity, to make of the person a privileged element of adaptation and evolution. It is for this reason that the main responses chosen by this present 'white paper' are, in the first place, to guarantee that each man and each women has access to *general culture* and, in the second place, to develop each person's vocation for *employment and being active*. (Cresson, 1996, p. 22)

In this context, it seems that the only path, one-dimensional, available is for pedagogy and knowledge to fall into the arms of performance, it being assumed at the same time that education should place individuals in an 'interesting' situation with regard to the labour market. We stress the word 'interesting' because the development of individual capacities, in this sense, appears to articulate itself with, and to articulate generally, a process of individualisation that not only makes the individual responsible for him/herself in finding a place on the labour market – meaning, within the network (Castells, 1996) – but also makes the individual responsible for his/her own failures. This way of centring the education process in the individual is, as we stated above, a form of condemnation; in being trained to be an individual, individuality becomes an onus for itself.

This critique of the reduction of the education process to individualisation and to articulation with the demands of the labour market has also been adopted by some educators who, as we have already mentioned, claim education as a form of rupture, i.e. non-articulation with the labour market and with the new demands of the so-called 'new economy'. All this apparently taking place as if the purpose of the educational process were the emancipatory delivery of the individual to him/herself, education being only concerned with the integral education/formation of the individual, with individuation, in the sense of emancipation.

> All know that the objective of education is to carry out the terrible
> transformation: do everything such that children forget the desire
> for pleasure that resides in their savage bodies, in order to
> transform them into domesticated ducks that waddle to the
> rhythm of social utility. Silent philosophy: each child is a means
> for obtaining that larger entity which is society.
> (Alves, 2000, p. 169)

The conception of an individual's education in the context of the network society does not appear to conjugate well with the dichotomy between individualisation, as a condemnation of the individual to his/her own dimension, with the simultaneous retraction of the mechanisms of social protection, and the integral education of the individual, as affirmation of him/herself as an emancipatory project. It is difficult to conceive of the integral education of the individual, in the development – for example – of the individual's identity(ies), exterior to the site of work. It is in this sense that one argues:

> the understanding necessary to produce practices capable of
> reducing the socio-economic constraints ... acting on (groups
> penalised by the school) depends upon an understanding of their
> direct relationship with material production and the world of
> work, but, also, upon an understanding of the way these groups
> 'live' and 'construct' their lives. ... In our opinion, only in this way
> can one avoid either an approach that blames the very 'victims' for
> the continued existence of these constraints ('they are dangerous',
> 'they have the wrong values', 'they are ignorant'), or an approach
> that reduces the analysis of these constraints (and the practices
> possible for overcoming them) to the class antagonism that exists
> between labour and capital. (Stoer, 1994, pp. 8-9)

Thus, the opposition between education as the articulation of the demands of the labour market and education as the integral formation of the individual independently of these demands reveals itself as unsustainable. It is unsustainable because, on the one hand, the projects of individuals are inseparable from the possibilities effectively available to them which, indeed, are those offered by a capitalist labour market that, at present, is undergoing global expansion and taking on distinct characteristics. The consequences of this expansion are still to be determined in their totality, there being available many possibilities, some of which, as we shall argue further on, are related to what Castells has called the network society (1996). On the other hand, work, even in its most commodified form, and in spite of determination in the first instance to which we referred above, is neither the only, nor a total, determination. There resides here, in fact, a strange paradox: at the same time that capitalism presents itself as the 'only' historical solution, and in this sense as the 'end of history', it becomes more volatile, widening the mesh of its determination and opening new possibilities for that which in other work, inspired by diverse authors, we have called new forms of social and cultural action (Stoer et al, 2003).

Knowledge, as a vehicle of education, and in this context, is configured in a double sense: as competencies, as essential competencies, that give rise to, at least in part, initiatives such as the 'flexible management of the curriculum'; *and* as the integral formation of the individual that is far from being determined by his/her relationship to work. With the rise of the network society, this duplicity appears to diminish, due to the fact that the opposition between knowledge as competencies and knowledge as the integral formation of the individual is itself being reconfigured as a result of changes in the nature of work, in the nature of the labour market, in the way one lives citizenship and in the unprecedented affirmation of personal and group identities.

Network Society, Knowledge and Education

In fact, as a result of the increasing centrality of information and knowledge in the processes of production, distribution and consumption, profound transformations have taken place in these processes. Bernstein (1990), for example, has emphasised the role of knowledge in the transition of a society based on physical resources (raw materials, workforce, installations, etc.) to another society based on information and knowledge. Harvey (1989) (and one could cite numerous other authors) has explained how access to information and to scientific and technical knowledge, although always important for capitalist production, has taken on renewed and central importance in what he calls flexible capitalism, due mainly to the fact that both information and knowledge not only are crucial for the flexible responses required by flexible markets but also because they have become key commodities themselves. The possession of informational and communicational capital has become a strategic aim of social classes traditionally more identified with functions of social reproduction. In this respect, Lash (1994) states:

> With the production of informational goods becoming the new
> axial principle of capital accumulation, the (new) new middle class
> is created. This new class embraces occupational places which
> have developed from the new principle of accumulation. But now
> the middle class is no longer a 'service class', that is, a class in the
> service of the reproduction needs of manufacturing capital. In its
> expanded form, it becomes more a 'served' than a service class, as

> its mainly information-processing labour is no longer subsumed
> under the needs of manufacturing accumulation. ... The key point
> is that the accumulation of information (and of capital) in the I &
> C (information and communication) structures becomes the
> driving force of reflexive modernity, just as the accumulation of
> manufacturing capital and its associated social structures had been
> in an earlier modernity. (Lash, 1994, pp. 129-130)

This results in an interesting new situation: if information and knowledge have now become the driving force of the production process, the groups linked to its creation and manipulation move from being reproducers to producers, or are simultaneously both.

In becoming informational and communicational capital, knowledge itself appears to change in nature. On the one hand, pronouncements on the world and on society are translated into information bytes for circulation on the network.[1] Among the implications of this phenomenon are those related to access to the network: if, in modern terms, citizenship was determined by its link to salaried work and to national identity, at present it appears to depend increasingly on integration into the network, that is, its determination widens to the cultural field. As a result, citizenship takes on new forms: instead of being 'attributed', it is 'claimed', or 'demanded' ('I have rights – for example, the right to indemnity for the effects of several centuries of slavery on my life chances – duties and special needs as a black lesbian that cannot be dealt with through national identity'), meaning that citizenship is structured not only through national identity but also through other identities, both local and supranational – see Magalhães & Stoer (2003). On the other hand, knowledge, above all its scientific version, is being reconfigured by reflexivity. Beck (1992) argues, with regard to this matter, that we are dealing with a second phase of scientisation that is based on confrontation with the first phase, that is, the scientisation of the natural and social worlds. The second phase of scientisation is, par excellence, reflexive: nobody is in a position to say 'I didn't know'. Knowledge on the social and natural worlds already has to be conscious of its own consequences on these same worlds. Just as Giddens (1990) has stated that after Chernobyl there can be no 'Others', Beck (1992) would argue that after this nuclear accident, science can never be the same.

The knowledge that is susceptible to be translated and to circulate in the form of bytes appears to be precisely the knowledge on which the concept of competencies is based. Further, the knowledge on which reflexivity is based appears to arise as that knowledge that articulates new forms of citizenship and processes of identity affirmation. It is in this latter sense that we can talk of a movement of knowledge from the school at the national level to the 'local' level. Still, it is important not to overestimate this opposition between knowledge founded in bytes and the knowledge based on reflexivity, because what takes place is an intertwining of the local and supranational levels. When one speaks here of the 'local', one is referring not only to the territorialised locality, frequently linked to the phenomenon of the reinvention of tradition (for example, the case of Barrancos and the killing of the bull in Portugal – see Stoer et al, 2003), a kind of recontextualisation in Giddens' terms. The 'local' arises, rather, as a pluralised claim that involves territory, but is not reduced to it. The 'local', such as we are using it here, is plural and pluralised. It is plural because it integrates multiple subjective and collective identity dimensions (for example, the 'samba' which, being globalised, has a very strong local identity) that can neither be reduced to territory nor to local community. It is pluralised because it is subject to multiple interpretations or appropriations (for example, the reinvention of 'traditional' Cuban music by Ry Cooder that is simultaneously an icon for the Left and a commodity).

Thus, when one talks of a movement of knowledge from the school at the national level to the 'local' level, one wishes to suggest that knowledge, as an essential factor of education/formation, is escaping the school to relocalise itself in different contexts and at various places in the local community. On the one hand, this cognitively and emotionally driven knowledge develops on the basis of the strategies of what we have referred to, in the wake of Bernstein, as the new middle class (Magalhães & Stoer, 2003), and which includes resorting to supplementary education, exterior to the school, in the form of paid lessons and guidance, cultural study visits and holidays, personalised computer equipment and computer expertise that allows one to be proactive with regard to the network, the transformation of parents into resource banks and agents of knowledge (Correia & Matos, 2001), and so on. This happens to such an extent that that which was part of the school's normal functions now appears to take place in other places, such as the family, on the basis of resources eventually less subject to democratic control and thus reinforcing processes linked to the possession of cultural and social capital (in Bourdieu's terms). On the other hand, and using a metaphor created by the North American researcher Linda McNeill, if the emphasis on essential competencies and their assessment leads to youth checking in their local knowledges before entering the classroom, much as the cowboys of the mythical Far West would do with their pistols before entering the saloon, the process of the relocalisation of knowledge that we are referring to appears to implicitly indicate an interpretation of the school–community relationship that suggests that this relationship should not only be sensitive to but even porous with regard to local knowledges and sociabilities, in the sense of a kind of reinvention of the so-called 'educational city'.

This latter interpretation arises precisely as an interpretation, that is, in the form of alternative proposals to official schooling, considered socially and cognitively unjust and incapable of guaranteeing knowledge as concerned with the integral education/formation of the individual. These proposals have taken on diverse forms that extend from the critique of 'school-centrism' (Correia & Matos, 2002) to the promotion of rural schools as the 'last' refuge of a potentially counter-hegemonic education, including along the way proposals (with a strong emphasis on local sociabilities) for community education, adult education, the education of groups that resist integration into the system (such as nomadic populations), and so on. The community appears, in these proposals, as a kind of 'transparent place' that is both anti-capitalist and anti-market, in opposition to the society based on work (the image that comes to mind is one of Huck Finn and Tom Sawyer floating on a raft down the Mississippi, enjoying complete happiness and authenticity).

In the same way, the idea of the 'network' should not arise as a 'transparent place'. It has been argued that some enthusiasts of the network society have been tempted to assume that information has definitively replaced knowledge and that, as such, it has gone beyond the need for epistemological and sociological legitimation. Castells has been interpellated precisely in this sense by Visvanathan (2001):

> Because of Castells' preoccupation with information, there is a strange silence about knowledge. Castells' network society is sociology of the informational paradigm without sociology of knowledge or theory of knowledge. ... As a result, Castells' network society is the gigantic civics of the transfer of technology paradigm, embodying a new relation between map and territory. What it lacks is a politics of knowledge and a politics of competing theories of knowledge. Castells' paradigm would see alternative epistemologies as 'noise'. For example, Africa is compulsively part of the Fourth World as a result of the failure of development. But apart from the breakdown of the state and the growth of a predatory elite, the failure might be a result of the models of science applied to it. It is often argued that African models of farming might embody different notions of community and science. It is this community of expertise that the official application of development might have destroyed. Within such a framework, African agriculture and systems of healing might be alternative paradigms, elusive and elliptical to current models of science. Viewed in this way, the Fourth World becomes not a void or a black box but an alternative list of diversities, possibilities, epistemologies. (Visvanathan, 2001, pp. 38-39)

Visvanathan's critique of Manuel Castells' 'grand sociology' ('one of the master narratives of the 20th century' where the hero of the twenty-first century 'is not the state, nor the non-governmental organisation, not organisations like the party and the trade union, but the network' [Visvanathan, 2001, p. 35]) emphasises the need to create alternative models of development outside the network. The network ('a fragment of the democratic imagination', *ibid*) in developing its own logic becomes a new form of totalitarianism, fixing the rules of the game in such a way that all other players are condemned to play according to these rules, thus erasing the possibility for other developmental paradigms that are not based on informationalism.

A major question that arises on the basis of Visvanathan's critique is if the network has become coincidental with the 'system', in this case the new global economy, is it possible to speak from a place that rests exterior to it? In other words, can a new game, that is, a new network, be invented? The concern with inclusion and human emancipation in general appears to make knowledge and the practices deriving from it more legitimate. It is as if Visvanathan were talking from a transparent place, so transparent that it becomes invisible even to those who inhabit it. Such transparency allows unquestionable liberty to speak of alternatives, alternatives that become crucial mechanisms of sociological analysis, but that lead one to a place absolutely exterior to the so-called 'system' ('network') within which they find their origin. In this sense, one can argue that it is necessary to demystify and unveil the place from which one wishes to propose alternatives.

Our approach is, rather, one of asking what are the implications of the network society for the development of individual capacities. To participate fully in the network brings important advantages that not only relate to the accumulation of social and communicational capital but also to the possibility of competencies being produced by network users themselves as network agents, and not simply as network users. As we have suggested above, the logic of the network is of the same kind as the type of knowledge, founded in information, that circulates on it. The critique of Visvanathan opposes knowledge to this process of informationalisation. But is informational knowledge susceptible to being reduced to the mere packages of competencies that are operationalised by institutions and educational actors? Is the so-called 'death of the teacher' (Nuyen, 1992), at the hands of 'bytified' competencies, an accomplished fact or one of the aspects of the ideological battlefield in which the outcome is still unknown? The opposition between knowledge as the education/formation of the individual and knowledge as competencies may dramatically reduce the educational debate, making it seem as if, parallel to the reduction of knowledge to bytes, social and personal reflexivity does not reconfigure the field of agency of the diverse social actors involved. The opposition that Visvanathan sets up appears to reproduce others such as emancipation versus regulation and pedagogy versus performance. Thus many educators, in a rather paradoxical fashion, see competencies as the enemy of pedagogy when they represent precisely a pedagogical input into the knowledge process, in other words, into the space of pedagogical agency. The Swiss sociologist Perrenoud states (2001, pp. 12-13), for example: 'Competency is surplus value added on to knowledges: the capacity to *use* knowledge to resolve problems, develop strategies, take decisions, act in the widest sense of the word (emphasis in original). The pedagogical process, thus, is enriched by a central concern with an increase in reflexivity as an individual process, in the sense that competencies should serve individuals. The opposite of this process, for example within the scope of the flexible management of the curriculum, would be the pupil conceived of as an 'object' of this management rather than as its 'subject'. In other words, the flexible management of the curriculum only fulfils its promises if it is capable of promoting reflexivity and not simply the competencies that, to a large extent, make it up. Thus, in not accepting the opposition between knowledge as the education/formation of the individual and knowledge as competencies, we insist that the conception of knowledge as reflexive education/formation must assume a central place in the educational context.

What appears to be happening is that with the movement that we mentioned above of the school from the national level to the local, there is a strong tendency to reduce the learning process within the school to the acquisition of competencies. In this sense, the flexible *management* of the curriculum becomes, rather, the flexible 'piloting', or even 'surfing', of the curriculum.[2]

Conclusion

In this article, we have traced the development of knowledge on the basis of a framework within which knowledge arises simultaneously as education for the formation/development of the individual (*Bildung*) and as a form of socialisation strongly marked by the demands of the consolidation of capitalism as the dominant mode of production of western societies. With the emergence of post-Fordism and with related transformations in the mode of producing, distributing and consuming, knowledge has changed, not only in terms of its nature but also with regard to its status. Indeed, knowledge has become reconfigured as a communicational and informational network and has assumed a central place in the productive process. With regard to the place and function of knowledge in the education process and, in particular, in individual development, this change appears to translate the tension between the upward and downward movements brought about by economic and cultural globalisation and by the development of the new information and communication technologies. This tension has been translated, in the educational debate, into the opposition between educating for competencies and education for the formation/development of the individual, as if the first corresponded to the top-down pressure resulting, above all, from the demands of the reconfigured labour market where only 'competent' individuals have a place and are able to circulate; and as if the second corresponded, above all, to the bottom-up pressure resulting from the demands for education as an ambiguous mixture of individual emancipation and local claims.

We have argued in recent works for the need to unravel these kinds of educational and political dichotomies between, for example, education as formation/individual development and education as competencies, between pedagogy and performance (Magalhães & Stoer, 2002) and between globalisation and localisation. In this article, we have tried to emphasise, in the wake of this previous work, the possibility that knowledge as the education/formation of the individual and knowledge as information are not polar opposites within the scope of individual development. As we said above, the development of individuals cannot be reduced either to economic determinations nor, in an idealist fashion, to cultural determinations. This perspective allows one to effectively complexify the relationship between different types of competencies and education as formation. For example, European construction and the Europeanisation of education appear to imply new forms of citizenship that take on different forms of 'localisation' ('gay' localisation, 'Barrancos' localisation, 'European' localisation, etc.), forms that are not untouched by the reconfiguration of the labour market within the European space (the dissolution of professions and of occupations into competencies occurs simultaneously with the construction and affirmation of multiple and diverse identities – take, for example, the 'green' business entrepreneur who assumes his concern with the environment at the same time that he tries to make a profit, or the 'fair trade' shops that abide by the rules of the capitalist market, etc.).[3]

On the other hand, and taking into account the perspective of pressure coming from below, the movement of knowledge to the local level, to the community, constitutes, in the first place, a reconfiguration of the social strategies of the new middle class in the sense of guaranteeing a solid education that can be easily translated into social and cultural capital; in the second place, it constitutes an appeal to the community for the reconfiguration of knowledge in terms of the locale, that is, if with regard to the modern school the locale itself was rarely present, or called upon, the present claim of communities appears to be the valorisation of knowledge produced locally (to retake the metaphor of Linda McNeill, local knowledge is no longer easily allowed to be left at the entrance to the classroom).

We think, however, that this latter type of the reconfiguration of knowledge is conditioned by the fact that it is simultaneously local and global, that is, the knowledge produced locally, given that it does not exist independently of globalised capitalism, clearly has a global dimension. In other words, due to the development of the network, the local production of knowledge is, at the same time, its global production, and vice versa. However, the effects of the network on knowledge should not be, as Visvanathan (2001) reminds us, underestimated. The Chiapas, for instance, by taking political action via the network, provide 'information' about their cause, but they do not necessarily provide 'knowledge' of their cause. Still, the gap between information and knowledge should not be understood here in absolute terms, but, rather, contextualised as an ideological battleground where the agency of researchers, teachers and social movements is activated. To assume the absolute character of the distinction, in our opinion, would be a collapse into unproductive and constraining dichotomies such as pedagogy–performance and knowledge as education/formation–knowledge as competencies, or, in more strictly political terms, critical action within the system as opposed to critical action exterior to the system. It is in this sense that one may interpret the statement by Carnoy that 'knowledge production plays a definitive role (in the *network state*) ... in managing and compensating the disequalising effects of globalisation locally' (2001, p. 31).

If one admits that a new mandate for education with respect to the development of individual capacities is underway, then what is the *locus* of our refusal to dichotomise the educational debate between these two poles? That which is, in Dale's terms (1989), desirable and possible to carry out by the education system, in the context of a network society and state, does not appear to us to arise as if one had to choose between a *corpus* of knowledge able to provide the 'truth' about nature, societies and social and human relations, and the enlightened nature of knowledge capable of inducing individual and group liberty. What is at stake here is, rather, the reconfiguration of the limits and potentialities of the very concept of 'mandate'. Education hardly arises today, in the research in the social and human sciences, as a privileged field for steering social change, nor does it appear to arise as universal and definitive content. The epistemological fragility of knowledge does not dilute its formative character and, simultaneously, informationalism, in itself, does not empty knowledge of its potential for political and social intervention.

Notes

[1] Although we wish to distance ourselves somewhat from Manuel Castells' apparent technological determinism, we take on, within the economy of this text and in operational terms, his definition of the network: 'networks constitute the new morphology of our societies, and the diffusion of network logic substantially modifies the operation and outcomes in processes of production, experience, power and culture. While the networking form of social organisation has existed in other times and places, the new informational technology paradigm provides the material base for its pervasive expansion throughout the entire social structure. Furthermore, I would argue that this networking logic induces a social determination of a higher level than that of specific social interests expressed through the networks: the power of flows takes precedence over the flows of power. ... Networks are open structures, able to expand without limits, integrating new nodes as long as they are able to communicate within the network, namely as long as they share the same communication codes (for example, values for performance goals). A network-based social structure is a highly dynamic, open system susceptible to innovating without upsetting its balance' (Castells, 1996, pp. 469-70).

[2] See Cortesão et al (2000) for the matrix of the conception of policy as susceptible to being managed, piloted or surfed.

[3] We know that the dichotomy between generic labour and self-programmable labour (Castells, 1996) introduces important nuances into this complex game,

such that that which we have affirmed here is more in accord with the latter than with the former (see Magalhães & Stoer, 2002).

References

Abrantes, Paulo (2001) Nota de apresentação in Ministério da Educação (Portugal). *Currículo Nacional do Ensino Básico: competências essenciais.* Lisbon: Ministério da Educação, Departamento do Ensino Básico.

Alaluf, M. (1993) *Formation professionnelle et emploi: transformation des acteurs et effets de structures.* Brussels: Point d'Appui.

Alves, Ruben (2000) *Por uma Educação Romântica.* Vila Nova de Famalicão: Centro de Formação Camilo Castelo Branco.

Barnett, Ronald (1997) *Higher Education: a critical business.* Buckingham: Society for Research into Higher Education and Open University Press.

Bauman, Zigmunt (2001) *The Individualized Society.* Cambridge: Polity Press.

Beck, Ulrich (1992) *The Risk Society.* London: Sage.

Bernstein, Basil (1990) *The Structuring of Pedagogic Discourse, Vol. IV. Class, Codes and Control.* London: Routledge.

Bernstein, Basil (1996) *Pedagogy, Symbolic Control and Identity.* London: Taylor & Francis.

Candeias, António (2002) Etat nation et éducation dans le contexte Européen: une approche socio-historique, in Jean-Marc Ferry & Séverine De Proost (Eds) *L'école au défi de l'Europe,* 17-33. Brussels: Editions Université de Bruxelles.

Carnoy, Martin (2001) The Role of the State in the New Global Economy, in Johan Muller, Nico Cloete & Shireen Badat (Eds) *Challanges of Globalisation: South African debates with Manuel Castells,* 22-34. Cape Town: Maskew Miller Longman.

Castells, Manuel (1996) *The Rise of the Network Society.* Cambridge: Blackwell.

Correia, José Alberto & Matos, Manuel (2001) *Solidões e solidariedades nos quotidianos dos professores.* Oporto: Edições ASA.

Correia, José Alberto & Matos, Manuel (2002) Da crise da escola ao escolocentrismo, in Stephen R. Stoer, Luiza Cortesão & José Alberto Correia (Eds) *Transnacionalização da Educação: da crise da educação à 'educação' da crise,* 91-117. Oporto: Edições Afrontamento.

Cortesão, Luiza, Magalhães, António M. & Stoer, Stephen R. (2000) Mapeando Decisões no Campo de Educaçãono Âmbito da Realização das Políticas Educativas, *Educação, Sociedade & Culturas,* 14, 45-58.

Cresson, Edith (1996) *Livro Branco: Ensinar e aprender. Rumo à sociedade cognitiva.* Luxemburg: Serviço das Publicações Oficiais das Comunidades Europeias.

Dale, Roger (1989) *The State and Education Policy.* Milton Keynes: Open University Press.

Giddens, Anthony (1990) *The Consequences of Modernity.* Cambridge: Polity Press.

Harvey, David (1989) *The Condition of Postmodernity: an inquiry into the origins of cultural change.* Oxford: Basil Blackwell.

Hegel, George W. Friedrich (1965) *Introduction aux leçons sur la philosophie de l'histoire.* Paris: Nouvelle Revue Française.

Lash, Scott (1994) Reflexivity and Its Doubles: structure, aesthetics, community, in Ulrich Beck, Anthony Giddens & Scott Lash (Eds) *Reflexive Modernization*, pp. 110-173. Cambridge: Polity Press.

Lyotard, Jean-François (1989) *A Condição Pós-Moderna.* Lisbon: Gradiva.

Magalhães, António M. & Stoer, Stephen R. (1998) *Orgulhosamente Filhos de Rousseau.* Oporto: Profedições.

Magalhães, António M. & Stoer, Stephen R. (2002) *A Escola para Todos e a Excelência Académica.* Oporto: Profedições.

Magalhães, António M. & Stoer, Stephen R. (2003) Performance, Citizenship and the Knowledge Society: a new mandate for European education policy, *Globalisation, Societies and Education*, 1, 41-66. http://dx.doi.org/10.1080/1476772032000061815

Ministry of Education (Portugal) (2001) *Currículo Nacional do Ensino Básico: competências essenciais.* Lisbon: Ministry of Education – Department of Basic Education.

Nóvoa, António (1998) L'Europe et l'éducation (analyse socio-historique des politiques éducatives européennes), in A. Nóvoa, *Histoire & comparaison (essais sur l'éducation)*, 85-120. Lisbon: Educa.

Nuyen, A. Tuan (1992) Lyotard on the Death of the Professor, *Educational Theory*, 42, 25-37. http://dx.doi.org/10.1111/j.1741-5446.1992.00025.x

Perrenoud, Philippe (2001) *Porquê construir competências a partir da escola?* Oporto: Edições ASA.

Santos, Boaventura de Sousa (1991) Ciência, in Manuel M. Carrilho (Ed.) *Dicionário do Pensamento Contemporâneo.* Lisbon: Publicações D. Quixote.

Stoer, Stephen R. (1994) Construindo A Escola Democrática Através do 'Campo da Recontextualização Pedagógica', *Educação, Sociedade & Culturas*, 1, 7-28.

Stoer, Stephen R., Rodrigues, David & Magalhães, António M. (2003) *Theories of Social Exclusion.* Frankfurt am Main: Peter Lang.

Visvanathan, Shiv (2001) The Grand Sociology of Manuel Castells, in Johan Muller, Nico Cloete & Shireen Badat (Eds) *Challanges of Globalisation: South African debates with Manuel Castells*, 35-49. Cape Town: Maskew Miller Longman.

CHAPTER 3

Europe, Competitiveness and Higher Education: an evolving project

SUSAN ROBERTSON

SUMMARY Europe's approach to internationalising higher education is a multi-facetted set of political strategies which, over time, have become more complex as an array of European-level actors, most importantly the European Commission, have responded to pressures in the regional and global economy. This chapter examines a series of projects that have been unfolding over time and contributing to 'making' Europe and a European Education Space. The author focuses specific attention on the more recent activities that have resulting in Europe projecting itself outward into the global sphere through higher education reforms. This globalising European project, to build a competitive Europe and European Higher Education area, is also viewed as an imperialising project. This strategy begs questions as to its legitimacy. At the same time, it undermines Europe's discourse about its distinctive social project.

Introduction

'Europe's' approach to internationalising higher education is a multifaceted set of political strategies that, over time, has become more complex as an array of both national and European-level actors, and most importantly the European Commission, respond to pressures in the regional and global economies. This chapter explores this complexity, suggesting that Europe's inter/nationalising of higher education is a longstanding set of projects: *culturally* – to contribute to the construction of Europe as a distinctive entity; *economically* – to construct a competitive Europe; and, *politically* – to locate greater power at the supranational scale that would enable European-level actors more control over regional and global affairs.

The discourse of 'internationalising' education suggests that the power to direct education is located with Member States. However, in this chapter I will be arguing that the internationalising of higher education in Europe – or in other words the discourses that have driven the intensification of transborder activity across Member State boundaries – are more accurately represented as processes of regionalisation and, more recently, globalisation, and are the outcomes of social forces, both governmental and non-governmental (Cox, 1996), engaged in the progressive restructuring of European social relations in the global political economy. These processes can be discerned through tracing out three distinct, dynamic and overlapping policy trajectories which I develop below.

Crossing National Boundaries: higher education as the mechanism for creating Europe and its elites (1955-92)

Standard accounts of the early years of Europe's internationalising of higher education tend to begin with the creation of student mobility programmes in the 1980s (see Neave, 1995). However, as Corbett (2003, 2005) argues, the period prior to the 1970s was a highly political and active one for policymaking in the area of higher education and thus 'an essential input into understanding the policy-making process that developed after 1971' (2003, p. 315). This history begins in June 1955, when senior ministers of the European Coal and Steel Community [1] (later to become the European Economic Community [EEC] in 1958) met to consider a basis for extending European integration. At this meeting a proposal was tabled to create a European University (Corbett, 2003, p. 317), the realisation of which took almost two decades (in 1971). The reason for this delay was that creating a European higher education institution at this particular historical juncture was highly problematic. The heads of state agreed that education was not to be part of the Community's competence, and that it was a 'national' affair. There were also fundamental differences of view amongst the six Member States over what a university should look like. Yet, at the same time, the proposed university offered the potential to advance particular nationally based political agendas. The French, for example, were attracted to the creation of a university as a vehicle for a European representation of science and research training, while the Italians wanted in on their soil. The universities, for their part, were keen to develop a European dimension to their mobility and exchange programmes (Corbett, 2003, p. 319). It was, as Corbett shows, a highly political process, as much shaped by already existing structures, the activities of policy entrepreneurs and unexpected events. In 1971, the ministers agreed to set up a European University Institute in Florence.

It was during this same period that a deal was made by the European partners on cooperation around education. The Hague Summit in November 1969 called for a widening and deepening of the EEC (Corbett, 2003, p. 319), including education, and was supported by more European-minded university associations. However, there was also an emerging view amongst Europhiles that there needed to be European-minded people to run the expanding Community and larger Commission [2], and that these individuals needed to be educated in such a way as to protect and progress the idea of a European culture and European values.

In 1974 the ministers of education set the principles of cooperation in motion. In 1976, following a Resolution of the Council and Ministers of Education, an action programme was established in the field of education (Huisman & van der Wende, 2004, p. 350). As Corbett (2005, p. 95) notes, 'the issue was no longer whether the community should play a role in higher education/education. Rather, it was "what the appropriate mechanisms were for advancing cooperation?"' These decisions and actions entailed cooperation on the development of closer relations between education systems in Europe, increased cooperation between institutions of higher education, possibilities for recognition of qualifications, and freer movement of teachers, students and research workers (Corbett, 2003, p. 321).

These proposals mirrored the preferred means of cooperation amongst the higher education institutions; that is, bottom-up, and willing to network on a European scale with no real interference at the supranational scale. In other words, implementation itself would reside with Member States rather than at this emerging regional scale. As Corbett details, the success of the Commission in moving into this new policy arena was the result of some very clever framing by Commission personnel; that the European Commission was a set of resources (soft governance) rather than a means of regulation (hard governance) (Corbett, 2005, p. 96). However, whether soft or hard, governance means governing (Borras & Jacobsson, 2003). Through soft governance, the EC had already begun to provide some direction to higher education policy and a higher education area. There was, however, deep suspicion by some Member States (e.g. Danes, British, French) that the EC was moving beyond its spheres of competence and intruding into areas of national sovereignty. Nevertheless, high-level Council initiatives continued to advance the idea of European integration (Corbett, 2005, p. 114) and regionalism.

Jacques Delors' appointment as President of the Commission in 1985 provided a fresh, more energetic and expansionary direction for the creation of Europe, especially in the face of more than two decades of relative stagnation (Bieler & Morton, 2001, p. 3). In 1985, the Commission published its famous White Paper, *Completing the Internal Market*, which proposed 300 measures designed to facilitate progress toward the completion of the internal market by 1992 through the abolition of non-tariff barriers (Bieler & Morton, 2001, p. 3). The Single European Act of 1987 not only spelled out the goals of the internal market – freedoms of goods, services, capital and labour – but it also strengthened a suite of European-level institutions, such as the European Court of Justice.

Delors [3] 'had a highly developed idea of education and the part it could play in his strategy for advancing European integration via the single market' (Corbett, 2005, p. 121). Two concerns came together which higher education programmes could mediate: how to create a single market on the one hand and a European citizen on the other whilst combating the narrow nationalism that would get in the way of the EC's territorialising project.

The Erasmus Programme, launched in 1987, was an ambitious response. Students could experience first-hand life in another Member State for a recognised period of study abroad; a pool of graduates would be produced with experience of regional cooperation; and the ties between citizens would be strengthened, consolidating the idea of a 'People's Europe' (Corbett, 2005, p. 130). The target number of students was 10% of the student population. While the rectors gave it their unanimous support, concerns were expressed at national level over jurisdiction and resources, and it was some time and with much high-level politicking that Erasmus was sealed as a deal.

This was a momentous occasion. For the first time, full Community authority was being exercised for higher education cooperation, with the agreement of the Member States. According to Teichler (1999, p. 11), Erasmus also 'triggered off a re-thinking in higher education' largely because it challenged the typical model of international movement of students (from the colonised south to the imperialising north). However, evidence would soon emerge that suggested there was a significant shortfall in reaching the target of 10%, and that 10 years on, little more than 1% of students had been involved (see Teichler, 1999). Recent figures suggest that this pattern has not changed much (Huisman & van der Wende, 2004, p. 350); in 2005, Erasmus scholarships had supported only 1.4 million students (European Commission, 2005a). However, as Teichler (1999) noted: 'The numbers were sufficiently large to lift student mobility within Europe from an exceptional activity of the individual to a phenomenon which forced institutions of higher education to reconsider their curricula and their services for these students' (p. 11). Mobility also revealed the diverse nature of national higher education systems across the Member States, and the complicated issue of credit transfer.

In reviewing this first phase or policy trajectory, the internationalising higher education discourse was distinctively regional in scope and ambition. Movements that were facilitated by programmes, such as Erasmus or the European University Institute, whilst contained within the borders of the Community, were to produce Europe as a region and an entity, and promote European values. That those borders were being redrawn over time to include new members [4] made the regionalising project – in particular its political dimensions and cultural challenges – more pressing. Culturally, the concern was to create a European citizen with a European sensibility and sense of responsibility to a bigger political entity – Europe. Economically, higher education would contribute a pool of graduates for the single market, while politically this pool of graduates would be the new intelligentsia for European governing. Erasmus, when it was finally launched, was to be the main vehicle for this regionalising project. Modelled on existing activity [5], it was supported by a network of university rectors and academics [6] who, in turn, became its advocates. This enabled the Commission to promote a European agenda for higher education without charges of it undermining national sovereignty – a strategy that it learnt to pursue later on. The production of Europe as a region, using institutional capacity within higher education and instruments such as Erasmus, was profoundly shaped by the politics of post-war reconstruction and economic survival. In that sense, regionalisation was intimately linked to the global, even if it had not yet come to be theorised in that way.

Creating the New Europe and Europe of Knowledge through Blurring National Boundaries

In 1992, a single market and European Union were created under the Treaty of the European Union (Maastricht Treaty). The Maastricht Treaty, for the first time, gave the European Union a direct role in education. Losing no time, the Commission made an internal assessment of its programmes and developed a new strategy. Whilst the Maastricht Treaty appeared to suggest that the role would be modest, the European Commission, still under the presidency of Jacques Delors, had other ambitions. A 1991 *Memorandum on Higher Education* shows that higher education 'had already become part of the Community's broader agenda of economic and social coherence' (Huisman & van der Wende, 2004, p. 350). The Commission also began to look outward beyond the region, establishing programmes with non-EU third countries, for example the ALPHA programme in Latin America, and the Asia–Europe Link with ASEAN [7] countries.

To make sense of the politics behind the Memorandum and the events that followed, it is critical that we consider the changing nature of the wider economic and geopolitical context. In 1991-92 the biggest economies (including Germany) experienced a recession which increased the number of unemployed graduates in Europe (Teichler & Kehm, 1995). This provided some legitimacy for the EC's higher education project. However, of greater significance were the wider changes taking place in the global economy as a result of economic globalisation: the transnationalisation of production and finance at the material level, and the shift from Keynesianism to neoliberalism at the ideological level (Cox, 1993, pp. 259-260). These structural changes in the global economy not only had important implications for the EU, but they directly affected the restructuring of the EU. To be competitive in the global economy, Europe had to transform itself along free trade and free market lines. As Bieler & Morton (2001) argue:

> the deregulation of the national financial markets was institutionalised in the Internal Market Programme ... while the shift toward neo-liberalism was expressed by the very nature of the Internal Market programme and its drive for liberalisation and the neo-liberal convergence criteria of EMU [European Monetary Union] focusing on low inflation and price stability. (p. 5)

The ascendancy of neoliberal theory in policymaking gave prominence to particular ways of looking at (higher) education – as human capital, as an engine for economic growth, as a private rather than public good, and as a new services sector within the economy. This was reflected in European-level policymaking and instruments such as a Europe of Knowledge, a European knowledge-based economy, technology policy, research and development, and so on. These policies aligned themselves with the view, long promoted by the Organisation for Economic and Cooperative Development (OECD) (see Mattelart, 2003), that post-industrial societies would be information or knowledge based.

Creating the 'New Europe' – to formally include a European Higher Education Area and European Research Area (ERA) – was both a response to and outcome of these wider dynamics. In January 2000, upon the proposal of the European Commission, a decision was taken to establish a European Research and Innovation Area (ERIA). The principal objective of the ERIA was to create a knowledge-based economy – the Europe of Knowledge. The mandate and agenda for doing this was articulated in the now-famous Lisbon Strategy, part of the EU's wider economic platform. That:

> the European Union must become the most competitive and dynamic knowledge-based economy in the world capable of sustainable economic growth with more and better jobs and greater social cohesion. (European Council, 2001, p. 1)

This meant extending the reach of Europe's constitutionally framed 'competence' deeper into national territory – education.

Like the Erasmus initiative, which grafted itself onto an existing scheme, the Lisbon Agenda also had a mechanism it could turn to: the Bologna Process (Bologna Declaration, 1999). Launched in 1999, the Bologna Process aimed at creating a European Higher Education Area. Like with the Erasmus negotiations, the Bologna Process had been set in train, not by the Commission but by the European Universities Association (EUA) and endorsed by the European ministers of education (Tomusk, 2004). Much is made of this fact, particularly by the Commission, who continue to be highly sensitive to charges of interference in 'national' affairs. However, the Commission is a key stakeholder in the process, and has been active in promoting the Process in the interests of the Lisbon Agenda and Europe's overall position in the global economy.

The Bologna Declaration committed an initial set of 29 signatories to six objectives which, together, aimed to establish a European Higher Education Area (EHEA) by 2010 (European Universities Association, 2006). Within the EHEA, staff and student mobility is to be enhanced by the alignment of national quality assurance agencies, uniform degree structures, the adoption of a credit transfer system and a common way of describing the qualification (diploma supplement). Responsibility for implementing the goals of the Bologna Declaration in each signatory country lies with its academic institutions, student organisations and professional bodies. It is, however, a profoundly 'European Project' in ambition, substance and interests. The Bologna Follow-Up Group has overall steerage of the Bologna Process, it is chaired by the EU Presidency, and it is composed of representatives of the Member States along with the European Commission, the Council of Europe, the National Union of Students in Europe and the European Association of Institutions in Higher Education.

At one level, the Bologna Process appears to have none of the high drama that might be associated with such a revolutionary move. Sorting out a system of credit transfer for undergraduate and Master's-level courses (cycles 1 and 2), a means of making degrees readable, and determining mechanisms of quality assurance are, in themselves, technical procedures. However, like all technical matters, they are also highly political, and in a world where the higher education sector is increasingly viewed as an engine for the knowledge-based economy, the stakes are high. Yet, developing a supranational (or European) higher education system means running headlong into national and local interests. The language used to describe the Bologna Process, as a tool to *connect* education systems so as to ensure the diversity of national systems rather than producing harmonisation (see European Universities Association, 2006, p. 2), suggests how sensitive it is to charges of meddling in national affairs. Yet, in anyone's language, the realisation of a European higher education system is a dramatic change in the political and economic landscape of the region. The scale of the Bologna Process initiative can be appreciated in the following facts: that it involves around 5600 public and private institutions hosting 16 million students and is growing. The EHEA is conceptualised as a vast reservoir of talent for the economy and a vehicle through which a coherent 'European' sensibility could be built. By constructing an EHEA, it is also possible to make it intelligible as a single system (rather than the sum of many) and thus a destination and market for international students.

Indeed, the stakes were sufficiently high to cause the Australian government to release a paper entitled *The Bologna Process and Australia: next steps* (Bishop, 2006). It also put into place a series of projects [8] that might enable Australia to develop 'Bologna comparability' (Australian Vice-Chancellor's Committee, 2006, pp. 6, 9) and to assess whether any of the

Asia-Pacific governments are intending to implement the Bologna structures (p. 7) – for a significant proportion of Australia's education export income comes from European and Asian students studying graduate programmes in Australia. Australia has a huge share of the international student market (Australia Technology Network, 2005, p. 1) and to stay globally competitive it has to monitor developments that might undermine its position in the global marketplace.

The USA has also reacted to the Bologna Process, in part because of the sheer size of the EHEA and its mobilisation of various instruments to recruit brainpower for the European economy, but also because of ongoing concerns about the USA's global position in higher education (Robertson & Keeling, 2007). In 2006 US Education Secretary Margaret Spellings convened the Spellings Commission in order to stimulate a national dialogue on higher education. Whilst primarily focused upon national issues, such as the efficiency and effectiveness of higher education institutions in the USA, central to the Commission's remit was a concern over the ability of the USA to develop and attract the world's best minds for the economy.

The Bologna Process is also very expansionist. This has taken a number of forms (see Zgaga, 2007). The first is with membership of the EHEA. From the initial 29 signatories in 1999 the number rapidly rose to 45. The European Higher Education Area now includes Russia and southeast Europe, extending far beyond 'Europe' as a constitutional entity. The flexibility of the European boundary, so as to include bordering countries who are not members of the EU, suggests that Bologna is strategically deployed to: 1. limit the encroachment of foreign, for instance USA-based, private higher education providers into territories that border the EU (Scott, 2002); 2. expand the pool of educated labour beyond the EU boundary; 3. provide a template for quality for public and private higher education institutions in these post-communist countries (Fried et al, 2006), and give additional dynamism to the process (Tomusk, 2004, p. 86).

Second, projects like 'Tuning Educational Structures in Europe' have been incorporated into the Bologna Process as a solution to a particular kind of problem: how to 'translate' curriculum experiences from across diverse institutional and national settings into equivalents, enabling translatability, coherence and mobility.[9] 'Tuning', as it has come to be known, was funded under the Erasmus Thematic Network Programme of the EC and extends to all universities in the European Higher Education Area. The mechanism of translation developed by this network is the development of a hierarchical framework of general and specific competencies and learning outcomes. Much is made of the fact that tuning is driven by institutions in Member States. However, not only did the Commission choose to fund and then champion the Tuning Project, but other Erasmus Thematic Networks were required (in other words this was not negotiable) to 'tune' their curricula.

Third, under the auspices of the Bologna Process [10], new items have been added to the agenda intended to realise the aim of a European knowledge society (see European Universities Association, 2005). In the Berlin 2003 meeting, PhD programmes were included in the scope of the European Higher Education Area (Berlin Communique, 2003; European Universities Association, 2005). This resulted in the EUA sponsoring a project on doctoral careers [11] as well as running a series of workshops for universities on the organisation of doctoral/graduate schools in a European context.[12] This work has a strong pedagogical and governance thrust. This can be seen, for instance, in concerns over appropriate forms of supervision and viva arrangements, and in the recommendation that data on completion rates and career outcomes be collected. The idea of a European Doctorate (or Doctor Europaeus) is viewed by the EUA as a 'a powerful tool for making the Lisbon objectives more visible and for making the doctoral degree more attractive to young people as a symbol of European research collaboration'. In addition, '[a]n open debate on the European doctorate should be part of a wider discussion on internationalisation of higher education and research and on building a competitive European Higher Education Area' (European Universities Association, 2005, pp. 29-30). The focus on PhD training and programmes is viewed as a necessary bridge between the European Higher Education Area and the European Research and Innovation Area.

Two years later at the 2005 Bergen meeting, the Bologna Follow-Up Group (BFUG) adopted an overarching framework for qualifications and agreed upon a set of European standards and guidelines for quality assurance. This includes nationally based quality assurance agencies submitting themselves to a cycle of review; the development of a European register of quality assurance agencies 'making it easier to identify professional and creditable agencies' (European Universities Association, 2006, p. 6); the creation of a European Register Committee to oversee the inclusion of agencies on the register; and the establishment of an annual forum so that quality assurance agencies, universities and other stakeholders could meet and discuss ongoing issues (European Universities Association, 2006).

Developments under Bologna contribute to a thickening landscape of European structures, policies and programmes that register and translate the experiences of the European learner and worker. The European Qualifications Framework (launched in 2005) (European Commission, 2005b, p. 4) is a meta-framework consisting of common reference points (some developed by the Tuning Project) at eight levels. This enables users to see how qualifications embedded in national systems relate to each other (European Commission, 2005b, p. 12). It is also intended to capture the complexity of lifelong learning and promote the mobility of learners and workers (European Commission, 2005b, p. 7).

The Europass [13], on the other hand, is the individual's learning and working ID [14] and it is expected that three million Europeans (though this is less than a very modest 1%) will adopt this by 2010. 'It is designed to encourage mobility and lifelong learning in an enlarged Europe' (European Commission, 2005c). The Europass consists of five documents:

- Europass CV (common CV structure);
- Europass Mobility (record in a common format of transnational mobility for learning purposes);
- Europass Diploma Supplement (personal document which records the holder's educational record);
- Europass Certificate Supplement (supplement of vocational education and training), and Europass Language Portfolio (record of linguistic skills).[15]

While the Bologna Process (reform of structures), tuning (instrument for translation) and the European Qualifications Framework (hierarchy of qualifications) are mechanisms for making education experiences and education systems across Member States intelligible at a European scale, the Europass carries the individually encoded information on learning and workplace experiences. In other words, qualifications and competences are a currency that can be earned and spent across Europe.[16] Critics, however, argue that the Europass does not address more fundamental issues associated with barriers to mobility such as professional accreditation, language and xenophobia. Others suggest that the one-size-fits-all CV might well be jettisoned by more creative and competitive individuals, keen to show their difference from rather than adherence to a European script (see debate in Observatory on Borderless Higher Education, 2006, p. 2).

In reviewing the nature and consequences of the internationalising of higher education in this second policy trajectory, the discourse of a globally competitive knowledge economy, and obstacles to achieving that, provide the rationale and legitimacy for the creation of a European higher education system. The effect of this has been to force upon Member States, and invite, if not challenge, those beyond to engage in, dramatic structural changes in their higher education systems. Politically, regionalising education has blurred the boundaries around Member States' spheres of interest and opened up the higher education territory of Member States to the European-level governance sphere. And while the key actors insist that these processes are driven by Member States, there is considerable evidence that there is a coalition of social forces at the European scale who are shaping the regionalising project. What this second trajectory also reveals is the remarkable extension of the Bologna Process beyond the borders of constitutional Europe (Kwiek, 2004), to include those on the perimeter of an expanding Europe who see themselves as Europeans, whose inclusion limits access by global education firms, and who provide a pool of educated labour on the periphery of the region (see European Commission, 2006b).

This is not to suggest that the Bologna Process has been willingly or wittingly embraced at the institutional (or indeed national) levels, or that the discursive and the material are direct reflections of each other. Nor is there a coherent view of Europe, or what it means to be European. Indeed, there is considerable evidence that engagement with Bologna is highly uneven across the European Higher Education Area [17] and may require concessions for the Eastern European and Balkan countries (Kwiek, 2004, p. 760). Neither do I want to suggest that becoming a part of the European Higher Education Area will benefit those inside it equally. As Kwiek notes:

> the promotion of mobility in higher education is likely to benefit those affluent, generally Western countries; thus from a national perspective, there are gains and losses of such increasing movement of the best talent available; for the more 'exporting' (transition) than 'importing' (old EU) countries, the issue is not going to be uncontroversial in the long run. (Kwiek, 2004, p. 770)

In other words, mobility giving rise to charges of brain drain will have effects on national and sub-national economies and policies of Member States. This may well result in the reinstatement and reinforcement of views that national interests need protecting.[18]

Destination 'Europe':
the European Higher Education Area as lure

If the internationalisation of higher education in the two earlier policy trajectories has been oriented predominantly toward a regionalising project, from around 2003 the EU began to pursue a more explicit globalising strategy. In a speech delivered in 2003 to the opening of the World Education Market, Viviane Reding, Member of the European Commission responsible for Education and Culture, laid out the bases for 'Making the EU a Prominent Figure in the World Education Market', arguing that 'national governments alone cannot meet the challenges of globalisation, new technologies and the single market' (Reding, 2003, p. 2). This includes a new role for the private sector. Internationalising European higher education is now externally oriented, market driven and globalising.

From 2003, a suite of programme initiatives have been launched, all characterised by a strong emphasis on global competitiveness and the development of a European higher education market. Initiatives include the recruitment of talent from around the globe (Erasmus Mundus), the sale of the idea of Bologna globally through the Tuning and Asia-Link Projects, and the creation a European higher education market and industry. These are outlined below.

The shift toward the global must be seen in the light of huge competition for international students in the globalising education industry, and awareness by the European Commission that, to date, Europe has little presence in the global market as a preferred destination.[19] Over two million students are enrolled in higher education institutions outside of their country of citizenship, and these numbers are expected to rise in the future, with some pundits suggesting figures like 7.6 million by 2025 (European Commission, 2004, p. 16). This concern is also seen in a variety of Commission policies and initiatives, for instance in the Asia-Link programme, where the Commission is working hard to spark interest in Europe in the Asian Imaginary (see Robertson, 2006) and through a series of funded Asia Fairs.[20] The Commission is also an aggressive negotiator in the World Trade Organization's General Agreement on Trade in Services (GATS) processes, and has been pursuing the liberalisation of education services in the various round of trade talks (Oxfam, 2005). However, Europe appears a long way from being able to create a globally competitive higher education industry, able to lure full foreign fee-paying students to Europe as the preferred destination, though the Commission is now supporting a marketing strategy for the EHEA (European Commission, 2006b, p. 7).

In 2004 a Commission-commissioned report on the perceptions of European higher education in third countries argued that the EU would have to determine a brand for itself if it was going to be able to compete with the USA and Australia as the preferred destination for students. It notes: 'Overall, Europe is not perceived as a union as regards higher education. However, when it comes to cultural aspects and higher education, most students saw Europe as a range of very different countries' (European Commission, 2004, p. 10). Furthermore, the report notes that Asian students in particular have a weak preference for Europe. 'Beyond this, respondents saw the most substantial discrepancies regarding cost-related issues (both tuition and living costs) and student support' (European Commission, 2004, p. 11). The discrepancy in tuition fees across Europe is viewed as a serious problem by those hoping to generate a competitive higher education market at the level of Europe. In a EUA survey in 2005, seven of the 27 EU countries charged fees to all students, seven charged fees to some students, and 13 did not charge fees at all, including 'foreign' students. Implementing a regime of student fees, even for international students, is regarded as a very controversial move in a number of EU Member States (see Huisman & van de Wende, 2004, p. 354; Observatory on Borderless Higher Education, 2005). Proposals to the Finnish Parliament to charge international students tuition fees were overturned in 2006.

A second example is the Erasmus Mundus Programme. Erasmus Mundus is intended to recruit the best brains from around the world and was launched along with urgings to mobilise the brainpower of Europe (European Commission, 2005d). This programme funds joint Masters that must operate across at least three European Union universities and is open to European and non-European students, though there is a particular emphasis on recruiting Asian students. The hope is that the best overseas talent might be retained in the EU, and that the EU's expenditure on Master's research training programmes will generate greater research activity across the region. The first phase of Erasmus Mundus is now running (2004-08), with the hope that it will support 250 Master's programmes and around 5000 scholarships. Comparing it with the USA's Fulbright Programme established in 1946, the European Union of Students has been highly critical of Erasmus Mundus, arguing that it will exaggerate problems of brain drain. It has also resulted in the USA operating in crisis mode to restore US competitiveness, arguing that 'the best and the brightest are a sought after commodity' (NAFSA, 2006, p. 1). The USA's position, of course, has been seriously jeopardised with tight security and immigration laws following September 11.

Thirdly, the Bologna Process, and associated projects like the Tuning Project, are being globalised (as well as receiving a global reaction – see above). In a Communiqué in 2006, the Commission argued that: 'Ministers see the European Higher Education Area as a partner of higher education systems in other regions of the world' and noted that: 'The role and visibility of higher education in EU external relations is increasingly toward neighbouring countries (European Neighbourhood Policy), in relation to industrialised nations (OECD/G8) and with developing countries (Alban, Asia-Link etc.)' (European Commission, 2006a, p. 7; Europa, 2006). The BFUG have also been given the mandate to elaborate and agree on a strategy for the external dimension in order to strengthen the attractiveness of the EHEA (Bologna Follow-Up Group, 2006). This strategy, to be with other regions rather than countries (Bologna Follow-Up Group, 2005), is to be tabled at the London 2007 Ministerial meeting. The task ahead is to create the conditions for international mobility (mode 4 of the GATS agreement), recognition structures, cooperation and attractiveness (see, for example, the Nordic Bologna Process Official Seminar held in September 2006).

In 2003, the Tuning Group – supported by the European Commission – launched its Latin American venture Tuning America Latina, funded under the ALPHA programme. This is an ambitious initiative. It involves 18 countries (including Argentina, Bolivia, Cuba, Mexico and Venezuela) and 180 universities. The subject areas that are being dealt with include education, history, medicine, geology, physics and mathematics. The venture has involved surveying students', employers' and universities' views on learning outcomes and competencies in the specified subject area, and then assembling these competencies so as to develop a tool of translation within the Latin American region, and in relation to the EU (Wagenaar, 2006). As Wagenaar (2006) also shows, the scope of ambition is not confined to Latin America. Russia, Asia and Asia are all on the radar for Tuning.

Despite these rather ambitious global strategies, a Mid Term Review (European Commission, 2005b) concluded that the Lisbon Strategy had failed to deliver a satisfactory economic growth performance and that Europe was far from achieving the potential for change that the Lisbon Strategy offered (see also Dion, 2005). The Review gave further impetus to a direction that was already well in train [21], though now there is a new sense of urgency surrounding many Commission reports (European Commission, 2005d) around mobilising the brainpower of Europe.

Civilising or Imperialising Europe?
A Problematic Subject

Through locating internationalising higher education within Europe historically and spatially, we can see the changing nature, scale and scope of this geopolitical project. It is also possible to see the complex structure of internationalised reality over time, as it is reflected in the principles embraced by the higher education policy agenda. Throughout, however, there are important continuities in the project. One is that rhetorically, the project of internationalising has continued to be constructed as activity that is driven by Member States. Yet, as we can see, it is profoundly European, both in terms of the actors progressing these changes and in the overall purpose – to build a European region that is able to more effectively compete in the global economy. The delicate line to tread has been, and continues to be, how to construct a European higher education system without charges of interference. This is a highly political process that is being progressed by a coalition of interests who operate on multiple scales (supranational, national and institutional) and who have been able to progress a radical agenda for higher education change. The discontinuity with the past is the scale, scope and consequences of the ideological and political regionalising and globalising project for higher education. Under the rubric of the knowledge-based economy, higher education is valued for its economic rather than cultural contribution, as a lucrative market and as a means for generating new value through innovation and patents.

It is possible to discern two strategies that have been pursued over time, using the discourse of internationalisation of higher education. The first is a regionalising strategy; to build a coherent set of structures that enable a European higher education system, and Europe, to come into existence. The second is the more recent globalising strategy in higher education which, as we see in this current phase, both legitimates the European Commission as a state-like actor on the global stage and provides a springboard for Europe's discursive and material-based competition with the USA for the hearts, minds and pockets of individuals in different various spheres of the world. While for a long time Europe has legitimated its activities by presenting itself as a civilising rather than imperialising presence, its more explicit economic and transnational interests open it up to charges of modern-day colonialism and imperialism. The question remains, then, as to how long Europe will be able to promote itself as a political alternative to Anglo-Saxon models of capitalist imperialist development, and how the USA, Australia, China and India might respond as they ratchet up the stakes.

There are also major tensions and contradictions within Europe that will mediate progress. These include how the European Union's strategies will work with or against those of its Member States and how the cultural and economic dimensions will be balanced against each other. There are also tensions that will, if they have not already, emerge between the two spheres of Europe: a constitutionally anchored sphere that provides citizenship entitlements, and a more expansive education space that entitles citizens to a Europass and Europeanised qualification, but none of the benefits of citizenship (e.g. European fees as opposed to 'foreign' fees). This raises all kinds of issues around the relationship between education, citizenship and entitlement in the European space which are yet to be debated.

Notes

[1] The ECSC was composed of Belgium, France, Italy, Luxembourg, the Netherlands and West Germany. It was later renamed the European Community.

[2] In 1973, Denmark, Ireland and the United Kingdom joined, taking the number of Member States to nine. It also meant that the Commission itself had to play a larger role.

[3] Delors was President of the European Commission from 1985-95.

[4] Greece joined in 1981, Portugal and Spain joined in 1986, and in 1990, East Germany became part of a unified Germany.

[5] The Joint Study Programme was the predecessor of Erasmus.

[6] The expansion in the number of Erasmus Thematic Networks in the last 10 years is a case in point.

[7] ASEAN – Association of South East Asian Nations. In 1967 this included Singapore, Thailand, Indonesia, Malaysia and the Philippines.

[8] Curtin University of Technology in Perth, Western Australia, is currently undertaking a feasibility study of implementing the Diploma Supplement.

[9] See http://www.europeunit.ac.uk/qualifications/tuning_project.cfm

[10] See http://www.eua.be/eua/en/bologna_basics.jspx

[11] Though only 22 countries across Europe were involved.

[12] See http://www.eua.be/eua/en/publications.jspx

[13] Available at a dedicated Europass Portal, see http://europass.cedefop.edu.int

[14] It was launched in 2004 and ratified by the European Parliament and Council.

[15] See http://ec.europa.eu/education/programmes/europass/index_en.html

[16] See http://www.europeunit.ac.uk/qualifications/index.cfm

[17] Accession countries display greater levels of commitment to the EU's internationalising programmes, such as Erasmus (PriceWaterhouseCoopers, 2005).**2006?**

[18] There are highly uneven patterns of mobility across Europe: for example, the lowest outbound mobility ratios are the UK (1%) and Spain (1.4%), whilst France, Germany, Greece and Italy have the largest number of mobile students (Observatory on Borderless Higher Education, 2006, p. 2).

[19] The UK (British Council), Germany (DAAD) and France (EduFrance) are all active exporters in the global marketplace.

Susan Robertson

[20] A series of seven events to promote European higher education, funded by the European Commission's Asia-Link Programme, is taking place in China, India, Indonesia, Malaysia, the Philippines, Thailand and Vietnam between 2006 and 2008. The European Higher Education Fairs will be organised by a consortium of four European agencies led by EduFrance (France) and composed of DAAD (Germany), Nuffic (Netherlands) and the British Council (United Kingdom). The events aim to increase the attractiveness of Europe as a study and research centre for excellence, to strengthen Europe's economic and cultural presence in Asia and vice versa, to enhance mutual awareness and contribute to the further development of EU–Asian cooperation in the field of higher education. Each event will be composed of two components: an Asia-Link Symposium and a European Higher Education Fair. The Symposia will provide a platform for high-level dialogue on EU–Asian cooperation and for developing awareness of EU mechanisms and programmes, while the Fairs will provide a platform for representatives of national structures and higher education institutions from all 25 EU Member States to give information on study opportunities in Europe. Applications to take part in the fairs and/or Asia-Link Symposia must be made online with deadlines varying according to the event of interest.

[21] An earlier Kok Report (2004) pointed to a general unwillingness to engage in Lisbon, too broad an agenda, poor coordination and conflicting priorities.

References

Australian Technology Network (2005) The Bologna Process and Australia: next steps – response from the Australia Technology Network (ATN), Australian Technology Network of Universities.

Australian Vice-Chancellor's Committee (2006) *AVCC Response to Discussion Paper – the Bologna Process and Australia, next steps*. Canberra: AVCC.

Berlin Communiqué (2003) Realising the European Higher Education Area. Communiqué of Ministers Responsible for Higher Education, Berlin, 19 September.

Bieler, A. & Morton, A. (Eds) (2001) Introduction: Neo-Gramscian perspectives in international political economy and the relevance to European integration, in A. Bieler & A. Morton (Eds) *Social Forces in the Making of the New Europe*. Basingstoke: Palgrave.

Bishop, J. (2006) *The Bologna Process and Australia: next steps*. Canberra: Australian Federal Department of Education, Skills and Training.

Bologna Declaration (1999) The European Higher Education Area. Joint Declaration of the European Ministers of Education convened in Bologna, 19 June.

Bologna Follow-Up Group (2005) Possible Bologna Partnership with Other Regions. BFG 4 10.

Bologna Follow-Up Group (2006) BFGUB11 6: BFUG Work Programme 2005-2007. http://www.dfes.gov.uk/bologna/

Borras, S. & Jacobsson, K. (2004) The Open Method of Coordination and New Governance Patterns in the EU, *Journal of European Public Policy*, 11(2), 185-208. http://dx.doi.org/10.1080/1350176042000194395

Corbett, A. (2003) Ideas, Institutions and Policy Entrepreneurs: toward a new history of higher education in the European Community, *European Journal of Education*, 38(3), 315-330. http://dx.doi.org/10.1111/1467-3435.00150

Corbett, A. (2005) *Universities and the Europe of Knowledge: ideas, institutions and policy entrepreneurship in European Union higher education 1955-2005*. Basingstoke: Palgrave.

Cox, R. (1993) Structural Issues of Global Governance: implications for Europe, in S. Gill (Ed.) *Gramsci, Historical Materialism and International Relations*. Cambridge: Cambridge University Press.

Cox, R. (1996) *Approaches to World Order*. Cambridge: Cambridge University Press.

Dion, D.-P. (2005) The Lisbon Process: a European odyssey, *European Journal of Education*, 40(3), 295-313. http://dx.doi.org/10.1111/j.1465-3435.2005.00227.x

Europa (2006) Press Release – Higher Education: the Commission supports university reforms in neighbouring countries. IP/06/998, 17 July. http://europa.eu/rapid/pressReleasesAction.do?reference=IP/06/998&format=HTML&aged=0&language=EN&guiLanguage=en last accessed 17/08/2006.

European Commission (2004) *Perceptions of European Higher Education in Third Countries*. Final Report Project 2004-3924/001-001 MUN-MUNA31. Brussels: EC.

European Commission (2005a) Erasmus Networks now Cover Nine-tenths of Europe's Universities. Press Release, 20 October. IP/05/1313.

European Commission (2005b) *Mid-term Review of the Lisbon Strategy*. Brussels: EC.

European Commission (2005c) *Toward a European Qualifications Framework for Lifelong Learning*. Commission Staff Working Document, SEC(2005) 957. Brussels: European Commission.

European Commission (2005d) *Mobilising the Brainpower of Europe: enabling universities to make their full contribution to the Lisbon Strategy*. Brussels: EC.

European Commission (2006a) Higher Education: the Commission supports university reforms in neighbouring countries. Press release, 17 July. IP/06/998.

European Commission (2006b) *From Bergen to London: the EU contribution*. Brussels: EC.

European Council (2001) *The Concrete Future Objectives of Education and Training Systems*. A report to the European Council, 5980/01. Brussels: European Council.

European Universities Association (2005) *Doctoral Programmes for the European Knowledge Society: report on the EUA Doctoral Programmes Project 2004-2005*. Brussels: EUA.

European Universities Association (2006) *Europe's New Higher Education Landscape*. Brussels: EUA.

Fried, J., Glass, A. & Baumgartl, B. (2006) Summary of an Extended Comparative Analysis on European Private Higher Education, *Higher Education in Europe*, 31(1), 3-9. http://dx.doi.org/10.1080/03797720600859007

Huisman, J. & van der Wende, M. (2004) The EU and Bologna: are supra- and international initiatives threatening domestic agendas? *European Journal of Education*, 39(3), 349-357. http://dx.doi.org/10.1111/j.1465-3435.2004.00188.x

Kok Report (2004) *Facing the Challenge: the Lisbon Strategy for growth and employment.* Brussels: European Commission.

Kwiek, M. (2004) The Emergent European Educational Policies Under Scrutiny: the Bologna Process from a Central European perspective, *European Educational Research Journal*, 3(4), 759-776. http://dx.doi.org/10.2304/eerj.2004.3.4.3

Mattelart, A. (2003) *The Information Society.* London: Sage.

NAFSA (2006) *Restoring US Competitiveness for International Students and Scholars.* Washington: Association of International Educators.

Neave, G. (1995) On Living in Interesting Times: higher education in Western Europe 1985-1995, *European Journal of Education*, 30(4), 377-393. http://dx.doi.org/10.2307/1503512

Observatory on Borderless Higher Education (2006) Are Tertiary Students Really Becoming More Mobile? The Latest Findings from the UNESCO Institute for Statistics. Breaking News Article, 7 June. http://www.obhe.ac.uk/cgi-bin/news/article.pl?id+559&mode=month

Oxfam (2005) *What Happened in Hong Kong? Initial Analysis of the WTO Ministerial.* Oxfam Briefing Paper. London: Oxfam.

PriceWaterHouseCoopers (2006) *Review of the Erasmus Programme.* Twente: Center for Higher Education Policy Studies.

Reding, V. (2003) Making the EU a Prominent Figure in the World Education Market. SPEECH/03/254.

Robertson, S. (2006) Regionalism, 'Europe/Asia' and Higher Education, paper presented to the Association of American Geographers, 7-11 March, Chicago.

Robertson, S. & Keeling, R. (2007) Stirring the Lions: strategy and tactics in global higher education, European Union Studies Association Conference, Montreal, 18 May.

Scott, P. (2002) Reflections on the Reform of Higher Education in Central and Eastern Europe, *Higher Education in Europe*, XXVII(1-2), 137-152. http://dx.doi.org/10.1080/0379772022000003288

Teichler, U. (1999) Internationalisation as a Challenge for Higher Education in Europe, *Tertiary Education and Management*, 5, 5-23. http://dx.doi.org/10.1023/A:1018736718422

Teichler, U. & Kehm, B. (1995) Toward a New Understanding of the Relationship between Higher Education and Employment, *European Journal of Education*, 30(2), 115-132. http://dx.doi.org/10.2307/1503524

Tomusk, V. (2004) Three Bolognas and a Pizza Pie: notes on institutionalisation of the European higher education system, *International Studies in Sociology of Education*, 14(1), 75-95. http://dx.doi.org/10.1080/09620210400200120

Wagenaar, R. (2006) European and National Qualification Frameworks and the Contribution of Tuning: an overview of project outcomes, presentation to the Tuning Conference, Brussels, June.

Zgaga, P. (2007) *Looking Out: the Bologna Process in a global setting – on the external dimension of the Bologna Process*. Oslo: Norwegian Ministry of Education Research.

CHAPTER 4

Lifelong Learning as Social Need and as Policy Discourse

PALLE RASMUSSEN

SUMMARY Lifelong learning is a key concept in EU policy documents not only on education, but also on economic competitiveness and social cohesion. The discourse on lifelong learning has been strongly criticised by educational researchers, who document that it often reflects narrow notions of learning and neoliberal ideology. However, the concept of lifelong learning is basically sound and promising, because people in the contemporary world increasingly have and express needs to learn in order to handle the social transformations, opportunities and risks they experience. Drawing on Habermas' conceptualisation of systemic and communicative processes in modern society this chapter discusses the social need for learning and its policy implications. The development of lifelong learning provision under the conditions of globalisation and Europeanisation is traced and serious limitations in the policies of EU and other international actors are pointed out. The concept of lifelong learning needs to reinterpreted in order to connect to the social need for learning.

Introduction

Lifelong learning has emerged as an important issue in educational policy during the last two decades. UNESCO, the World Bank, the Organisation for Economic Co-operation and Development and the EU have all adopted and propagated the concept, and although there have been considerable differences between their versions of lifelong learning, they all see it as a positive and necessary response to the challenges of economic and social modernisation. National governments have followed suit, most visibly in Europe, and have placed lifelong learning firmly on their policy agendas. Implementation in educational practices has been uneven and sometimes slow, but participation in adult education and training has generally increased (Larson, 2006).

The steady flow of policy discourse on lifelong learning has met with much criticism from educational research. In the words of one researcher this has become 'something of a growth industry' (Rubenson, 2006, p. 152). The keenness of the criticism is probably not unrelated to the fact that the policies have been disseminated by powerful transnational agencies and have often been perceived as impositions in national educational contexts. Critics have documented how official versions of lifelong learning policy are often permeated with narrow utilitarian and technological notions of learning, neoliberal ideology and undocumented assumptions about the competences needed in modern economies. I share much of this criticism, as will become evident below, but I think that it is often allowed to overshadow the positive potential and promise of lifelong learning. In my view the focus on lifelong learning is not a superficial twist of policy; it reflects the fact that people in the contemporary world have and express an increasing need for learning in order to handle the social transformations they are experiencing. The purpose of this paper is on one hand to elucidate the character of the human and social need for lifelong learning, on the other hand to illustrate how educational policies for lifelong learning are developed without sufficient awareness of these needs and often institutionalised in narrow ways that do not really address the situations and potentials of the learners.

Education, Learning, Lifelong

Until fairly recently the predominant themes in discourses on education concerned questions of curriculum, teaching and control in primary and (to a lesser extent) secondary schooling. Sometimes issues in higher education were also debated by more limited audiences, but the focus was on educational institutions, on 'the school'. During the last one or two decades this has partially changed. Today much interest is also taken in learning and acquisition of skills outside school, in training schemes, on the job or in other areas of adult life. Policies are being developed that do not focus primarily on educational institutions but rather on learning in different settings over the life course. This represents a change in both policy and educational theory, a change that has sometimes misleadingly been labelled 'from education to learning'. However, it is not a question of giving up the concept of education and the institutions linked to it; it is a question of seeing institutional education as an element (and a vital element) in processes of learning that also include other elements.

Learning can be defined as a process of creating change through the accumulation of knowledge and competence. This process is cognitive as well as emotional and social, and it goes all through the human life course. But learning does not only change individuals; through the individuals it also affects and changes the organisations and institutions which the individuals are part of. Learning takes place both in educational institutions and in many other contexts, and the interaction and coordination of different learning contexts is very important to the quality of learning.

Today the concept of learning is used in many more areas than the educational sector. A prime example is the idea of 'learning organisations', which has been widely taken up in private business as well as in public administration. Another example is concepts of learning cities and regions, which have had considerable impact in regional development policies. The popularity of the word 'learning' and its inclusion in the rhetoric of both policymakers and business gurus does not help to clarify the implications of the concept. But in my view it reflects an important paradigmatic change in the conceptualisation of educational phenomena and the implementation of educational practices.

The widespread acceptance and use of the concept of lifelong learning also signals this paradigmatic change. To be sure the concept is most often used in a restricted sense, covering programmes and practices in adult education and training that have generally existed on the margins of educational systems. But the logic of lifelong learning implies that all stages of education (preschool, primary and secondary schooling, vocational education, higher education, adult education) as well as contexts for learning outside institutionalised education should be seen and developed within a common framework. The European Commission's recent initiative to place all its educational programmes under the umbrella of lifelong learning (European Commission, 2006) is an example of this logic, as are the various attempts to develop common frameworks for describing and recognising competencies acquired in education and in other contexts. I emphasise that these examples serve to illustrate the implications of the concept of lifelong learning, not as a claim that these implications are generally being realised in educational and social policy.

Using the concept of lifelong learning instead of education or training also implies that the responsibility for developing persons' knowledge, skills and identity does not rest solely or even primarily with the educational institutions. If this is taken seriously it demands two qualities of institutions and persons who are to support learning. Firstly, they must see learning in the context of the whole life course. Secondly, they should not be rooted in only one area of learning, no matter how important this area may seem.

Nevertheless, educational institutions are still crucial to lifelong learning. Much experience in organising and supporting processes of learning has been accumulated in educational institutions, and institutions in other areas of social life (like workplaces) have not been used to taking responsibility for learning in more than a very narrow sense. But educational institutions and teachers will increasingly have to use their professional knowledge and experience in new and more versatile ways; in supporting the interaction of learning in schools, workplaces and other sites they are increasingly called on not only to teach, but also to supervise, coach, plan, mediate and coordinate.

One risk in the current focus on learning is that it may partly obscure the social differences and conflicts in which learning and education are embedded. In many discourses learning appears primarily as a process of growth in cognitive or technical competence, more or less independent of values or social interests. The fact that the concept of learning is not directly linked with the traditional educational institutions and their cultures may contribute to this. The same types of discourse have of course flourished around the concept of the knowledge society. However, this picture has to be corrected. Learning is no less a social process than education. On the contrary; learning takes place through many more social contexts than schools and other educational institutions, and processes of learning reflect the social differences of all these contexts.

The Social Need for Lifelong Learning

The second half of the twentieth century was characterised by a massive growth in educational participation. The patterns of growth depended on the pre-existing levels of education, the available resources and the educational structures in different nations and regions. In many developing nations emphasis was on extending real participation in primary education to all children and young people; in many western nations the emphasis was on accommodating increasing enrolments in secondary and higher education. It has been argued by some (for instance Archer, 1982) that existing educational systems played a crucial role in educational expansion by instituting principles of 'sequence' that enabled and encouraged students to pass on to higher levels of education and thus stay in the system. However, one area of educational expansion is difficult to explain in this way – the proliferation of adult education schemes and the growing participation in them. Regardless of their level of education adult persons have been outside the educational system for some time and are more or less tied up by work, family obligations and other activities. Although educational institutions may try to attract them, their decision to participate in education will primarily be based on experienced needs for learning and/or educational credentials. The character of these needs will of course depend on the frameworks within which they are experienced; for instance, some employees may have need of training in certain skills not because they have experienced this need in their daily work but because their employer has decided that these skills are a precondition for holding the job.

When persons express their perceived need for education and learning, it is often conceptualised as a 'social demand' for education. This is probably a reasonable representation of how manifested needs look from the side of the suppliers of education. I use the term 'social need' here not with reference to any specific model or hierarchy of human needs, but in order to highlight the background to educational participation in adults' lives.

The existence of a fundamental social need for learning has been highlighted by many scholars of adult education and learning (see Jarvis, 2006). This need is evident in a multitude of specific situations in adults' lives as employees, as citizens, as family members and parents, as consumers and other areas. In order to state the need for learning in more general terms I shall draw on Habermas's theory of communicative action.

In Habermas's conceptualisation of modern society, which he has presented most comprehensively in his massive *Theory of Communicative Action* (Habermas, 1984-87), different types of rationality are embedded in cultural and social contexts and are reproduced through different types of action. Communicative rationality, which has the potential to humanise the social order, is anchored in the life-world and upheld through communicative action. Reflexive learning is an important part of this process.

The concept of rationality is a controversial one in social theory. It has often been denounced as a obsolete residue of idealist philosophy. Habermas, however, maintains that a critical theory of society must include a theory of rationality, because the world we live in is still in many ways determined by the process which Weber called 'the disenchantment of the Western world'. Social theory must be able to grasp this process of rationalisation.

Habermas conceptualises the development of rationality as an inter-subjective process in which the human subject relates to a world of objects but also to other subjects, with whom it may communicate over ways to relate to the world of objects. The learning of communicative rationality must be seen as a continuous process where participants improve their competence in offering and responding to communicative acts, and at the same time confirm their attachment to the community. The availability of communication 'tools', mainly in the form of linguistic systems of communication, makes it possible to stabilise the outcomes of learning, both in social organisation and in the minds of subjects. In Habermas's theory, the 'place' of this stabilised learning is the life-world. This concept signifies the horizon of communication, the frame of reference which is common to speaker and listener, and which enables them to understand each other. Thus, the life-world mainly consists of 'tacit knowledge' founded in everyday life. The life-world is continuously reproduced through communicative action. If distortion of communication takes place it threatens the reproduction of the life-world. Because of changes and crises in social life communicative rationality is not something learned once and for all; it will often have to be recontextualised and relearned.

At a very general level Habermas's theory indicates how learning is needed to develop and uphold life-worlds and communicative rationality and how this need is present throughout human life courses.

At a less general level the social need for lifelong learning manifests itself in the challenges adult persons encounter in different areas of life in contemporary society. Changing and increasing demands for job skills make it necessary to supplement on-the-job training with more systematic and general education. There are also increasing demands for skills in other areas of life, for instance maintaining your rights in contacts with public authorities. Adult learning for people without jobs is not only a question of enhancing skills and preparing for work, but also of providing meaningful activity. Furthermore increasing individualisation and rapid social change mean that a growing part of the adult population tries to practise some type of 'life planning' in partly unknown contexts. Education becomes an important part of this.

However, it is obvious that there are marked social divisions both in the perceived needs for and in the resources for participation in organised learning. People with low skills have fewer resources and less motivation to participate in education and training, especially more general types of education. Well-educated people have resources and motivation to educate themselves further (and further). Low skills are found more often in groups that are socially marginalised in other respects, like many groups of immigrants. Access to educational opportunities for adults is spatially unevenly distributed, being concentrated around urban centres and far less available in, for instance, rural areas with outflow of young people and falling populations. Companies are much more willing to contribute (with funds and organised opportunities) to the education of professionals than the training of low-skilled employees.

Globalisation, Europeanisation and the Need for Lifelong Learning

How do the processes of globalisation and Europeanisation impact on the express social need for lifelong learning? Mainly in two ways. Firstly they serve to accentuate the needs and the social divisions outlined above. Secondly they reinforce the trend to have social needs for learning articulated and met through the institution of the market. This is true not only for globalisation, but also for Europeanisation, because at the level of everyday life the main impact of the EU is through the realisation of the single European market.

The increased cooperation and competition between companies on a global scale does not mean that labour markets are lifted out of their national contexts. The main mobile elements are capital and jobs, and the combination of market liberalisation, information and communications technology (ICT) and cheap transport has made it increasingly feasible for companies to relocate activities to places where conditions are most inviting. In Europe the most obvious result of this has been the displacement of many skilled and unskilled jobs, especially in manufacturing, towards Asia and Eastern Europe. International career paths are there, to be sure, but they are mostly open to a small group of well-educated managers and specialists.

However, the character of work in developed countries is changing. Many work processes involve international cooperation with customers, partners and subcontractors. For instance, a survey found that by the end of the Nineties about one-fourth of Danish manufacturing companies were involved in transnational cooperation on product innovation (Lundvall, 2002). In such processes some employees have to communicate in foreign languages (mostly English) and with persons in the same line of work but rooted in other cultures.

The changes in everyday life and culture are more visible and perhaps also more far-reaching than the changes in the world of work. Everyday life in the modern world is a combination of local and international elements. The slogan 'Think globally, act locally' originally launched by the Brundtland Commission may in fact be seen as a principle of modern life; many people have quick access to information on events and developments all over the world. They may form strong opinions on global issues; but their chances of influencing decisions on these issues are almost non-existent. There is a strong polarisation between the greater part of the population whose radius of action is almost entirely local, and the small elites who move and act internationally.

On a formal level, developments in culture and everyday life have had little impact on education. Whereas education is confronted with the demand for skills in the world of work through the mediation of labour markets, the skills required in other life areas are not made visible in this way. But they still influence education. One example is that the mass of information available on the Internet becomes an important source for student learning, but the lack of structure and quality indicators for this information becomes a problem. Another example is the fact that pupils' and students' attachment to global youth cultures influences their perception of the school curriculum and their choices of themes and subjects.

From Adult Education to Lifelong Learning

The institutional strategies for lifelong learning being pursued in different countries are shaped on the one hand by the policy discourses and models developed and circulated internationally, on the other hand by the historical trajectories of adult education in each country. As an example I shall briefly describe the historical development of adult education in Denmark, my country of origin (Olesen & Rasmussen, 1996; Illeris, 2004).

The evolution of educational provision for adults in Denmark can be described in three main phases. The first phase was the establishment of independent and liberal adult education through the folk high schools during the nineteenth century. These were boarding schools for young adults representing a popular and non-academic type of adult education rooted most often in rural communities. The teaching mainly consisted mainly of oral narration and discussion in the Danish language with history and literature as important subjects. The folk high school soon inspired the establishment of many types of evening classes leading to a liberal system of leisure-time teaching funded generously by the state. Many voluntary educational associations were established, partly linked to the main political parties, offering evening courses in both practical subjects (like housekeeping), general subjects (like languages) and ideological issues.

The second phase started around 1960, when new educational structures were created in two areas that had previously been left to the popular enlightenment associations. One area was general adult education aimed at preparing adults for examinations in general school subjects like mathematics, Danish and foreign languages. Originally these courses were mostly given at ordinary primary and secondary schools, but later they were organised in independent institutions. The other area was vocational training, which was introduced through an act on training of adult semi-skilled workers. The system of courses for workers assumed an important role in the development of industrial skills and worker mobility, and special schools were established for this purpose and grew steadily.

Danish adult education is currently in its third phase of development, which started some 20 years ago and marks a gradual transition to the logic of lifelong learning. It is characterised by an increasing focus on the acquisition of vocational qualifications, a stronger political emphasis on educational opportunities for adults and a policy of establishing comprehensive institutional frameworks for adult education and its interfaces with the ordinary educational system. The main result up to now has been a reform introduced in 2000 which created a new system of part-time vocational adult education with programmes corresponding to the main levels in full-time education. For instance 'continuing adult education' corresponds to upper-secondary vocational education. A certain amount of previous relevant work experience is required to enter part-time study at a given level.

In this new Danish system of adult education the logic of lifelong learning is present to some degree, visible in the fact that the possibility of adult education is included at different levels of education and that skills learned in other contexts are recognised in the educational system. In other ways, however, the lifelong perspective is not present. The institutional frameworks are structured in modules and the content elements may be quite fragmented. For the individual learner, the system consists of building blocks of vocational competence that have to be pieced together, and there is little guidance and counselling available to help the learner. Adult education receives considerable public funding, but users still have to pay fees, and it is easier to get support for courses closely linked to the labour market. The question of personal growth and development is given little official attention.

Seen through the lens of Habermas's theory the evolution of Danish adult education illustrates the complex relationship between life-world and social system. I have used the concept of life-world to elucidate the social need for learning, but Habermas's concept of society has two faces, conceived not only in terms of the life-world but also in terms of social systems (Habermas, 1984-87). This is because the organisation of social life is not only achieved through mutual understanding between individuals; many social processes have to be coordinated through social systems, where media constitute common measures for individual evaluations of the consequences of action.

In the course of social evolution, differentiation occurs both in social systems (in the form of growing complexity) and in life-world contexts (in the form of rationalisation). Through rationalisation, the knowledge transmitted within the life-world increasingly becomes the object of discussion. Through a parallel process, the reproduction of society increasingly comes to rest on subsystems of goal-oriented action, organised through media like money and power. The problem is that in developed western societies, the social systems come to dominate or undermine the processes of rationalisation in the life-world. This 'colonisation of the life-world' implies a systematic distortion of communicative action. One of the examples Habermas offers is the legal regulation of social relations in the family and in the school. School law originates as a supplementary regulation; the processes of education are expected to 'run themselves', drawing on the potential of communicative action. But when the formal structures of legal regulation come to dominate educational institutions, the capacity for symbolic reproduction of the life-world suffers. As educational institutions are entrusted with the development of skills aimed at the labour market, they are tied to the system perspective. The economic system demands that education be disconnected from the ideal of education as a general civil right, and connected to the system of employment. This contributes to the colonisation of the life-world.

The parallel with the development of lifelong learning is easy to see. In the Danish case, phase three marks the definitive transition to a situation where different types of adult education do not 'run themselves'. To respond to the increased social need for learning their rationality has to be developed and their activities supported through institutional regulation (Rasmussen, 2006b); but this increases the risk that processes of learning may be colonised by instrumental system logics with resulting deformation of the life-world. It is in this delicate balance between rationalisation and colonisation that policy discourses and instruments in the area of lifelong learning intervene.

Globalisation and Lifelong Learning Policy

Globalisation impacts on lifelong learning policy in several ways (Rasmussen, 2006a). It involves education, which has until recently been the more or less exclusive domain of nation states, in international negotiations on and regulations of rights and conditions, for instance when education is included in charters on human rights and when education as a service is included in trade regulation. It also spurs an increased awareness of and responsiveness to inter-nation competition, as has been evidenced for instance by the intense debates on the results of the PISA surveys. National publics and professionals are constantly confronted with the achievements of major players on the world stage, be it the United States or the 'Asian tigers'.

The increased awareness of inter-nation competition in education can be illustrated by a report on lifelong learning brought out by the World Bank a few years ago. The report emphasised that lifelong learning is becoming a necessity in many countries and that opportunities for learning throughout one's lifetime are becoming critical for competitiveness in the knowledge economy. The report concerned itself especially with the contemporary educational challenges for the developing countries, and it summarised these challenges in the following way:

> Developing countries and countries with transition economies risk being further marginalized in a competitive global knowledge economy because their education and training systems are not equipping learners with the skills they need. To respond to the problem, policymakers need to make fundamental changes. They need to replace the information-based, teacher-directed rote learning provided within a formal education system governed by directives with a new type of learning that emphasizes creating, applying, analyzing, and synthesizing knowledge and engaging in collaborative learning throughout the lifespan. (World Bank, 2003, pp. 18-19)

Here lifelong learning is seen primarily as a means to develop the skills necessary for economic competitiveness and global relations are seen primarily as market relations.

A prominent actor in the process of globalisation is the World Trade Organization, which may be described as a political initiative focused on strengthening market mechanisms across national boundaries and removing trade barriers. In the context of lifelong learning the agreements on trade in services (GATS) are of particular interest. These agreements adhere to the general principles of the free market, like the transparency principle, demanding that GATS member states make public all measures and decisions relating to market access, or the most favoured nation principle, which says that no nation should have less favourable trade principles than the most favoured one. Education is a type of service, but it is only in the most recent negotiations that trade in educational services has been treated seriously.

The GATS agreements consist of both a general framework, to which all members must adhere, and bilateral agreements between individual members on the more specific areas of liberalisation. As regards educational sectors the focus seems to be on higher education and adult education, while no countries seem willing to involve GATS in their primary education systems.

Unsurprisingly, the USA launched the most radical suggestions for liberalising educational services, especially in trade with Asian and Latin American partners. The USA, and probably also the EU, seem to be using the GATS to get easier access to markets in the developing countries. Against this background actors from the developing countries have voiced strong views on the danger of trade in educational services. The Minister of Education in South Africa has stated that 'it is important that we remain vigilant to ensure that increased trade in education does not undermine our national efforts to transform higher education and in particular to strengthen the public sector so that it can effectively participate in increasing education' (quoted from Knight, 2003, p. 10). And the Vice-Chancellor of the University of Mauritius worries that developing countries may be 'flooded with foreign and private providers delivering essentially profitable subjects ... and in these areas they will pose as serious competitors to local universities, leaving the latter to deal with non-profitable subjects in arts, humanities, science and technology, so vital for a country's development' (quoted from Knight, 2003, p. 11).

The impact of GATS regulations and negotiations in the area of education and more specifically lifelong learning is still difficult to assess. But it seems probable that the more public educational activities are being co-funded by private means (like participants' fees or contributions from foundations or business), the more they must follow the principles laid down by GATS (Rikowski, 2003). And adult and continuing education is probably the sector of the educational system where these types of mixed funding are most widespread. In their analysis of the prospects for trade in education Larsen & Vincent-Lacrain (2002) suggested that this will have a deeper impact on the lifelong learning market than on traditional higher education.

Throughout modernity education and learning have mainly been linked to and run by nation states, and they still are today. This has not prevented the existence of international markets for education, and these markets seem to have grown in recent years. Still, markets are not the dominant way of regulating the production and distribution of education, not even adult and continuing education. The actors on the international markets for education are as often public institutions as private entrepreneurs. Fredriksson (2004) has tried to illustrate the potential impact of GATS regulation through hypothetical scenarios that illustrate how the interplay of contextual factors (such as public–private co-funding schemes introduced nationally to improve the quality of education) may open education systems to GATS regulation through decisions in Trade Dispute Panels. He points out that although the decisions of such panels cannot be predicted, '[t]he problem is that decisions taken by governments in questions related to education will be regarded in a trade perspective' (Fredriksson, 2004, p. 432).

The development of educational markets is of course a question of demand, supply and profitability. But it is also a question of policy, not least of the general free trade policy pursued by the USA and other western nations in the GATS framework and its impact on education.

Europeanisation and Lifelong Learning Policy

Since the mid-nineties the EU has increasingly tried to develop common educational policies. This is a logical development given the movement towards a more politically defined union, which means that EU bodies (especially the Commission) have acquired a more valid legal basis for initiatives in education. This also means that members of the professional staff of the EU are in a position to play a more active role in policymaking, a role for which they have undoubtedly been socialised by working in the international environment of the EU headquarters. The failure to mobilise popular support for the proposed EU constitution does not seem to have seriously affected the legitimacy of such common EU policies.

One area in which new initiatives have been taken is lifelong learning. During the last few years the European Commission has issued several policy documents in this area. Some of the most important elements in these documents are:

- linking lifelong learning to the needs of the knowledge-based economy and society;
- emphasising the necessity of new basic skills (like IT skills, foreign languages and social skills) to live and work in the knowledge society;
- securing access to learning throughout the life course;
- recognition of adults' non-formal learning and qualifications;
- emphasising the use of ICT in lifelong learning;
- recognition (in a very general way) of the role of lifelong learning in the strengthening of citizenship, democracy and intercultural understanding.

In general the EU documents on lifelong learning are characterised by a harmonising discourse, in which concepts like social inclusion and cohesion are prominent, while the logically related concepts of social exclusion and division are rarely mentioned (cf. Borg & Mayo, 2005; Rasmussen, 2006a).

While the Commission actively tries to develop policies for lifelong learning it is not easy to assess the actual impact of these efforts on the national policies of the Member States. An early survey of national initiatives to implement lifelong learning in the EU Member States (Eurydice & Cedefop, 2001) showed that many initiatives taken in different European countries were largely in agreement with the principles laid out in the EU Memorandum on Lifelong Learning. But 'largely' meant that the initiatives did not precisely follow or refer to the EU recommendations – which would indeed have been difficult, as the recommendations were not very precise or specific. The 2006 report *Progress Towards the Lisbon Objectives in Education and Training* also acknowledges that in a number of EU member countries participation in adult education lags behind expectations and that more comprehensive and coherent educational strategies are necessary (European Commission, 2006). At the general policy level, however, the status of the concept of lifelong learning has been boosted by the 2006 action programme in the field of lifelong learning, which has formally included the previous programmes in preschool and school education, adult education, vocational education and higher education as sub-programmes (European Union, 2006).

The primary effect of the EU efforts in this area has up to now probably not been to develop specific policies, but rather to legitimise trends already visible in developed western societies and to generalise these trends inside the EU area. In the EU policy documents on education and learning, a European citizen is pictured as a learner, not through being a student, but through being actively engaged in learning in professional contexts as well as in other areas and aspects of life. He or she moves effortlessly between informal, non-formal and formal learning and is an enthusiastic ICT user. The citizen participates in tightly knit communities and is active in shaping individual life as well as communities and society at large. But if one looks closer, taking the perspective of the majority of Europeans, the picture of the learning citizen is distorted. The meaning of 'learning' changes from context to context and slips between the fingers like sand. Risk, conflict and impoverishment appear in communities and in individual lives. The attempts to install learning as an aspect of European citizenship creates a cultural model which will not serve to include the majority of Europeans in active learning because it takes little account of the reality of learning and education in present-day European societies.

Conclusion

People need to learn. Life in the modern world – in which I include not only those regions and countries that regard themselves as 'developed' – confronts people with many opportunities, but also with risks and contradictions. To cope, to seize opportunities, to improve their quality of life people need to be able to acquire relevant skills and knowledge. When governments adopt the concept of lifelong learning, they make a promise: public authorities at all levels will support citizens, regardless of age, in their efforts to learn. This is the positive content and potential of the concept of lifelong learning and the work of the EU and other international organisations can help unfold this potential. But there is also the risk that the lifelong learning policies developed by these organisations and national governments can pervert the idea of lifelong learning and block its potential. Much of the policy discourse produced and disseminated by the powerful actors of globalisation and Europeanisation tends to disconnect learning from people's real-life contexts and experiences, because the policymakers implicitly regard these as barriers to modernity, competitiveness, innovativeness and so on. It is an urgent task to reinterpret the concept of lifelong learning in ways that connect it to the real challenges of life in the modern world.

References

Archer, M. (1982) Introduction: theorizing about the expansion of educational systems, in M. Archer (Ed.) *The Sociology of Educational Expansion*, 3-64. Beverley Hills: Sage.

Borg, C. & Mayo, P. (2005) The EU Memorandum on Lifelong Learning. Old Wine in New Bottles? *Globalisation, Societies and Education*, 3(2), 257-278. http://dx.doi.org/10.1080/14767720500167082

European Commission (2006) Progress Towards the Lisbon Objectives in Education and Training. 2006 Report. Brussels.

European Union (2006) Establishing an Action Programme in the Field of Lifelong Learning. Decision of the European Parliament and of the Council of 15 November 2006. Brussels.

Eurydice & Cedefop (2001) *National Actions to Implement Lifelong Learning in Europe.* Brussels: Eurydice.

Fredriksson, U. (2004) Studying the Supra-national in Education: GATS, education and teacher union policies? *European Educational Research Journal*, 3(2), 415-441. http://dx.doi.org/10.2304/eerj.2004.3.2.1

Habermas, J. (1984-87) *The Theory of Communicative Action*, vols 1-2. Cambridge: Polity Press.

Illeris, K. (2004) *Adult Education and Adult Learning.* Copenhagen: Roskilde University Press.

Jarvis, P. (2006) *Towards a Comprehensive Theory of Human Learning.* London: Routledge.

Knight, J. (2003) *GATS, Trade and Higher Education. Perspective 2003 – where are we?* London: Observatory on Borderless Higher Education.

Larsen, K. & Vincent-Lacrain, S. (2002) International Trade in Educational Services – good or bad? *Higher Education Management and Policy*, 14(3), 8-47.

Larson, A. (2006) Participation and Non-participation in Adult Education and Training, in S. Ehlers (Ed.) *Milestones – towards lifelong learning systems*, 47-61. Copenhagen: Danish University of Education Press.

Lundvall, B.-Å. (2002) *Innovation, Growth and Social Cohesion. The Danish Model.* Cheltenham: Edward Elgar.

Olesen, H.S. & Rasmussen, P. (Eds) (1996) *Theoretical Issues in Adult Education. Danish Research and Experiences.* Copenhagen: Roskilde University Press.

Rasmussen, P. (2006a) Globalisation and Lifelong Learning, in S. Ehlers (Ed.) *Milestones – towards lifelong learning systems*, 171-185. Copenhagen: Danish University of Education Press.

Rasmussen, P. (2006b) Danish Learning Traditions in the Context of the European Union, in M. Kuhn & R. Sultana (Eds) *Homo Sapiens Europæus. Creating the European Learning Citizen*, 47-67. New York: Peter Lang.

Rikowski, G. (2003) Schools and the GATS Enigma, *Journal for Critical Education Policy Studies*, 1(1).
http://www.jceps.com/index.php?pageID=article&articleID=8

Rubenson, K. (2006) Constructing the Lifelong Learning Paradigm: competing visions from the OECD and UNESCO, in S. Ehlers (Ed.) *Milestones – towards lifelong learning systems*, 151-170. Copenhagen: Danish University of Education Press.

World Bank (2003) Lifelong Learning in the Global Knowledge Economy: challenges for developing countries. Washington: World Bank.

CHAPTER 5

Unravelling the Politics of Public Private Partnerships in Education in Europe

SUSAN ROBERTSON

SUMMARY Europe's engagement with the education sector is shaped by the idea of subsidiarity; that is, that autonomy over public sector activities, such as education, should be located at the closest point to delivery. However, since 2000, and the adoption of the Lisbon agenda - to make Europe the most competitive, knowledge-based economy in the world - there has been considerable activity at the European scale in the area of compulsory education. One form this has taken is in the area of implementing new governance arrangements in the area of digital technologies and learning. This chapter explores the way in which Public-Private-Partnerships (PPPs) have emerged to enable to development. The author argues that this generates capacity for the European Commission, on the one hand, and provides a window for the entry of the private sector into education governance, on the other.

Introduction

Analysts following European Union education policymaking are more than familiar with the strategic goals for Europe as set out in the 2000 Lisbon Council – 'to become the most competitive and dynamic knowledge-based economy in the world capable of sustainable economic growth with more and better jobs and greater social cohesion' (European Council, 2000, para. 5). Analysts are also likely to be able to identify the Commission's strategies to generate structural reform across Europe and develop its policymaking capacity, as well as the development of actions around lifelong learning, information and communications technology (ICT), and so on. These goals,

101

strategies and actions are, in the words of the Commission, a European response to the challenges posed by globalisation, specifically the means to ensure the transition to a digital, knowledge-based economy and society (cf. Lisbon European Council, 2000; European Commission, 2001a, b).

What we are less familiar with is a particular governance mechanism to bring this about: Public Private Partnerships (PPPs). This is because much of the work on governance has tended to focus on the Open Method of Coordination (Walters & Haahr, 2005). In this chapter I want to fill in this gap by unravelling PPPs as a key mechanism to develop the eSociety/eLearning strategy. In the view of the Commission, a viable education strategy must involve the business sector if it is to respond to the demands of a knowledge economy. Through a close reading of: 1. key eLearning and related policy documents published between 1996-2002 when the policy was being developed and embedded; 2. a later review of PPPs by the European Investment Bank (2004); and 3. an analysis of PPPs in the education sector in England, we can see that this new governance arrangement opens up education to the private sector on a scale, and in a form, not seen before. I will also argue that the mechanisms for regulating private interests in the investment of education at the European level are not sufficiently developed to be able to protect social equality, despite the weight given to it by the various EU bodies. It is therefore unlikely that the eLearning strategy will generate outcomes that contribute to the Lisbon goals of social cohesion.

The European eLearning Summit and PPPs

In the Summit Declaration held in La Hulpe, Belgium, on 10 and 11 May 2001, the eLearning Summit Taskforce laid out the challenges facing 'Europe' in meeting the goals of the Lisbon Council (2000): 'to become the most competitive and knowledge-based economy in the world capable of sustainable economic growth with more and better jobs and greater social cohesion' (European Council, 2000, para. 5). The purpose of the Summit was to take forward the European Commission's Action Plan presented by the Council of the European Union in March 2001 to the Member States:

- to develop the comprehensive integration of ICT into education and training;
- to create flexible infrastructures that will make eLearning available to all;
- to develop universal digital literacy;
- to create a culture of lifelong learning;
- to develop a high-quality European educational content.
  (European eLearning Summit Taskforce, 2001, p. 2)

According to the Summit report, 'to meet these goals, Europe needs to expand its educational opportunity' (ibid, p. 2). Educational opportunity is viewed as each individual having access to ICT and a means of developing digital literacy which will enable them to keep pace with economic, social and technological changes and thus ensure each person will be able to secure their own future through a process of lifelong learning.

The Summit Declaration identified a number of key challenges facing 'Europe'. First, in order to meet the demands of the knowledge economy, there is a need to accelerate the process of change and innovation. However, the Summit Taskforce argues that attempts by Member States to generate these changes through bringing teachers alongside are failing to progress sufficiently rapidly to ensure the realisation of the eLearning strategy. The Taskforce observes: 'In many European countries the conditions needed for developing the role of the teacher and enhancing the status of the profession are simply not progressing at a pace that will allow pedagogical innovation to be spread rapidly so that it becomes a systemic part of the education system' (ibid, p. 2).

Second, according to the eLearning Summit Taskforce, eLearning requires immediate and substantial investments by governments and education and training bodies to generate universal digital literacy. Again, the Taskforce note that the necessary pace of change and the scale of investment in infrastructure, tools, services and content that will be required 'must be significantly increased' (ibid, p. 2). From there the solution for the Taskforce is an inevitable alternative: that in order to 'provide a step change in the implementation of innovative models of eLearning, the transformation of learning institutions, and the social perception of the role and status of educational practitioners' (p. 3), PPPs should be explored as offering considerable potential as a mechanism for delivering education and training into the future given the capital shortages Member States face in investing in the public sector. In the view of the Summit Taskforce: 'Active private sector participation in eLearning and ongoing dialogue with the public sector is no longer a viable option but an urgent necessity' (ibid, p. 3) and 'a precursor to preparing a fresh stage in sustainable European cooperation' (ibid, p. 3). The Taskforce Declaration concluded with the recommendation to the Commission that it should 'explore the potential of public private partnerships' (ibid, p. 6).

In many respects, the Summit Taskforce report is a remarkable one. To begin, the Summit Taskforce, chaired by IBM Europe, was composed of five companies: IBM, Cisco, Nokia, SanomaWSOY and Smartforce. It was this group, too, who had led the development of the Summit and who have had a significant role in subsequent developments including the development of Career Space, an initiative I will look at in closer detail later in this chapter. The Summit, hosted at the IBM International Training Centre, La hulpe, Belgium, attracted over 350 participants from the public and the private sectors, including policy makers from national ministries of education and employment, senior officials from the European Commission, and ICT industry representatives. At the Summit a further 25 companies (including

3Com, Apex Interactive, Apple, Auralog, British Telecom, Centra, CEPIUS, Ge.world, Transware, CompTIA, Courseware Factory, De Wilde CBT, Digital Brain, EDS, EdskillsNTO, European Education Partnership, Granada Media, Intel, Interact Group, Manpower, Marconi, Oracle, Sonera), then formed a Steering Group who agreed to take the conclusions and recommendations of the Summit forward. These transnational firms have huge interests in the information technology world, including the provision of hardware, software and education and training. Second, the Summit Report observes that education, as we have known it, must be recast. According to the Taskforce, no longer will education be necessarily delivered via an education system and its teachers. Rather, educators' roles, pedagogical practices and educational spaces will be redefined within the framework of a partnership between the public and the private sectors.

If one were to read the report of the eLearning Summit Taskforce disconnected from other events and agendas within the EU, it might be easy to conclude that key interests within the private sector had hijacked the agenda of the eLearning Summit and inserted a seemingly tentative claim to the need for (exploring) Public Private Partnerships as a means for creating capacity. However, as early as 1996, the Commission – in setting out the guidelines for future Community action 2000-06 in *Toward a Europe of Knowledge* (European Commission, 1997) – had linked the idea of knowledge and skills for a knowledge economy with the specification of a particular means for bring this about – the private sector. For example, in paragraph 3 of the Report, under the section 'The Parties Involved', the Commission notes that 'there needs to be a commitment to securing greater involvement of the business sector ... the dividing line between the world of education and that of the information society is fluid and connections need to be established in both directions' (European Commission, 1997, para 3).

The evidence suggests that by the mid-1990s the Commission had a preferred ideological position of how the European knowledge economy education space should be developed. This ideological preference, of the liberalisation of markets and the conditions of trade, was later given structural weight with the Stability Pact (European Council, 1999), negotiated in Cologne in June 1999 as part of the Commission's conditions for widening the Union to include South Eastern Europe (European Commission, 1999). Linked to the Treaty of Maastricht (European Council, 1991) with its emphasis on the management of public spending, the Stability Pact commits EU members and acceding countries to principles of market liberalisation (European Council, 1999, p. 3) while reigning in public expenditure:

- public spending must be in surplus – 1 to 2.5% of gross domestic product (GDP) in 2002;
- central government spending must be in balance;
- overall central government spending must be lower than the growth of the overall budget (European Council, 2000).

While the Stability Pact is invoked as the reason for pressing Member States and acceding countries into consideration of private financing of previously publicly funded activity [1], the Commission had made clear its ideological position and determined that its capacity to construct and govern a European Education Space in line with the 1991 Treaty of Maastricht [2] and the Commission's economic strategy would require substantial support from the business sector.

Embedding a European Education Space – the Lisbon Council

Embedding education in a European space is no straightforward process, particularly as ideas like 'European education' are neither pre-existing nor common-sense categories with identifiable activities and institutions, and because the Commission has had limited desire (largely because of its commitment to the principle of subsidiarity) and limited capacity to govern that space in policy terms. However, within the context of creating a competitive European knowledge economy, creating a European Education Space with a particular mandate and capacity that could be governed was critical. The Presidency Conclusions of the European Council in Lisbon, 23-24 March 2000, can be seen as a watershed in this regard (Barcelona European Council, 2001). Here the Council specified a clear mandate for education and training, as well as the means for bringing this about. ICT was high on the agenda. According to the Council, investments in ICT infrastructure and digital literacy were critical to developing the services sector and to overcoming the widening skills gap in information technology. The means to do this was along partnership lines.

The Council identified two kinds of partnership. One kind of partnership was for multi-partners establishing multipurposed education centres (Barcelona European Council, 2001, para. 26). This type of partnership was to open up the previously closed world of provision of education to a range of new providers, along with those traditionally in the education sector, as well as being a site that was accessible to different types of (lifelong) learners. A second kind of partnership referred to the means through which the new European Education Space might be achieved. Under the heading 'Mobilising the Necessary Means' (para. 41), the Council stated that:

> Achieving the new strategic goal will rely primarily on the private sector, as well as on Public-Private-Partnerships. It will depend on mobilizing the resources available on the markets as well as on efforts by Member States. The Union's role is to act as a catalyst in this process, by establishing an effective framework for mobilizing all available resources for the transition to the knowledge based economy and by adding its own contribution to this effort under existing Community policies while respecting Agenda 2000.

In 2001 the European Commission, in its *European Report on the Quality of School Education*, laid down a framework for guiding action and mobilising resources –16 Quality Indicators for catalysing change in the direction envisaged by the Commission. In the area of ICT the key indicator was the 'number of students per computer' – a benchmark that according to the Commission would 'provide an introduction to policy discussion by raising a number of questions about the future place, purpose and practice of ICT in European schools' (European Commission, 2001d, p. 7) and because 'ICT is already having a far-reaching effect on people's lives and pupils' learning, with, for example, 40% of all UK market shares in ICT' (p. 7). While in reality the 'number of students per computer' benchmark of 'quality' tells us little about the conditions of access [3] for pupils in schools, it would seem that its presence as a benchmark was to register the centrality of ICT in the creation of a European Education Space as part of the European knowledge economy. As Shore put it, while Euro-statistics are themselves indices of opinion based upon little more than aggregated data, they:

> are not only powerful political instruments for creating a
> knowable, quantifiable and hence more tangible and governable
> 'European population' and 'European space': rather, they are also
> powerful moulders of consciousness that furnish the meta-
> classifications within which identities and subjectivities are
> formed. (Shore, 2000, p. 31)

The European Commission report also raised questions about the costs/benefits of alternative forms of provision: for example, how much learning can be independent, teacher led, peer group led, or, home-school or community based (European Commission, 2001c, p. 7). Like previous Commission reports, the *European Report* also argues:

> The information explosion demands fundamental rethinking of
> traditional conceptions of knowledge, its transmission, delivery by
> teachers and acquisition by students. ... All of these areas of
> knowledge and skills present major challenges to the teaching
> profession ... Change requires rethinking, reappraisal, reevaluation
> of accepted practices, challenging what has always been done and
> accepted. Change often requires *restructuring* and *re-culturing of
> organizations*. It poses new demands on hierarchies, status and
> relationships. (European Commission, 2001d, p. 9, emphasis
> added)

The Commission report turns to the difficult question of resources. It suggests that requests for more resources is a typical response and adds that 'more' is not feasible, especially when governments are faced with providing for an increased number of learners in education settings for a longer period of time. In essence, the report argues the resource challenge has to be looked at in a different way particularly as 'young people see school structures, curricula and the learning environment' (European Commission, 2001d, p. 9) as irrelevant to their lives.

Like previous declarations and reports, the Commission identifies the threats to the development of the knowledge economy strategy as lying in both the forces (teachers) and the means (access to computing) of production. That is, teachers lack skills and resist using ICT as they see it as a threat to their jobs (European Commission, 2001d, p. 24); the ratio of pupils per computer is still very uneven (p. 52), and in many cases computers in schools are simply not sufficiently up to date to enable them to access programs that have been developed (p. 53). A preferred solution follows: the flexible knowledge economy means provision should be less institutionalised, with individuals assembling their own building blocks of knowledge and qualifications in informal ways and in new contexts (p. 10). The report observes:

> All member states are realizing that the future brings a
> monumental challenge to traditional structures of education
> institutions. This means finding ways of educating people beyond
> school and outside the classroom, helping them to acquire the
> skills and competencies that will make them less vulnerable in the
> global economy. (p. 11) The question then posed is: How would
> it be possible to create partnership with institutions or
> organisations which could help to increase the availability of
> computers in schools? How can schools be guaranteed a real long-
> term benefit from such an approach?

Following the Council Resolution on eLearning in July 2001 (Council of the European Union, 2001), an Interim Report– *eLearning: designing tomorrow's schools* – was released by the European Commission in February 2002, which sought to 'lay the foundations for concrete and sustainable actions' (European Commission, 2002, p. 2) to meet the Commission's knowledge economy goals with an ICT and digital literacy strategy. With enhancing quality and improving access constantly narrated as the keystones for building the European knowledge society, the report then proceeds to lay out a set of preferred options for what quality and access might mean: flexible and virtual universities, multipurpose places for learning, the development of an ICT curriculum for the twenty-first century, Public Private Partnerships. Again the issue of resources and the means through which resources might be made available is considered: 'This need is ever more pressing in a more difficult economic environment' (p. 11) while 'Public-Private Partnerships need to be explored' (p. 11). At the same time, that this European space is more than a 'learning space' in a more traditional sense becomes evident at several points in the report. While recognising the recent downturn in the ICT sector and consolidations in the market for eLearning products, the report observes: 'The global market for eLearning and services is expected to grow strongly in the forthcoming years, providing both a challenge and an opportunity to European education systems and to related economic sectors such as multimedia publishing' (p. 5). The report concludes with: 'it is clear that the eLearning initiative is playing an important role in helping Europe to exploit the use of ICT for education and training, and to realize its potential to be a world leader in learning products and services, and in terms of successfully sharing resources and know-how in education and training' (p. 7).

A European Knowledge Economy Education Space: scale and the politics of territorialisation

Before moving to examine the Commission's privileging of Public Private Partnerships as a means through which the European knowledge economy education space is to be realised, I want to consider the social and political processes at work in creating this territory. The work of the critical geographers and their analysis of space, scale and territorialisation, as well as work on the idea of 'Europe' and the 'European economy' as a social imaginary is particularly useful for this purpose. Ways of thinking about the active construction of space and territory at a supranational scale enable us to see how a complex and particular regime of economic governance is developed as part of an embryonic Euro-polity.

As Shore (2000) and Rosamond (2002) point out, categories such as 'the European economy' and 'European competitiveness' are not self-evident entities. Rather, they are social constructions that are worked at discursively and materially to embed a set of social relations at a new scale – the supranational. This way of thinking about space and scale (Europe versus National States) and the identities of those who inhabit that space (such as the 'competitive European', an 'educated European') owes much to the work of writers like Lefebvre (1991), Harvey (1982, 1999), Smith (1993) and Brenner (1998, 1999, 2003). These writers argue that human activities are located on multiple territories and that the geography of a territory, its nature and meanings, is both produced and reproduced. Territories, thus, can be viewed as spatial configurations and treated as an active moment within the overall temporal dynamic of accumulation and social reproduction (Harvey, 1999). In other words spaces and their territories, like the 'global' or the 'national', 'are not neutral containers; they are themselves constructed and reconstructed, spaces that are mapped as places which are, on the one hand, governed and, on the other, lived in and through social relationships and social relations' (Robertson et al, 2002, p. 474). Similarly, Rosamond (2002), in an analysis of the construction of a competitive Europe, argues that 'imagining the European economy' is a rhetorical strategy as part of a more complex process of constructing a regime of economic governance being developed around the European Union. Rosamond shows how an 'idea' like 'competitiveness' can become 'sedimented and "banal" in the sense of becoming commonsensical and barely discussed' (p. 158), yet in the process is constructing identities and subjectivities.

In the same way, we can see how the narration of ideas like a 'European Education Space', a 'competitive and knowledge-based economy' and 'Public Private Partnerships', as well as the institutions engaged with their narration, come to be viewed as common-sense ideas at a scale that sits beyond the national and the local. We can also see the way these ideas are scaffolded into existence and sedimented into institutions and operative networks as material practices through additional policy manoeuvres such as benchmarking. Finally we can see how these strategies privilege particular kinds of interests and institutional arrangements (as in the eLearning Summit Taskforce and the subsequent development of Career Space) and embed a particular kind of framework for action, a particular type of common sense. In Robert Cox's (1996, p. 97) view, a framework for action or historical structure is 'a particular combination of thought patterns, material conditions, and human institutions which has certain coherence among its elements. These structures do not determine people's actions in any mechanical sense but constitute the context of habits, pressures, expectations and constraints within which action takes place'. This process is co-constitutive. That is, the construction of space as a particular type of territory, shaped by particular types of ideas, is both the object of and the outcome of struggles between agents that operate at different scales.

In the case that I am concerned with here, understanding the creation of a 'European knowledge economy' through the construction of a 'European Education Space', this means engaging in a set of strategic manoeuvres that legitimates the right of a set of supranational institutions (European Commission, Council of Europe, Organisation for Economic and Co-operative Development) and transnational firms, all operating at a supranational scale, to imagine, produce, make visible, and govern this space. The strategy of the Commission through its various reports involves drawing on common-sense discourses of globalisation to elaborate upon the external threats to this imagined 'Europe' while promoting the uniqueness of the European space. It thus legitimises policymaking in this area and the means for bringing this about. In relation to threats, the Commission and key economic actors point to:

- the inability of national states to generate the level of investment in ICT and education required to keep up to date;
- the entrenched interests of teachers in national education systems thus making rapid progress difficult; and
- the difficulties posed by changes in the governance of education systems (devolution) thus limiting the capacity of nation states to direct education systems and ensure equity of access.

With regard to uniqueness, the Commission argues that it is only at the European level that the scale and pace of investment is possible. In relation to means, the Commission is insistent that the private sector must be involved in the development of education policy and provision. The identification of imperatives means Commission actors are 'then able to offer powerful cases for the development of European-level solutions, delivered through European-level policy instruments and institutions' (Rosamond, 2002, p. 162). He further observes:

> Such patterns of rhetorical practice are perhaps particular to the
> Commission and may indeed be part and parcel of the distinctive
> policymaking dynamics of the EU where supranational
> entrepreneurs produce analyses of possibilities, ongoing
> deliberation and interaction. This is especially true of the
> Commission which, as Thomas Christiansen notes, has developed
> over time sophisticated strategies for the achievement of its
> institutional purpose: the expansion of its policy competence.
> (p. 162)

Key economic actors, like the large transnational firms IBM, Cisco and Nokia, have been actively participating in the creation of a European Education Space through generating the conditions for their ongoing and future investment in the lucrative education market without the impediments of existing institutional arrangements, problems of state regulation, or pressures from civil society, about the role of large private for-profit firms in the education sector. [4] However, for the European Commission to foray into education and training on such an unprecedented scale, unhindered by the local and national politics of the Member States, it must develop its own system of innovation enabling it to realise a 'quantum shift' in the capacity to bring this about. This means developing the means to go beyond the establishment of objectives and benchmarks. It means drawing upon a set of resources made available through the private sector to provide a particular kind of education that is not dependent upon place but, rather, uses new technologies to operate across boundaries. The construction of this knowledge economy education space carries all of the hallmarks of the emerging EU economic space, which, as Rosamond observes, is quite distinctive: 'It amounts to a quite particular form of economic internationalisation involving the freeing of trade and significant deregulation, combined with new rule setting, the development of common policies, the transfer of power to central institutions and the development of redistributive mechanisms' (2002, p. 162). However, the question to be posed is whether the EC has sufficient regulatory apparatus in place, aside from crude measures of quality like 'the number of computers per pupil', to ensure that social equality is not undermined when the education space is exposed to private for-profit interests.

The Role of the European Investment Bank in Bankrolling PPPs and Smoothing the Regulatory Environment

A key agent for helping advance PPPs in Europe was the European Investment Bank (EIB). It is instructive, therefore, to look at the review by the EIB on its own role in PPPs (European Investment Bank, 2004), particularly its reflections on the financial, legislative, and other policy issues that needed to be addressed to develop national PPP programmes.

The European Commission, the European Council and the EIB, key movers of the PPP policy at the European scale, articulated the mandate of PPPs as 'improving value for money' for the public sector. Inserting PPPs into the governance regimes of Member States required: 1. not only financial incentives from the Bank to push the policy along; but 2. changes in the regulatory environment in ways that would impact on national regulatory spaces; and 3. the development of institutional linkages in national spaces, such as with the National PPP Task Forces. Thus, the early focus was on the:

> creation of the right regulatory, financial and administrative
> conditions to boost private investment as well as the mobilization
> of Community funding, allied with an invitation to Member States
> to continue refocusing public expenditure towards growth
> enhancing areas without increasing public budgets. (European
> Investment Bank, 2004, p. 2)

The EIB report notes no typical model of PPP being advanced across Europe (European Investment Bank, 2004, p. 3). Nor are PPPs specific to a sector, such as transport. What we see is the EIB opportunistically involving itself in PPPs ranging from public infrastructures (airports, railways and so on) to public buildings, such as schools and prisons. The objective of Europe's PPP programme is to 'harness private sector skills in support of improved public services. This is achieved by moving away from the direct procurement by the public sector of physical assets and towards the procurement of services from the private sector under public sector regulation/contract' (p. 3), whilst the reasons advanced for the promotion of PPPs is that private sector interests/resources and the transfer of risk to the private sector will improve the efficiency and quality of public services, thereby generating greater value for money. However, the EIB (2004, p. 5) notes that value for money or the transfer of risk is not automatic, and should be reviewed on a case-by-case basis. 'Achieving the optimal allocation of risk is the most important single factor in structuring a PPP' (European Investment Bank, 2005, 2004? p. 5). This is not an easy task, largely as specifying risk in complex contracts involving a range of players is very difficult. Adding to this difficulty is that many in the public sector have little to no experience of specifying contracts in ways that would protect the public interest and public investment. Despite this, Europe has pressed forward on this project so that by 2003, upward of

111

3000 EIB PPP signatures per year were being registered (European Investment Bank, 2004, p. 6). Out of a total of 14,721 million, investment in social infrastructure (health and education) totalled 819 million, or 5% of the overall total, with the UK registering almost 25% of that, followed by Portugal (19%), Spain (18%), Greece (14%) and Austria (10%) (p. 7).

To aid national governments, the EU Commission injected structural/cohesion funds to part-finance the public sector contribution, including collaborating with National PPP Taskforces (European Investment Bank, 2004, p. 10). The Commission also has progressively put into place initiatives under public procurement law to both clarify the legal framework of PPPs (European Commission, 2000, p. 5, 2004) and to advance the basis of an internal, or regional, market.

PPPs – articulating and aligning European and national projects

So far I have been tracing the advance of PPPs by key actors located at the European scale to further the internal market and to advance a way of thinking about education that opens it to new providers. As crucial aspects of the provision of education take place at the level of the national (and presided over by Member States), for Europe's PPP project to take hold it must articulate with political projects already underway at the level of the national. From the figures outlined above about the extent of PPPs within Member States, we can see considerable resonance with 'Third Way', 'Neue Mitte' and other restructuring and modernisation programmes taking place across Europe, including Germany, Spain and Greece (see Giddens, 2001; Mouzelis, 2001). Like arguments for PPPs as a new mechanism of governance at the European scale, a fundamental idea within Member States is that the state should not dominate the provision of public services; rather a range of patterns including the market and civil society should emerge that enables consumer choice and market competition though, as Giddens argues (2001, p. 6), the state needs to regulate and intervene in both to ensure both quality and social equality. The appeal of the idea of partnership for national governments committed to neoliberal policies is that it is a powerful discourse of inclusion and collaboration. In talking about the partnership politics in the UK under Blair, Newman argues that it was Labour's attempt to forge a consensual style of politics. It signified 'an harmonious, non-conflict-based form of relationship. In particular the language of partnership was adopted in place of the language of competition to re-label contractual or outsourcing arrangements between the public and the private sectors' (Newman, 2001, p. 166).

For the European Commission, the idea of partnership has a number of purposes: it enables considerable leverage over a particular type of capacity in the ICT field, the ability to draw upon financial resources/expertise to enhance its territorialising agendas in relation to Member States while at the same time suggesting a continuation of the Commission's partnership strategy with Member States (see Rodrigues & Stoer, 2001). In the process, the idea of partnership conceals the extent to which the Commission has sought to be an environment maker rather than an environment taker (Rosamond, 2002, p. 163) in key economic and social policy areas.

The insertion of private interests into the European Education Space is potentially problematic, particularly in the case of the ICT strategy if we are talking about the introduction of private for-profit interests in the partnership. In order to think through this in more detail, it is instructive to look at a number of examples of Public Private Partnerships. In the EU, the most high-profile PPP is the development of Career Space (http:www.eui-net.org/Project_documents?KoM_files/Curriculum_Development_Guidelines .pdf). Career Space is a consortium of major ICT companies – BT, Cisco Systems, IBM Europe, Microsoft, Intel, Nokia, Nortel Neworks, Philips Semiconductors, Siemens AG, Telefonia S.A and Thales – plus the European Information and Communications Technology Industry Association. Career Space is conceptualised as an alternative site that, it proposes, is critical to help develop the knowledge economy (it argues that ICT accounts for more than 6.3% of GDP). The purpose of Career Space is:

> To develop a framework for students, education institutions and governments that describes the roles, skills and competencies required by the ICT industry in Europe. The first step has been to develop generic skills profiles relevant to key jobs in ICT and to create a dedicated website (www.career-space.com) and use other communication tools to make this information widely available. The generic skills profiles described in this document cover the main job areas for which the ICT industry is experiencing skills shortages. These core profiles describe the jobs, setting out the vision, role and lifestyle associated with them. The specific technology areas and tasks associated with each job are also outlined, as well as the level of behavioural and technical skills required to carry out the profiled jobs.

The large transnational ICT firms' interest in creating an ICT curriculum framework that gives substance to and which operates in a virtual European education and training space is tied to their own needs to generate profits and to shape the conditions that give rise to profitability. The curriculum, however, as Apple (1982) reminds us more than two decades ago in his work on teachers and texts and the logic of curricular control, is no neutral space. Rather, the curriculum is a particular set of discourses, shaped by particular sets of ideas about the world and proper social relationships.

The question of the nature of private sector interests in PPPs has emerged in England – especially as Labour has relentlessly (and in the face of considerable public opposition – see Freedland, 2002) used PPPs in key public sector areas of expenditure like health, education and transport.[5] An early model of PPPs in the education sector is City Technology Colleges (CTCs); an individual, a company or an organisation acts as a sponsor and sets up a charitable foundation to run a school on a not-for-profit basis.[6] The sponsor contributes to the capital costs of the school, they may well own the land, and are expected to contribute to the ongoing capital costs for the school. CTCs are pedagogical spaces; where the curriculum is more keenly oriented toward the world of 'business', teachers' labour contracts are different to those of other teachers employed in the schooling system (longer hours, individual contracts, and the traditional hierarchy of 'central government–Local Education Authority–local school' is replaced with a governance structure run by the 'private sector' interests in the school. This has not, in the main, been a successful PPP strategy, largely as it is based upon a not-for-profit model. This model has deterred the private sector from investing in this initiative; instead, the government has ended up providing the funds itself while losing considerable control over the governance of the school.

Later versions of PPPs within the schooling sector have emerged under the Private Finance Initiative (PFI) (see Robertson, 2002, for an extended analysis of PPPs in England). The immediate perceived benefit of PFIs to the government is that services can be provided on an 'off-balance sheet' basis. This practice, in theory, enables governments to avoid public sector controls – some of which, as discussed earlier, are imposed at the supranational level, while relocating the risks of investment with the private sector.[7] However, as Ball et al (2002) show, while the case made for introducing PFIs was to ensure that means other than public sector borrowing should be found to finance worthwhile public sector investments (particularly capital investments in infrastructure), long-run analyses demonstrate a different effect: that public sector borrowing falls by the full amount in the first year and after that the fall disappears over time. The upshot of this is that PFIs permit less and less extra investment as time goes by. For the state to increase levels of funding, it then must do it through higher taxes.

Education Action Zones (EAZs) are the most visible example of PPPs within education currently. The model being pursued in EAZs is largely not for profit, though some activities within the zone, like ICT investments, operate under the for-profit model through the PFI. Again, evidence suggests that where the model of PPPs is not for profit, there has been little significant investment of private funds.[8] Further, Hallgarten & Watling (2000, pp. 26-27), in a publication issued by the Institute for Public Policy Research, show that where the private sector has invested, there is an alarming level of opaqueness and lack of accountability.

PPPs in education raise questions about the nature of private interests. These interests might be directed toward: 1. profit making, 2. shaping the behaviour of young people and families, or 3. managing the image of the firm as a responsible corporate citizen within the community. In relation to the first of these, profit, analysts point to national and international companies making investments in ICT in schools (hardware and software) with a major interest in securing their interests in the competitive ICT market. Alternatively, companies like Jarvis, Cambridge Education Associates, the Council for British Teachers, or Arthur Andersen and Ernst and Young have secured PPPs to variously manage or build schools, or manage Local Education Authorities, all with a view to making a profit (Monbiot, 2000). In each of these cases, profits are central. As can be seen in systems that were previously publicly owned, such as transport, profit making and delivery of high-quality services to the wider public are often in conflict (Pollock et al, 2001). While it is argued that for-profit contracts can be set out with sufficient clarity and detail to ensure the provision of quality and accountable services, to date there have not been the mechanisms of public accountability for services delivered by private companies to ensure that this is actually the case.

Changing Governance, Changing Equality?

So far my concerns have been with the question of the nature of the private sector's interest in PPPs in education and the capacity of states to regulate those partnerships sufficiently to ensure transparency and public accountability. However, ideas like 'quality', 'transparency' and 'accountability' operate within a given framework of action. If we take a given structure or framework for granted, our actions are to make things more or less better, rather than question the overall framework. The EC's education policymaking in ICT operates within this framework. Investments in ICT infrastructure, education and training are directed at transforming both the forces and the means of production (Harvey, 1999, p. 101). Streeck (1999, p. 2) argues that:

> It is this dialectic that, in the face of new technologies, expanded
> markets and reorganized companies, forces public money to
> search for a new balance between protection and risk, security and
> opportunity, collective solidarity and individual responsibility,
> public authority and private exchange. The dominant logic in the
> European education space is supply side egalitarianism which is
> oriented toward equal marketability.

Streeck also suggests that large-scale reliance on private investment for infrastructural purposes will not, in the long run, bring about a level of inequality that is incompatible with supply-side egalitarianism. This is presumably as there will be a cost imposed on the 'consumer' in the form of fees unless the Commission is able to develop mechanisms of redistribution or other forms of regulation. For Streeck, Third Way social democracy seems to become indistinguishable from an activist liberalism that pursues social justice through intervention in the distribution, not of market outcomes, but of the capacities for successful market participation (Streeck, 1999, p. 3). In this set of arrangements, education loses its public good function. As a private good acquired to ensure equal marketability, education in the European space will have limited capacity to contribute to societal cohesion.

It is difficult to see how ideas like partnership can operate with any sense of symmetry of power between the public and the private, especially when it involves powerful companies like Apple, IBM and Cisco Systems, in short ICT versions of media owner Rupert Murdoch. As Mouzelis (2001, p. 447) observes in his comments on Giddens' (2001) proposed Third Way, a characteristic of late modern societies is that economic interests have penetrated the cultural realm and that this process has reached unprecedented dimensions. He calls for a regulatory approach that would democratise cultural production by bringing it into the sphere of 'civil society' where it would function neither on profit nor on state/party logic (Mouzelis, 2001, pp. 447-449). If not, he says, we are drifting from a market economy to a market society, and one that needs to be reversed. However, not only will it be increasingly problematic to reverse this policy tendency given the protections private investors are seeking under the terms of the World Trade Organization/GATS agreements (see Robertson et al, 2002), but it assumes a national focus in its analysis. The real challenge such scalar shifts present us with, and evident in the case that I have been analysing here, is that these are political manoeuvres by political and economic actors to conceal or reveal particular types of politics. Not only is it difficult to contest what is increasingly viewed as a common-sense solution to the challenges of globalisation, but the frameworks which structure the social relations of the European Education Space are (intentionally) less visible in the political arenas of everyday life. As a consequence, the rescaled functional division of labour and the creation of a European Education Space are less accessible to challenge.

Notes

[1] See, for example, the controversy in the UK when British Chancellor of the Exchequer Gordon Brown announced in May 2001 that public spending in health and education would increase. The EU reminded the UK that it must meet the terms of the Stability Pact in terms of its public sector spending (see Elliot, 2001).

[2] Under the 1991 Maastricht Treaty, countries that wish to join the Euro must meet certain criteria which include keeping their budget deficits under 3% of GDP, keeping their budgets close to balance over the medium term, and keeping their government debt under 60% of GDP (Ball et al, 2002, p. 58).

[3] In its benchmarking report *European Youth in the Digital Age* (November, 2001) based on Eurobarometer surveys carried out in 2001, the Commission notes that the level of computer equipment in EU schools is relatively high – with on average 12 offline computers per pupil. However, it adds that there

are vast differences between EU Member States, varying from 3 to 25 (European Commission, 2001d, p. 2).

[4] It should be noted that these developments are taking place at the same time that education is an important site of investment and a means of potential profit in the global economy (see Heyneman, 2001; Robertson et al, 2002; Ball, 2007).

[5] The Labour Party, through its policy 'think-tank' the Institute for Public Policy Research, commissioned a report on Public Private Partnerships (Commission on Public Private Partnerships, 2001). The report remains committed to PPPs, though recognises some of the shortcomings in particular public good sectors, like health and education.

[6] It is important to point out though that the idea of 'partnership' is not a new feature of public policy and practice in England. Through the late 1980s and early 1990s, though the form and approach have varied considerably, the Conservative government had introduced Public Private Partnerships as a means of unlocking the dominance of public sector power, a strategy not dissimilar to the way in which the EC is seeking to unlock the dominance of the nationally located institutional fix in education.

[7] If public sector bodies have to pay for assets, accounting rules say the full costs must be added to government expenditure in the year of implementation. Private financing, however, ostensibly provides an alternate means for the state of raising capital for investment in the public sector, sidestepping political controls and the political damage associated with it.

[8] Established in 1999 in disadvantaged inner city areas to respond to the problem of 'failing schools', around 10-12 schools formed to make up a zone intended to raise standards and link education innovations to wider social initiatives. Features of note are that the zone had to raise funds from the business sector to be matched by government; it was governed by a local forum hence avoiding the Local Education Authority; the focus in the curriculum was on ICT as a resource for learning; and new rules were invoked for employing teachers and administrative staff.

References

Apple, M. (1982) Curricular Form and the Logic of Technical Control: building the possessive individual, in M. Apple (Ed.) *Cultural and Economic Reproduction in Education.* London: Routledge & Kegan Paul.

Ball, R., Heafey, M. & King, D. (2002) The Private Finance Initiative and Public Sector Finance, *Environment and Planning C: Government and Planning 2002*, 20, 57-74. http://dx.doi.org/10.1068/c0045

Ball, S. (2007) *Education plc.* London: Routledge.

Barcelona European Council (2001) Presidency Conclusions. http://ue.eu/int/en.info.eurocouncil/index.htm

Brenner, N. (1998) Between Fixity and Motion: accumulation, territorial organisation and the historical geography of spatial scale, *Environment and Planning D: Society and Space*, 16(1), 459-481. http://dx.doi.org/10.1068/d160459

Brenner, N. (1999) Globalisation as Reterritorialisation: the rescaling of urban governance in the European Union, *Urban Studies*, 36(3), 431-451. http://dx.doi.org/10.1080/0042098993466

Brenner, N. (2003) *New State Spaces*. Oxford: Oxford University Press.

Commission on Public Private Partnerships (2001) *Building Better Partnerships: a final report*. London: Institute for Public Policy Research.

Council of the European Union (2001) Council Resolution July 2001. 2001/C 204/02.

Cox, R. (1996) *Approaches to World Order*. Cambridge: Cambridge University Press.

Elliot, L. (Ed.) (2001) Brown's Hands off Warning to Brussels, *The Guardian*, 7 May.

European Commission (1997) Toward a Europe of Knowledge. http://Europe.eu.int/comm./education/orient/orie-en.html

European Commission (2000) Toward a Europe of Knowledge, 2000-6. Brussels: European Commission. http://europa.eu/scadplus/leg/en/cha/c11040.htm

European Commission (2001a) Designing Tomorrow's Education. An Interim Report. Commission Staff Working Paper. http://europa.eu.int/comm/education/elearning/doc_en.html

European Commission (2001b) Designing Tomorrow's Education. http://europa.eu.int/comm/education/elearning/doc_en.html

European Commission (2001c) European Report on the Quality of School Education 1 – 16 quality indicators. http://europa.eu.int/comm/education/life/15indicators_en.pdf

European Commission (2001d) *European Youth in the Digital Age*. Brussels: European Commission.

European Commission (2004) *Green Paper on Public-private Partnerships and Community Law on Public Contracts and Concessions*. COM (2004) 327 final. Brussels: EC.

European Council (1991) The Treaty of Maastricht. http://www.uni-mannheim.de/users/ddz/edz/doku/vertrag/engl/m_engl.html

European Council (1999) The Stability Pact for South Eastern Europe. Cologne, June. http://www.stabilitypact.org/default.asp

European Council (2000) Conclusions of the European Lisbon Council, March 23-24, SN100/00. http://www.europarl.europa.eu/summits/lis1_en.htm

European Council (2000) Update of the Luxembourg Stability Programme for 1999-2003. http://www/etat.lu/FI/

European eLearning Summit Taskforce (2001) Summit Declaration. http://europa.eu.int/comm/education/elearning/summit.pdf

European Investment Bank (2004) *The EIB's Role in Public Private Partnerships (PPPs)*. Brussels: EIB.

Freedland, J. (2002) These Hybrid Monsters, *The Guardian*, 27 March.

Giddens, A. (Ed.) (2001) *The Global Third Way Debate*. Cambridge: Polity Press.

Hallgarten, J. & Watling, R. (2000) Zones of Contention, in R. Lissauer & P. Robinson (Eds) *A Learning Process: public-private partnerships in education*. London: Institute for Public Policy Research.

Harvey, D. (1982) *The Limits of Capital*. London: Verso.

Harvey, D. (1989) *The Condition of Postmodernity*. Oxford: Blackwell.

Harvey, D. (1999) *The Limits to Capital*, 2nd edn. London: Verso.

Heyneman, S. (2001) The Growing International Commercial Market for Educational Goods and Services, *International Journal of Educational Development*, 21, 345-359. http://dx.doi.org/10.1016/S0738-0593(00)00056-0

Lefebvre, H. (1991) *The Production of Space*, tr. D. Nicholson Smith. Oxford: Blackwell.

Monbiot, G. (2000) *Captive State: the corporate takeover of Britain*. London: Pan Books.

Mouzelis, N. (2001) Reflexive Modernization and the Third Way: the impasses of Giddens' social democratic politics, *The Sociological Review*, 49(3), 436-456. http://dx.doi.org/10.1111/1467-954X.00340

Newman, J. (2001) *Modernising Governance: New Labour, policy and society*. London: Sage.

Pollock, A., Shaoul, J., Rowland, D. & Player, S. (2001) *Public Services and the Private Sector: a response to the IPPR*. A Catalyst Working Paper. London: Catalyst Trust.

Robertson, S. (2002) Hybrid Monsters or Synergistic Solutions? The State of Public Private Partnerships in the Education Sector in England, paper presented to the Conference hosted by the Fundacao Joao Pinheiro and the British Council Belo Horizonte, Minas Gerais, 21-22 March.

Robertson, S., Bonal, X. & Dale, R. (2002) GATS and the Education Service Industry: the politics of scale and global re-territorialisation, *Comparative Education Review*, 43(3), 472-495. http://dx.doi.org/10.1086/343122

Rodrigues, F. & Stoer, S. (2001) Partnership and Local Development in Portugal: from 'globalised localism' to a new form of collective action, in M. Geddes & J. Benington (Eds) *Local Partnerships and Social Exclusion in the European Union: new forms of local social governance*. London: Routledge.

Rosamond, B. (2002) Imagining the European Economy: 'competitiveness' and the social construction of 'Europe' as an economic space, *New Political Economy*, 7(2), 157-177. http://dx.doi.org/10.1080/13563460220138826

Shore, C. (2000) *Building Europe: the cultural politics of European integration*. London: Routledge.

Smith, N. (1993) Homeless/Global: scaling places, in J. Bird et al (Eds) *Mapping the Futures: local cultures, global change*. London: Routledge.

Streeck, W. (1999) Competitive Solidarity: rethinking the 'European Social Model'. Society for the Advancement of Socio-Economics Presidential Address, Madison, 8-11 June. http://www.scase.org/conf1999/streeck.html

Walters, W. & Haahr, J. (2005) *Governing Europe: discourse, governmentality and European integration*. London: Routledge.

CHAPTER 6

Studying Globalisation and Europeanisation in Education: Lisbon, the Open Method of Coordination and beyond

ROGER DALE

SUMMARY This chapter begins by discussing the nature and implications of recent changes in the nature and place of education policy in a globalising world, through a discussion of the consequences of operating through existing tendencies towards methodological nationalism, statism and educationism, each of which it seeks to elaborate in the context of a growing European role in education. The main focus of the chapter is the relationship between the Open Method of Coordination (OMC) and the development of education related activities at the European level. It is suggested that its mediation through the OMC means that education policy will: take the form of policy paradigms (in Peter Hall's sense); focus on programme ontologies rather than programmes; be 'depoliticised', though not 'apolitical; and be directed at member states education systems rather than their education policies. The chapter concludes with speculation about the possible development of a distinct European education sector.

This chapter falls essentially into two halves. The first half elaborates some of the themes of Chapter 1, focusing in particular on the theoretical and methodological discussions of the qualitative distinction that has to be made between the analysis of national and European education policies. It does this through a consideration of the assumptions that lie behind analyses of national education systems, and the ways in which they relate to analyses of European Education Policy (EEP). In the second half of the chapter, I take up the question of the Open Method of Coordination, the means designated for the 'implementation' of the Lisbon Agenda in education. Here, I argue that the OMC works as a 'paradigm' and a 'programme ontology' rather than in the 'programme' mode which we have come to expect – even assume – will characterise 'policymaking' in education. The chapter concludes with some speculations about the emergence of a separate 'education' sector at European level.

Europe and National Education Systems

The assumptions in terms of European education on which this chapter is based tend to run against what seem to be taken – frequently implicitly – as common currency in discussions around the question, and may be most usefully disclosed through comparison with those common assumptions.

The first piece of common currency is the assumption that, as elaborated in Chapter 1, EEP is in most relevant dimensions similar to national education policies. Policies are made in the same way, by similar bodies, for similar purposes, and cover similar kinds of areas, and occupy the same place and space as they do in national systems. This means that the national can be scaled up to the regional with no loss of meaning.

The second piece of common currency is that the main purpose/goal/objective of EEP is to replace or at least (more commonly) to modify national education policies, in whole or in part, in the sense of having effects on them that would not otherwise have come about (in other words, very much like the highly popular academic tendency to see, and/or look for, evidence of 'Europe's' influence through its effects on domestic policies). This is not to say either that there are no such effects, or that they are not important, or that it is not important to look for them; it is, though, to say that confining ourselves to such searches unnecessarily, and misleadingly, limits our capacity to understand the nature of EEP.

This leads directly to the third assumption, that EEP exists only in so far as it can be shown to have achieved these things.

And finally, implicit in all the above is a zero-sum assumption about the relationship between Europe and Member States' education policies; they are either European or national.

By contrast, the approach advanced here suggests that, as argued in Chapter 1, we need to see the relationship as not only 'both and' as well as not 'either or', but also that we have to be open to the emergence of a new entity, a European Education Space (EES) and EEP, which are qualitatively distinct from Member States' national education systems, in terms of their scope, mandate, capacity and governance. So, the entity we intend to approach is EES and EEP, and not education policy (or policies) in Europe. As we argued in Chapter 1, the EES is formed by the unique governance system of the European Union; it overlaps with, but is not confined to, the education spaces of Member States, individually or collectively. EEP is a response to – or rather, as will be argued in this chapter – a shaping or framing of, problems perceived as distinctively 'European', or of distinctively

'European' elements of other problems encountered in common by Member States.

Perhaps the best way of developing this argument is to contrast the EES and EEP with each of the components of the common term, *national, education, system*. In elaborating this argument I will draw on the need to identify and go beyond what Susan Robertson and I have referred to as methodological 'isms' in the study of 'education': these are methodological nationalism, methodological statism and methodological 'educationism' (Dale & Robertson, 2007; Robertson & Dale, 2008).

First, and almost by definition, it is difficult to see EEP as 'national'; there may be issues of whether it is multinational or transnational, but it clearly cannot be 'national', especially if we accept Chernilo's argument that methodological nationalism 'can be simply defined as the all-pervasive equation between the idea of society and the formation of the nation-state in modernity' (2007, p. 1). However, the tendency to scale up the national to the regional in studies of EEP does run a severe danger of adopting methodological nationalist assumptions at a regional level, whenever and in so far as it identifies the 'society' that hosts or is 'affected by' 'education policy' with a territorial-political entity. This results from what Ruggie has called 'an extraordinarily impoverished mind-set ... that is able to visualise long-term challenges to the system of states only in terms of entities that are institutionally substitutable for the state' (1993, p. 143).

We should also note that, as was pointed out in Chapter 1, this tendency is likely to be reinforced by the fact that a major element of EEP is precisely the attempt to promote and thicken the idea of Europe as a distinct 'society', different from its individual Member States and from the sum of their parts. And we should also note that it is not 'methodologically nationalist' to recognise the fundamental importance of national education systems, or to appreciate 'Europe's' ambitions in this area. Problematising methodological nationalism does not mean ignoring and reducing the importance of what occurs at a national level; it concerns the equation of 'society' with a particular politico-territorial entity. It is as important to emphasise methodologically as it is to do so theoretically and empirically that national education policies will persist, and may well *look* very much as they did in the last quarter of the last century. However, though they may appear and be experienced similarly, they will not mean the same in all respects. Gavin Smith's suggestion that 'a whole series of key concepts for the understanding of society derive their power from appearing to be just what they always were and derive their instrumentality from taking on quite different forms' (Smith, 2006, p. 628) is probably nowhere more true or more relevant than in the case of education, which is everywhere enormously important to, intensely debated by, and utterly familiar to, more people within national societies than any other topic – which means that we have to be all the more aware of, and responsive to, Smith's point.

When we move to consider education *systems* we become vulnerable to methodological statism, because education systems are not only seen as nationally located but also as organised in a more or less common set of political, administrative and organisational arrangements that commonly are regarded as comprising 'the state'; it is their state basis which adds 'system' to national education systems. However, once again, it is crucial to interrogate and expose that nature of the assumptions on which this idea of 'state system' rests.

By 'methodological statism', I refer to the assumption that the state is the source and means of all governing activity, which, though it is typically taken for granted, is essentially contingent. Fundamental to methodological statism is the idea that it is the state that (necessarily) governs 'its' society, with an assumed unity between territory, society and political organisation. One implication of methodological statism is the assumption that the state continues to govern not only the same territory, but the same things and in the same ways that it has done historically – which in this case has been taken to be the 'Golden Age' of the post-war social democratic state form found in Western Europe until its gradual and accelerating erosion that began in around 1975 (see Zurn & Leibfried, 2005, p. 11).

While this was pre-eminently a national state, the scope of state activity was very wide, from intervention in the economy, to the monopoly of provision of welfare services. The state would mitigate the worst excesses of capitalism and ensure at least a minimum of social protection. It governed, from above, implicitly alone, and primarily through making policy. What is surprising is that despite the thorough critiques of this view of the state, some of these central assumptions continue to inform academic accounts, especially perhaps the idea that the state governs through policy; if things are to be changed, it is to the state that we expect to look to bring about those changes.

As was pointed out in Chapter 1, none of these things holds in the current era. For instance, the state can no longer be assumed to hold sovereignty over 'its' territory; sovereignty and territory no longer necessarily reinforce each other (see Dale, 2003). The state now governs through means other than 'policy' and in concert with a range of other institutions rather than alone. This has given rise to the term 'governance rather than government'. And this leads to a need to make the state *explanans* rather than *explanandum* in our analyses (see Dale, 2007)

We may infer two main points from this discussion. First, and less relevant in this context, it suggests that some well-established approaches to studying education policy at a national level might need to be reviewed. Second, empirically and theoretically, it is readily apparent that we are not dealing with an entity like the Golden Age state when we discuss the EU and its relationship to education policy, and hence that different theoretical assumptions and tools are necessary.

I pointed out in Chapter 1 that the EES is strongly framed by the EU's formal competence under Article 149 of the Treaty, which makes it clear that education (apart from vocational education) is a national competence, subject to subsidiarity, and in that sense, it does not act like a 'conventional' state. However, if we separate out the methodological nationalist and statist assumptions and instead focus on the activities that formal competence has been used to generate around education, it becomes clear that it has constructed an EES and has ambitions to fill it with an EEP. This is largely brought about by the Open Method of Coordination, which we will discuss in the second half of this chapter.

What this brief consideration of the 'system'-like nature of EEP leads us to recognise, then, is that once we shed the shackles of methodological statism in thinking about what counts as education policy and how it is made – if we do not assume that it has to be scaled-up national policy making – we are in a position to consider the possible substance of EEP – but again, only if we problematise the methodological educationism that has characterised thinking about education policy.

So, the final element to be discussed is what is meant by 'education' when we speak of national education systems. This, too, may be rendered in the form of an 'ism'; 'educationism' refers to the tendency to regard 'education' as a single category for purposes of analysis, with an assumed common scope, and a set of implicitly shared knowledges, practices and assumptions. It occurs when education is treated as abstract, fixed, absolute, ahistorical and universal, when no distinctions are made between its use to describe purpose, process, practice and outcomes. Particular representations of education are treated in isolation from each other, and addressed discretely rather than as part of a wider assemblage of representations – for there is no suggestion that the different representations of education have nothing in common with each other, or that the label is randomly attached. At the same time, 'Education' has accreted an extremely wide range of responsibilities that have little in common with each other except that education is the means of solving them. And this in turn means that education develops a range of solutions that have little in common with each other, that are selectively incorporated into education as a set of discourses and practices. Over the centuries, these practices have become themselves solidified into what has been called the 'grammar' of schooling (Tyack & Tobin, 1994), which pervades certainly all western education systems.

The central point here is that in that time, 'education' has become identified with the dominant organisational means of delivering some of its more salient responsibilities effectively and efficiently, that is to say, 'schooling' (Dale & Robertson, 2007).

However, this is an inappropriate guide to, or means of considering, what education might mean at the level of the EU, if only because the key differentia specifica of EU education space and policy is precisely that it is not confronted with 'an extremely wide range of responsibilities that have little in common with each other except that education is the means of solving them'. This is especially important when we consider that 'schooling' has emerged as the means of dealing with the whole congeries of problems accreted by education systems, and that therefore it may be seen as a poor guide to what might be attempted/achieved in the quite different context of an education project with a quantitatively and qualitatively different set of responsibilities and emergent issues.

However, while the policy space of education may be framed and filled in very different ways, it will do so following the same basic analytic format. 'Education'–and any other collectively provided and focused activity – must necessarily, and however tacitly, contain three distinct moments: a mandate, what it is considered desirable for it to achieve/attain; a capacity, the feasibility of achieving that mandate; and a means of governance, coordinating the activities seen as desirable and feasible.

The argument is, then, not to suggest that the EU does not have something that might be seen as an education policy, both formally and substantively. Formally, it might be seen as taking 'education' at a rather different level; at its most fundamental level, the place held by 'education' in EU policy is the fundamental formal contribution it makes to modernity, as the best available means of bringing about forms of social change, the key modernist institution for installing modernist values and practices. Substantively, it is based on the achievement of what have been identified in these chapters as its key goals: maximising the contribution of 'education' to the Lisbon Process, strengthening the European Social Model and thickening the idea of Europe.

In terms of the latter, it is interesting to note the approach to the substance of education policy within the European Commission. Interestingly, the mandate for an EES has been since the Lisbon Declaration considerably more explicit than might seem possible on the basis of the Treaty. That declaration not only advanced three 'Concrete Future Objectives' of education systems, but insisted that they could only be met at the level of the Community, rather than Member State level. Those objectives were attached to, and seen as the means through which education could contribute to, the achievement of the goals of the famous Lisbon Agenda – that 'by 2010, Europe would become the most competitive, dynamic, knowledge-based economy in the world, capable of sustained growth, with more and better jobs and greater social cohesion' (Council of the Communities, 2000, p. 1).

The Lisbon Agenda evidently set a multiple, and potentially contradictory, mandate for education systems, around the themes of competitiveness and social cohesion, though again we should note how comparatively narrow it is vis-à-vis Member States' education systems.

Extremely briefly (because this has been the topic of a large number of papers on education in the EU), its mandate is essentially organised around a view that sees Member States' education systems as deficient in a range of ways related to the achievement of the Lisbon goals (it should be noted that here I refer to the *intrinsic* shortcomings of the orthodox and taken-as-universal *form* of education *sectors* of Member States, i.e. educationism, rather than of policies adopted). The need to change is 'urgent'; the failure to do so threatens the achievement of the Lisbon goals (see Council of the European Union, 2004). The nature of change is also quite fundamental; the old solutions do not work any longer. This requires quite different capacity from Member States' education systems, but the claim is that that capacity has to be organised by, and can only be delivered at, the level of the Union, not of the Member States, individually or collectively. Here, the EU, like all Member State governments, runs up against the practices taken as constituting 'education' as set out in the discussion of educationism. Recognising educationism does not mean rejecting wholesale the 'traditional' assumptions on which it rests, which are deeply embedded in national social fabrics, especially their annual timetables; just think of *la rentrée*. The practices based on those assumptions are the basis of the professional identity of the education profession, and hence very difficult to budge. To a considerable degree, any attempt to change the assumptions of educationism will run up against the embedded assumptions of what 'education' consists of and entails. (Interestingly, this provides some common ground between politicians at regional and national levels, who share the frustration at the difficulty of changing education. And it also goes some way to explaining Member States' governments' relative lack of affront at having their education systems criticised, or identified as deficient, as they are in many EU documents; they may be quite happy to use 'disappointing' results from international comparisons as a stick with which to beat their education systems, and to deploy such criticism as leverage to bring about changes that have previously been resisted by the education profession.)

And third, in terms of governance, the EU will be the coordinator in chief, simultaneously driving the 'repair' project and establishing its own competence (in both senses of the word) in the area of education – largely through the Open Method of Coordination, to which we now turn.

The Open Method of Coordination

The OMC was the means chosen for the implementation of the Lisbon Agenda, but its influence is very much wider than might be assumed from that statement, both politically and theoretically. In particular, in both these areas the complexities of the OMC expose the limitations of 'implementation' as a means of conceiving of the 'policy process', where a 'policy' is devised by groups legitimated to do that, and 'implemented' in a polity through the capacities of a governing body with legitimate authority and sovereignty. None of these features is found in the OMC, and approaching it and seeing it as a form of implementation in this 'traditional' sense is somewhat misleading. And while we do recognise something that can be referred to as an EEP, its relationship to the OMC is qualitatively different from 'policy implementation' as traditionally conceived. Indeed, it is probably incorrect to think of it as merely 'implementing' the Lisbon Agenda, or even to see its consequences restricted to its association with that agenda. As was argued in Chapter 1, the OMC shapes both the EES, and how it can be filled. The position taken here is that, certainly as far as education is concerned, the OMC in effect is a central means of defining relationships between the EU and Member States, and of shaping the scope of the Union itself. Thus Radaelli's suggestion that the OMC 'constitutes convergence at the level of beliefs about what the European Social Model should be' (2003, p. 54) is quite correct but the statement's implications have to be traced out with care, for the OMC does not, and could not, fulfil that role as a 'mere' instrument. On the one hand, 'convergence' is a relatively distinct term in the Euro-lexicon, differentiated from harmonisation and regulation, for instance. However, we also need, as Colin Hay (2000) has pointed out, to ask *what* is converging – in addition to Radaelli's 'beliefs', he mentions inputs, outputs, processes, policies – and over what period. On the other hand it requires us to reflect on the assumptions it contains about the nature of 'Europe' as an entity capable of defining the overarching aims and structure of social policy among Member States, and claiming the authority to do so.

It is very revealing in the case of the OMC, in education as elsewhere, to ask Hay's question, 'what is converging?' The OMC in education clearly seeks greater convergence in outputs, such as the percentage of early school leavers, and seeks to influence inputs, at least rhetorically, through urging Member States to spend more on education. At the same time, there is an explicit emphasis on 'common goals, divergent means', which seems to rule out attempts to seek process convergence. However, in this context the issue of *policy* convergence is paramount, and it is here that the OMC most crucially shapes the European Education Policy Space.

It might be objected that, strictly, policy convergence is excluded not only by subsidiarity rules but also by the 'divergent means' argument. However, the nature of EU governance also imposes a further responsibility on the OMC, a strategic responsibility. As Renaud Dehousse points out, the OMC's

> purpose is not simply to permit the implementation of reforms in a number of domains but also a balanced progress toward sometimes contradictory goals: economic competitiveness, social cohesion and environmental protection. This ambition, which is the source of the complex architecture put into place at Lisbon, is itself the sign of weakness. Unable to agree on clear priorities, Europeans decided to tackle a number of issues at once. Thus, the attention directed at methodological questions: it was intended not only to insure the coherence of the whole construction, but also to conceal behind an innovative discourse, the difficulty to

make clear political choices in a system of decision by consensus like the EU. (Dehousse, 2002, p. 6)

The response to this dilemma might be seen as effectively threefold. First, the problems the OMC was set up to address (essentially the Lisbon Agenda) are represented not as Member States' individual national problems, or even the aggregate of those separate problems, but as *common* problems, shared at the level of the Union; here, any convergence is around the identification of those common problems. Second, the ability to act on common problem identification also involves convergence around the idea that 'Europe' is the appropriate level to develop policy to address those common issues, that is, that there should be some form of 'European Education Policy'. And third, any response should not be overtly 'political'. The argument to be made here is that it is those three convergences, especially the first two, since the third is essentially conditional, that set the parameters of the EES.

The parameters of the EES are made up of three elements: *formally*, they are bounded by the rules of subsidiarity; *substantively*, they are shaped by the dual agenda set for education at Lisbon, pursuing the Lisbon goals and contributing to the European Social Model; and *processually*, through the importance of embedding the message that 'Europe' is a key actor in these matters.

The first of these was spelled out in Chapter 1, where possible flexibilities in the Treaty clauses relating to education were discussed. The second, substantive, parameter both limits and directs legitimate European intervention in education We have already emphasised the centrality of the 'master discourse' of Lisbon, competitiveness, as far as education policy and efforts are concerned. However, we should recall that Lisbon also saw a key role for education in contributing to the European Social Model and European Social Policy, where the central features are 'investment in people' and 'building an active welfare state'. The first of these means that 'Europe's education and training systems need to adapt both to the demands of the knowledge society and to the need of an improved level and quality of employment' (Council of the European Communities, 2000, para. 25).

The OMC, the EES and the EEP

We turn now to examine in more detail the nature and consequences of the relationship between the OMC and education. There are four elements to the argument here. First, that the framing conditions just set out mean that anything 'policy-like' will be in the form of 'policy paradigms' rather than policy reforms. Second, that EEP developed through the OMC will take the form not of 'programmes', but of 'programme ontologies'. Third, that such outputs, though necessarily 'political', will be 'depoliticised'. And fourth, that they will be directed at the level of Member States' education systems not at education policies in Member States, with national education systems 'recontextualising' policies rather than constructing them anew.

The OMC as Paradigm

In an extremely influential article, Peter Hall, from an explicitly Kuhnian perspective, contrasts two models of policy making, what he calls 'normal policymaking' and 'paradigm shift' (Hall, 1993). As he puts it:

> policymakers customarily work within a framework of ideas and standards that specifies not only the goals of policy and the kind of instruments that can be used to attain them, but also the very nature of the problems they are meant to be addressing ... I am going to call this interpretive framework a policy paradigm.
> (p. 279)

He identifies two kinds of changes to this model, what he calls 'normal policymaking', by which he means a process that adjusts policy without challenging the overall terms of a given policy paradigm, much like 'normal science'. By contrast, what he refers to as a 'paradigm shift in policymaking' 'is likely to reflect a very different process, marked by the radical changes in the overarching terms of policy discourse' (Hall, 1993, p. 279).

This form of policy making seems to fit very well with both the aims and the necessary processes of EU Education Policy. (A similar argument has been advanced by Mabbett, 2007.) It reflects the necessity of constructing 'policy' that does not and cannot seek either to implement or to modify existing paradigms, or to cover the same areas that they do. And while Hall talks about *replacement* of one paradigm by another, that is not what is being suggested here. Rather, what we might see is the attempt to construct a 'parallel' paradigm, which is restricted both in its mandate and capacity by the fundamental differences in scope between EU and Member State education policies that we have mentioned above. 'Europe' here is less an external context with the potential to affect national policies, which is how it is typically perceived in the literature, and more a common space where Member States (under the coordination of the European Commission) shape and frame not so much distinct education policies but a parallel sector.

It is, of course, crucial to note that this does not mean that the activities associated with the 'EU paradigm' will be fundamentally different from those associated with existing Member States' policies. It does, though, mean that they are likely to be embedded in a different discourse, one that prioritises the Lisbon Agenda and seeks to associate all activities with the pursuit of that Agenda. And, of course, as will be elaborated below, the clearest example of this paradigm shift is the development of the EU education agenda under the umbrella of lifelong learning, which fulfils all the characteristics of a paradigm shift that does not cause upheavals in practice, the fundamental condition of EEP.

Two consequences flow from this, one theoretical, one methodological. Theoretically, it means that we need to distinguish not only which type of convergence and policy we are studying, why, where it comes from, what it seeks to do, but also *how it is conceived to achieve its ends*. This last point is especially important, and somewhat neglected in studies of European policy making, which tend not to have well-developed theories of how the European level will influence the national. This gap is especially significant in studies of the OMC and education; how might a European Education Policy work (given the parameters within which it is located)? This question is, of course, extremely important methodologically as well as theoretically. If we do not know how the OMC is supposed to work, how is it possible to analyse it? More fundamentally, we might ask what is the status of the OMC in the policy-making process – is it itself to be seen as a policy, an instrument, a programme? We need also to consider the consequences of the OMC operating as paradigmatic rather than normal policy making. Are the mechanisms through which it is to work (as set out in its original specification) assumed to work through exhortation, pressure, incentives, persuasion – all of which might be found in the 'normal' mode. The methodological consequences of this are that we need to know how the instruments/mechanisms relate to how the OMC itself works, recognising: (a) that instruments do not mean the same thing in all circumstances (e.g. benchmarking), and that (b) the OMC is in any case more than the sum of, and not reducible to, its mechanisms.

OMC as Programme Ontology

One very effective approach to tracking these issues is through the concept of 'Programme Ontology', which was developed by Ray Pawson (2002), originally in the context of evaluation research. Briefly, Pawson's argument is that in attempting to find a basis for generalisation of successful (or rejection of unsuccessful) social interventions and innovations, such as anti-crime initiatives, it is crucial to distinguish between what he calls the 'Programme' and the 'Programme Ontology'. Basically, the Programme is the intervention, or policy, or innovation that is being introduced or implemented with the intention of bringing about beneficial changes in some social phenomenon. The 'Programme Ontology', by contrast, accounts for *how* programmes, policies, and so on, actually work. It is essentially the 'theory' of the programme as opposed to its content (and the 'theory' is typically quite likely to be implicit). According to this perspective,

> it is not 'programmes' that work: rather it is the underlying
> reasons or resources that they offer subjects that generate change.
> Causation is also reckoned to be contingent. Whether the choices
> or capacities on offer in an initiative are acted upon depends on
> the nature of their subjects and the circumstances of the initiative.
> The vital ingredients of programme ontology are thus its
> 'generative mechanisms' and its 'contiguous context'.
> (Pawson, 2002, p. 342)

The argument we want to make from here, then, is that the OMC does not work only as either a paradigmatic means of making policy, or as a set of instruments that enable that, but can itself be seen as a programme ontology in the terms in which Pawson describes it. That is to say, it is more usefully seen as 'offering subjects (here, Member States) reasons and resources that will enable them to generate change', given: (a) their 'nature' as subjects (political entities with discretion to act), and (b) the circumstances of the initiative (Lisbon), than as either a particular programme package or a collection of instruments and mechanisms. The way that this works may become clearer if we translate the 'vital ingredients' of programme ontology, its generative mechanisms and contiguous contexts, into the structure and logic of the OMC.

We can deal quite quickly with the contiguous contexts, as they have effectively been addressed through the discussions of the EES and EEP in Chapter 1. However, it will be important to consider the 'generative mechanisms' in more detail. They might be seen to be made up of the 'reasons and resources'.

(a) The underlying reasons are: (i) above all, *the desire to proceed with Lisbon as far as possible*. The cognitive and normative framework of the OMC is very powerfully informed by the Lisbon Agenda, and particularly by the 'master discourse' of 'competitiveness' (Radaelli, 2003). It frames a conception of the European Social Model that ties it closely to the idea of productive social policy, and it is largely through this means that attempts to address the apparent contradictions in the Lisbon Agenda between economic and social aims are to be addressed. As Caroline de la Porte points out:

> the areas dealt with under the auspices of the OMC are politically
> linked to the overall strategic objective of the EU as defined at
> Lisbon. Therefore, although the social dimension of the Union
> has been boosted, it continues to be linked to the economic
> project of the Union. Indeed, it appears there is a tension between
> the top-down objectives agreed during the successive sessions of
> the European Council, and the need for the OMC to take on a life
> of its own in their individual spheres. (2001, p. 360)

(ii) the need to establish Europe as a competent (in both senses) actor but in circumstances where, given the impossibility of using the Community method, the EU lacks the political and possibly administrative capacity to do that.

This has possibly been the main area of research scrutiny around education policy. The contribution most directly linked to the EES has been made by Ase Gornitzka (2006). She argues that the European level in areas like education is essentially brought into being by the activities promoted by the OMC; without the OMC, 'Europe' would not exist in the form(s) that it does. Similarly, the same devices of benchmarking, sharing of best practice, and so on, are not only the means through which the national and European 'universes' are constructed, but also the means through which they are linked to each other; the OMC provides the means of both constructing (European) 'unity' and enabling (national) 'diversity' in subscribing to that unity.

Gornitzka (2006) also provides detailed evidence of how the European level is constructed in education through the OMC. She points out, for instance, that the five benchmarks for the improvement of education and training in Europe up to 2010 (reducing rates of early school leaving and of poor academic performance; increasing the numbers of graduates in mathematics, science and technology, of the proportion of the population completing upper secondary education, and of rates of participation in lifelong learning) 'are not concrete targets for *individual* countries to be reached by 2010. They are defined by the Council as "reference levels for the European *average* performance"' (2005, p. 17, emphasis in original).

She also makes the crucial point alluded to above that with the OMC, the question has shifted from the desirability to the feasibility of European education cooperation (2006, pp. 48-49).

(b) *The 'resources' element of the generative mechanisms.* We might see the *resources* to generate change that the OMC offers as comprising the list of its five characteristics, as stated in the Bulletin on the Conclusions of the Portuguese Presidency:

> the open method of coordination, which is designed to help the
> Member States to progressively develop their own policies,
> involves:
> 1. fixing *guidelines* for the Union combined with *specific timetables*
> for achieving the *goals* which they set in the short, medium and
> long terms;
> 2. establishing, where appropriate, quantitative and qualitative
> *indicators* and *benchmarks* against the best in the world and tailored
> to the needs of different Member States and sectors as a means of
> *comparing best practice*;
> 3. translating these European guidelines into *national and regional*
> *policies* by setting *specific targets and adopting measures*, taking into
> account national and regional differences;
> 4. periodic monitoring, evaluation and peer review as *mutual*
> *learning* processes. (Council of the European Communities, 2000,
> para. 37, emphases added)

It is important to note though these are set out in forms that seem to privilege quantification of strategies and outcomes, it is the taxonomy contained within, and reflected by, the indicators, benchmarks, and so on, that is crucial rather than the quantification itself (see Desrosieres, 2002). The OMC principles have the effect of putting all Member States on a single metric – they are all compared against the same standards. Above all, it makes all Member State education systems commensurable and makes them susceptible to the possibilities of comparison, which, as Nóvoa & Yariv-Mashal (2003) point out, makes comparison a powerful tool of governance. Bruno Theret makes a similar point:

> International comparison is for the Commission an essential weapon in the competitive struggle it wages with Member States over developing its political competences. It implies the construction of a common language of definition of problems chosen for the possibility of their becoming an object of joint action at Community level, a language that makes Member States comparable, if not homogeneous.
> (2005, p. 78, author's translation)

The Political Nature of the Outputs

As Renaud Dehousse suggests, differences between Member States in areas of policy meant that something that was relatively 'content free', and (apparently) non-political, was necessary to ensure a common platform (see Dehousse, 2002, pp. 9, 10).

This was in a sense intrinsic to the OMC and was a feature particularly of the numerical/statistical approaches at the core of the OMC. The fact is that 'objective indicators, typically drawn up by 'a-national' experts, have led many people (including me at an earlier stage) to infer that the process was somehow 'apolitical', or 'depoliticised'. However, as Radaelli put it:

> To choose a set of indicators, to designate an innovation as 'good practice', to undertake a benchmarking exercise, and to write guidelines are all political processes. They establish hierarchies of domestic solutions, they put pressure on some versions of the 'European social model' but not on others, or, in the case of taxation, they alter the comparative advantage of all Member States. To assume that a depoliticised, positive-sum game learning is the most common feature of the OMC is simply wrong.
> (2003, p. 40)

That is to say, indicators and benchmarks necessarily have 'political' consequences, even if (which may be unlikely) they are not chosen with a view to 'political' advantage, or structuring of the playing field – though, given the pervasiveness and taken-for-grantedness of the dominant paradigm, this would be done 'unconsciously'. However, Barbier argues that:

> increasingly, EU policies ... contribute to the *de-coupling* of the sphere of policies from the sphere of politics. More and more, at the EU level, cognitive and normative frameworks are established, which have an important cognitive influence on the way national programmes and policies are designed. (2007, p. 8)

Though, as he points out elsewhere, to assume that this means that they can be seen as merely 'technical', or 'a-political' is wrong' (Barbier, 2004, p. 3). Writing about the European employment sector, but with clear resonances for Education and all other social sectors, Barbier argues that:

> the standard political discourse is very appropriately consistent with what has come to be the mainstream policy-mix in Europe. This discourse is anything but neutral, anything but technical and it conveys a specific normative choice among other possible policies, including macroeconomic policies. However, as the EES discourse *exemplifies a consensus* which has been shared by all governments since the 'paradigm' change in economic policy (Hall 1993; Jobert 1994), it has been possible to present it as a relatively *de-politicized discourse*, irrespective of the partisan colours of the national governments in place. (Barbier, 2007, p. 14, emphases in original)

However, Dehousse suggests that there was some convergence at a political – possibly a paradigm – level:

> The symbolic value of the Lisbon strategy should also be underlined. After having invested much political capital in monetary unification, it was important for the left of centre governments (which were in the majority during the second half of the 1990s) to display their commitment to social issues. In this context, it was obviously tempting to develop a method which would borrow its vocabulary and its instruments from the EMU [European Monetary Union]. (Dehousse, 2002, p. 7)

System Management or Policy?

Here, we draw again on the work of Gábor Halász. He argues that the Treaty makes the harmonisation of systems of education, in the sense of curriculum or school organisation, impossible, but suggests that what happens instead is 'the harmonisation of policies directed to systems of education' (Halász, 2003, p. 2), what we may see as a kind of 'meta-harmonisation'. He extends this argument to the use of the idea of quality in EC education work, suggesting in particular the need to 'make a clear distinction between the indicators of educational quality and the indicators of the quality of education policy' (p. 10), suggesting that the use of indicators in the OMC is directed very much towards the latter rather than the former. And he concludes from this that 'the question of applying OMC in education could be seen ... not only as a question of how far we go with the Europeanisation of our national education policies, but also one that can help us renew our national ways of governing our own education systems' (p. 6). This fits well with the suggestions above about the 'paradigm' nature of the OMC's contribution, and the treatment of it as a programme ontology.

Towards a New Sector?

I want, finally, to offer some brief speculation about the possible future of the governance of European education. As hinted above, that speculation involves suggesting that the combination of the problems EU 'Education' is to address, and the means available for addressing them, may lead to the construction (whether formally or effectively) of a separate sector at the European level, which would in a sense run parallel with the education sectors of Member States. To put it another way, the EES and EEP may come together to form a new European education sector.

There are a number of reasons supporting this speculation:

1. The difference in the scope and range of responsibilities of European education makes it unnecessary, and unhelpful, for it to attempt to follow Member States' sectoral definitions and boundaries. At EU level, education is not part of state building and group identity and placement as at national level, but provides the underpinnings for a European project based around competitiveness and the European Social Model.
2. European education is strongly circumscribed by its Treaty status. Consequently, to be effective requires finding ways around the difficulties posed by that status.
3. It is confronted by the same embedded assumptions and practices in the sector that are experienced by Member States' education systems.
4. At the European level sectors become themselves what is at stake, as existing Member State education systems are perceived to be 'unfit for purpose' in a global knowledge economy. It is for this reason that we see the development of a European capacity in education, with a particular agenda to reform, reconstruct or transform the representation, the governance and the technology of education.
5. The OMC is intrinsically sector based and consequently has the capacity to reshape the sector.

Very briefly, Reason 1 suggests that the basis of a distinct sector already exists and that it would be more effective to be able to concentrate on that. The construction of a new sector that does not exist in any Member State is encouraged by Reason 2. Similarly, Reason 3 points to advantages to be gained by breaking away from difficulties that are entrenched in the existing sector. Reason 4 suggests that the value of continuing with existing sectors is doubtful, and that there is a strong case for reconstructing them. And finally, the OMC process in education is effectively concerned with a process of assembling a separate set of common definitions and roles, not reducible to the aggregate or average of Member State practices. It is the key means of demonstrating EU competence in education, of identifying European-level problems (or redefining existing problems by shifting their scale) that can only be addressed at European level. It thus offers a means through which such reconstruction might be organised, particularly if it is seen in the ways suggested above, as being concerned less with 'implementing programmes' and more with operating through the creation of new paradigms, taxonomies and programme ontologies.

This is by no means a wholly original argument. Similar ideas have been advanced for the social policy sector. Daly, for instance, has argued that 'the significance of EU social policy lies in how it serves to construct and create a social sphere or space for EU action which in turn has dynamic effects on European identity and European society' (2006, pp. 465-466). This creates new areas of EU activity and competence, while avoiding issues of subsidiarity and enables added 'Euro-value' by synergising national capacities. Savio & Palola (2004) have suggested that:

> the Lisbon strategy and the open method of co-ordination (OMC)
> can be regarded as signs which show us that the EU social policy
> has left its customary place and has *become a project to invent the*
> *social within the confines of the European Union* ... [and that] After
> Lisbon, it has no longer been relevant to make a distinction
> between EU-level and national level social policy, as this division,
> based on the Treaties' definition of competences in the area of
> social policy, is not recognised in the efforts to modernise social
> protection by means of the OMC. (pp. 2, 4, emphasis in original)

Moreover, there is clear evidence that such a project may be in course, in the form of what might be called a 'Knowledge Economy and Lifelong Learning' (KnELL) sector, with different purposes, substance and values from those of Member States' 'education' sectors, and linking (different forms of) education to social policy and knowledge policy sectors (see Dale, 2007). Strategically, lifelong learning (LLL) is not a 'sector' in any Member State (and may be distributed across different sectors in some of them), and the new generation of EU Directorate General for Education and Culture programmes is being coordinated under the heading of LLL (see e.g. European Community, 2006). A key element of the LLL agenda is its capacity to weld together the competitiveness and social cohesion components of the Lisbon Agenda through 'productive social policy'. The EU's Memorandum on Lifelong Learning states that: 'Lifelong Learning is no longer just one aspect of Education and Training; it *must become the guiding principle* for participation across the full continuum of learning contexts (Commission of the European Communities, 2000, p. 3, emphasis in original). The 2006 report on progress towards attaining the Commission's goals for education emphasises the need to accelerate the pace of reform in lifelong learning, which is seen as a 'sine qua non of achieving the Lisbon goals while strengthening the European Social Model', and calls for 'Effective inter-Ministerial synergy between 'knowledge policies' (education, training, employment/social affairs, research)(Commission of the European Communities, 2006, pp.10-11).

The intention that the sector should mark a shift away from existing conceptions of education sectors is also evident in the clear content intentions that the LLL documents contain and assume, where what is advanced differs from the national sectors in several respects. In terms of focus, it is concerned with (see Dale, 2007):

- 'learning' rather than 'education';
- competence not content;
- the key importance of its involvement of/with ICT;
- a specific, employment-related focus rather than comprehensive social policy, nation-building (etc.) scope;
- a 'Lifelong' system of provision that is confined neither to specified age-defined stages of an educational career, nor to existing 'educational' institutions.

Finally, we might speculate further, and suggest that the possible new sector will be linked with existing sectors through an emergent functional, scalar and sectoral division of the labour of education governance (see Dale, 2003). Here, we might expect issues around economic competitiveness and the European Social Model (respectively the 'knowledge sector' and 'social policy sector') to shift 'upwards' to become part of the new KnELL sector, and issues around education's role in the distribution of opportunities within national societies remain at the national level, or move 'downwards' to sub-national levels.

Thus, overall, we might suggest that the changes brought about by the construction of an EES and EEP have involved a movement from 'Education' as an exclusively and taken-for-grantedly distinctive knowledge/administrative space, deriving from and reinforcing coherence and cohesiveness within a national (and often provincial)-historical formation and division of labour of governance (e.g. ministries of education) to 'KnELL' as also possibly a distinctive knowledge/administrative space, deriving from and reinforcing coherence and cohesiveness within a supra- or sub-national division of labour of governance (e.g. European Education Space).

References

Barbier, Jean-Claude (2004) Research on 'Open Methods of Coordination' and National Social Policies: what sociological theories and methods?, paper for the Research Committee 19 international conference, Paris, 2-4 September.

Barbier, Jean-Claude (2007) The European Social Model (ESM) and Cultural Diversity in Europe, Inaugural lecture as adjungeret professor, University of Aalborg, 4 March.

Chernilo, Daniel (2007) *Social Theory and the State*. London: Routledge.

Commission of the European Communities (2000) *A Memorandum on Lifelong Learning*. Brussels: Commission Staff Working Paper.

Commission of the European Communities (2006) Communication from the Commission: modernising education and training: a vital contribution to prosperity and social cohesion in europe. Draft 2006 joint progress report of the

Council and the Commission on the implementation of the 'Education & Training 2010 work programme' [SEC(2005) 1415].

Council of the European Communities (2000) *Presidency Conclusions, Lisbon European Council, 23-24 March.* Brussels: CEC.

Council of the European Union (2004) *Education & Training 2010. The Success of the Lisbon Strategy Hinges on Urgent Reforms.* Joint interim report of the Council and the Commission on the implementation of the detailed work programme on the follow-up of the objectives of education and training systems in Europe. Brussels: European Union.

Dale, Roger (2003) The Lisbon Declaration, the Reconceptualisation of Governance and the Reconfiguration of European Educational Space, paper presented to RAPPE seminar, University of London Institute of Education, March.

Dale, Roger (2007) The EU's Lifelong Learning Strategy and the Reshaping of the Education Sector, paper presented at Keele University, Education Department, 2 May.

Dale, Roger & Robertson, Susan L. (2007) Beyond Methodological 'isms' in Comparative Education in an Era of Globalisation, in R. Cowen & A. Kazamias (Eds) *International Handbook of Comparative Education*, pp. 1099-1113. Springer.

Daly, Mary (2006) EU Social Policy after Lisbon, *Journal of Common Market Studies*, 44(3), 461-481. http://dx.doi.org/10.1111/j.1468-5965.2006.00631.x

Dehousse, Renaud (2002) *The Lisbon Strategy: the costs of non delegation.* http://www.mzes.uni-mannheim.de/projekte/typo3/site/fileadmin/research%20groups/6/reader/Dehousse_Connex_Paris.pdf

de la Porte, Caroline (2001) The Soft Open Method of Co-ordination in Social Protection, in *European Trade Union Yearbook 2001*, 339-361. Brussels: Observatoire Social Européen.

Desrosières, A. (2002) *The Politics of Large Numbers: a history of statistical reasoning.* Cambridge, MA: Harvard University Press.

European Community (2006) Decision No 1720/2006/Ec of the European Parliament and of the Council of 15 November 2006 establishing an action programme in the field of lifelong learning 24 November 2006, *Official Journal of the European Union*, L 327/45.

Gornitzka, Å. (2005) Coordinating Policies for a 'Europe of Knowledge': emerging practices of the open method of coordination in education and research, Arena Working Papers 05/16. Oslo: Arena.

Gornitzka, Å. (2006) The Open Method of Coordination as Practice: a watershed in European education policy? University of Oslo, Arena Working Paper No. 16.

Halász, Gábor (2003) European Co-ordination of National Education Policies from the Perspective of the New Member Countries, in *CIDREE Yearbook*. http://www.cidree.org/nieuwsflits/65/

Hall, Peter A. (1993) Policy Paradigms, Social Learning, and the State: the case of economic policymaking in Britain, *Comparative Politics*, 25(3), 275-329. http://dx.doi.org/10.2307/422246

Hay, Colin (2000) Contemporary Capitalism, Globalisation, Regionalisation and Persistence of National Variation, *Review of International Studies*, 26, 509-531. http://dx.doi.org/10.1017/S026021050000509X

Jobert, B. (1994) *Le tournant néo-libéral en Europe*. Paris: L'Harmattan.

Mabbett, Deborah (2007) Learning by Numbers? The Use of Indicators in the Co-ordination of Social Inclusion Policies in Europe, *Journal of European Public Policy*, 14(1), 78-95. http://dx.doi.org/10.1080/13501760601071786

Nóvoa, A. & Yariv-Mashal, T. (2003) Comparative Research in Education: a mode of governance or a historical journey? *Comparative Education*, 39(4), 423-438. http://dx.doi.org/10.1080/0305006032000162002

Pawson, Ray (2002) Evidence-based Policy: the promise of realist synthesis, *Evaluation*, 8(3), 340-358. http://dx.doi.org/10.1177/135638902401462448

Radaelli, C.M. (2003) *The Open Method of Coordination: a new governance architecture for the European Union?* Report 2003:1. Stockholm: Swedish Institute for European Studies.

Robertson, S. & Dale. R (2008) researching education in a globalising era: beyond methodological nationalism, methodological statism, methodological educationism and spatial fetishism, in J. Resnik (Ed.) *The Production of Educational Knowledge in the Global Era*. Rotterdam: Sense Publications.

Ruggie, John Gerard (1993) Territoriality and Beyond: problematising modernity in international relations, *International Organization*, 47(1), 139-174.

Savio, Anniki & Palola, Elina (2004) Post-Lisbon Social Policy – inventing the social in the confines of the European Union, paper presented at the ESPAnet annual conference, Oxford, 9-11 September.

Smith, Gavin (2006) When 'the Logic of Capital Is the Real Which Lurks in the Background': programme and practice in European 'regional economies', *Current Anthropology*, 47(4), 621-639. http://dx.doi.org/10.1086/504164

Theret, Bruno (2005) Comparisons internationales. La place de la dimension politique, in J.-C. Barbier & M.-L. Latablier (Eds) *Politiques Sociales: Enjeux methodologiques et epistemologiques des comparaisons internationales*, 71-95. Brussels: Peter Lang.

Tyack, David & Tobin, Henry (1994) The 'Grammar' of Schooling: why has it been so hard to change? *American Educational Research Journal*, 31(3), 453-479.

Zurn, Michael & Leibfried, Stephan (2005) Reconfiguring the National Constellation, *European Review*, 13, 1-36. http://dx.doi.org/10.1017/S1062798705000177

PART TWO

Citizenship, Identity and Language

CHAPTER 7

'In the Name of Globalisation': southern and northern paradigms of educational development[1]

XAVIER BONAL & XAVIER RAMBLA

SUMMARY This chapter compares the prevailing, official discourses on education and development in Latin America and the European Union. It highlights that in both cases the normative and explanatory frameworks have shifted from the national towards the global context. However, this initial shift was imposed in many Latin American countries (so that they paid back their debts in the 1980s), whereas it is a matter of harmonisation in Europe (since the Open Method of Coordination has been operating).

Introduction

In *The Structure of Scientific Revolutions*, the philosopher Thomas Kuhn defined a paradigm as 'the set of universally recognised scientific achievements which, for a certain time, provided models of problems and solutions to a scientific community' (Kuhn, 1971, p. 13). The establishment of a paradigm is a first step towards the existence of the 'normal science' phase, in which the paradigm is consolidated as a framework for research practice firmly shared by the scientific community. The paradigm may go into crisis in the presence of new paradigms that manage to superimpose themselves on the old ones, giving rise to new models and formulations redefining the research practices of the scientific community.

In the last few decades, if any factor seems to have given rise to changes in the paradigm in the explanatory frameworks of education and development, it is globalisation. Although it is a complex, multidimensional and polycentric concept, the phenomenon of globalisation has been the factor in whose name new approaches, new needs and new policies for development have been justified. It is possible that the concept of globalisation has not substantially modified the instruments with which the scientific community has studied educational development, but there is no doubt that, from the ideological point of view, globalisation has served as a catalyst for the introduction of new discourses, new practices and new agendas. The agents taking part in the production and circulation of these discourses are many and diverse: developing countries, certain non-governmental organisations, governments of rich countries paying out official aid to poor countries and, above all, supranational bodies channelling the majority of development aid and generating great scientific production providing legitimacy to the establishment of priorities and political strategies. The most important agencies in this field are the World Bank, the International Monetary Fund and the World Trade Organization, but there are also a large number of regional development banks and United Nations organisations.

It is no coincidence that it is the international bodies which make use of globalisation who lead changes in the paradigm. Ultimately, the process of globalisation itself gives them a much greater role in the development policy scenario than was intended at Bretton Woods, a leading role which they themselves are responsible for maintaining, emphasising the importance of reviewing the priorities and strategies necessary for incorporating less developed countries into the global economy. In order to do this, they have powerful research departments and systems for publicising analysis and political recommendations, with a clear vocation for hegemony. In the last few years, for example, the World Bank has been using the expression 'Knowledge Bank' to consolidate its image of an institution encouraging 'best practices' in development issues. Using strategies of this kind, the Bank manages not only to make its interpretation of development problems and solutions hegemonic, but also to become the reference point for providing answers to critics or for leading the changes in the required analysis methods and priorities.

So, in the name of globalisation we have seen the replacement and emergence of paradigms in the field of development policies, changes which have also affected the sphere of educational investment priorities and strategies. In the last few decades, the most important turning point in this sense has been the consolidation of the Washington Consensus as a basic frame of reference for marking out the problems relevant for development and as a set of political prescriptions necessary for achieving inclusion in the network of the countries most excluded from it. As indicated by Gore, the Washington Consensus involves the introduction of a new paradigm in as much as it alters the frames of reference for defining development problems and suggesting possible solutions to them.

The structure of the revolution in thinking that occurred with the introduction of Washington Consensus policies is usually seen as a

shift from state-led *dirigisme* to market-oriented policies. Such a
shift undoubtedly occurred. But it is not a sufficient description of
the nature of the change as a paradigm shift. As Kuhn shows,
when paradigms change, there are usually significant changes in
the 'methods, problem-field, and standards of solution' which are
accepted by a community of practitioners. (Gore, 2000, p. 790)

This study attempts to position itself before and after the Washington
Consensus so it can observe which changes to paradigms incorporate its
hegemony and in what way this consensus has been altered and modified in
the educational field, down to the appearance of the so-called Post-
Washington Consensus. Taking as a reference the work of Gore (2000),
developed for the general analysis of development policies, our analysis goes
into depth specifically in the field of educational policy to observe the
development of paradigms in education and development. We will firstly
apply this analysis to the case of less developed countries, the principal
recipients of Washington Consensus policies and of the imposition of certain
political agendas. Secondly, we will carry out the exercise of transferring the
same analytical methodology to the recent development of dominant
educational policies in the area of Europe. This analysis will allow us to make
it clear that, far from following the same patterns fed by the dominant
education and development paradigm, the use of the concept of globalisation
in Europe has given rise to a type of political response differing substantially
from the recipes provided for the countries of the South. Finally, by way of
conclusion, we will compare the two processes, to illustrate that the
polycentric nature of globalisation gives rise to different political logics in
areas characterised by different power relationships.

The Normative and Explanatory
Frameworks for Development Policies

According to Gore (2000), we can state that 'specifying development policy
problems involves both explanations of development trends and normative
judgements about how the world should be' (Gore, 2000, p. 790). In the
field of debates on development, a crucial aspect of these frames of reference
is their national or global nature. In effect, normative and explanatory
judgements can be made from exclusively global frames of reference,
exclusively national ones or from those corresponding to a combination of
the two. Figure 1 summarises these possibilities.

Gore applies his pattern to the analysis of development policies from
before and after the Washington Consensus. This allows him to position the
different currents of thought in the different quadrants, combining the
different normative and explanatory frames of reference and to go into depth
on the characteristics of each current. Gore's pattern makes it possible to
observe, above all, the transition of normative judgements from the national
level to the global level. Concerning the dominant paradigms, the dominant

framework for explaining the causes of underdevelopment remains at a national level, while political priorities and needs are changing, coming to be elaborated at a global level. The Washington Consensus constitutes the consolidation of a paradigm identifying the causes of underdevelopment in the inefficiency of national policies to successfully achieve incorporation into the global economy. This differentiates it fundamentally from the previous currents, such as modernisation theory, which also puts the causes of underdevelopment at national level, but which suggests policies adapted to the different stages of development in the different countries.

		Normative Framework	
		National	Global
Explanatory Framework	National	Wholly National	Global Norms/ National Explanations
	Global	Global Explanations/ National Norms	Wholly Global

Figure 1. Combination of explanatory and normative framework
in development policy analysis. Source: Gore (2000, p. 791).

Gore places the critical approaches of Latin American structuralism and the theory of dependence – theories which place the causes of underdevelopment at a world level (seeing it as a consequence of the economic imperialism of the metropolis) and suggest national policies (like import substitution policies) as a reply to the economic oppression of the north against the south – as concurrent with modernisation theories, but with a very different approach to development policies. Gore wonders how far we are seeing the appearance of a new paradigm with the emergence of the Post-Washington Consensus, a frame of reference maintaining the need for strategies designed globally to incorporate societies into the global economy. But, in contrast to the previous dominant model, the new 'paradigm' also considers that a good part of the causes of the failure of development policies resides in the exclusively national approach to the factors explaining underdevelopment. Because of this, it is necessary to consider the failures of global policy deriving from the uniform design of structural adjustment programmes and move forward towards understanding how globalisation itself is an explanatory part of societies' development problems. Figure 2 places the theories mentioned on the previous pattern.

		Normative Framework	
		National	Global
Explanatory Framework	**National**	Competing Mainstream Development Paradigms Pre-1982 *Modernisation Theories*	Dominant Development Paradigm Post-1982 *Washington Consensus*
	Global	Main Counter-currents Pre-1982 *Latin American Structuralism and Dependency Theory*	Coming Paradigm Shift? *Post-Washington Consensus*

Figure 2. The configuration of development policy analysis.
Source: adapted from Gore (2000, p. 792).

Southern Globalisation:
shifting paradigms in educational development

Gore's approach can be extended to the study of the relationships between education and development. Ultimately, educational policy is a fundamental sphere for development strategies and it is therefore logical that its explanatory and normative frames of reference should coincide. Figure 3 includes what, in our judgement, has been a correspondence of education with the evolution of development paradigms. The theory which has dominated the area of educational policies for development has undoubtedly been Human Capital Theory (HCT). Since it was formulated at the beginning of the 1960s, HCT has been the fundamental frame of reference for the establishment of priorities and education policy strategies. Seeing education as an investment providing social benefits was not, of course, new from a conceptual point of view, but its formulation as a frame of reference for decision making by states and international bodies, like the World Bank, was new. Before 1968 the World Bank had incorporated educational investment projects into its portfolio of loans to developing countries and, since then, not only has it not interrupted them but rather it has increased the sectorial distribution of all the loans granted by the Bank (Mundy, 2002).

The correspondence of HCT with modernisation theory's view of development is clear: educational investment is, from the social point of view, the best investment to ensure a workforce capable of driving the growth and modernisation of backward societies. Both approaches share an exclusively national character, both in the diagnosis of the development problems and in the initiatives to be carried out to solve them. It is no coincidence, therefore, that, based on this frame of reference, the version of HCT dominating the scene in the 1970s was the national planning of the workforce. Based on identifying the least advanced economic sectors considered crucial for development, HCT provides the basis for determining how and how much to invest in education. The World Bank, for example, established its educational loan priorities in professional technical education, ahead of investment in basic education (Heyneman, 2003).

Approaches critical of HCT in the area of education and development also emerged throughout the 1970s. The so-called theories of reproduction and correspondence provided an alternative explanatory framework for the causes of educational inequalities, functional inequalities in the unequal power relationships between social groups, whether cultural or economic. Outstanding among this set of critical positions were the criticism of HCT by Bowles & Gintis (1983) and, in the area of education for development, the work of Martín Carnoy (1974), *Education as Cultural Imperialism,* a work that illustrates as no other does that the causes of educational inequalities must be sought not in what the more backward countries were lacking but in the relationships of dependency between the periphery and the imperialist centre of the metropolis. These and other works, however, are mainly concerned with exposing the supposed social function of education for social mobility and go into very little or no depth in constructing normative frameworks, based on which power relationships and oppression in education can be overcome through struggle.

Changes could be seen in the normative frames of reference in the variants of HCT from the 1980s onwards. Undoubtedly the most outstanding change was the move in the method of calculating education investment priorities from planning the needs of the workforce to calculating rates of return on educational investment. In the space we have for this study, we cannot give an account of the set of causes that led to this change.[2] It is enough to indicate that the new logic based on rates of return on educational investment involved a substantial change of course in the World Bank's priorities and strategies (visible, for example, in the *Education Sector Policy Paper,* World Bank, 1980). In effect, the new educational investment paradigm justified the reorientation of the Bank's loans and recommendations in the direction of prioritising investment in basic education over other educational sectors (such as vocational education or higher education). From the point of view of analysis that interests us in this study, it should be highlighted that, in the same way that the Washington Consensus formed a set of prescriptions intended to be applicable regardless

148

of the context, the calculation method based on rates of return also served as a technique exclusively for global application. Any review of scientific production in the field of education and development from the 1980s onwards allows us to see the proliferation of studies on rates of return on educational investment in Zimbabwe, Bolivia, India or Malaysia. While problems of educational underdevelopment were still identified at national level, the normative framework came to be globalised thanks to the hegemony of the new version of HCT. Educational 'best practices' are, then, the result of a calculation method determining where to invest (in basic education) and give rise to a menu of policies 'consequent' on the calculation method and, of course, with the prescriptions laid down by the Washington Consensus. Heyneman (2003) has referred to this as the 'short education policy menu', characterised by the priority for investment in basic education, the incorporation of cost recovery policies, the increase in the range of private education and decentralisation.

		Normative Framework	
		National	Global
Explanatory Framework	National	Human Capital Theory *Manpower Planning Forecast*	Human Capital Theory *Rates of Return Basic Education*
	Global	Reproduction in Education *Education as Cultural Imperialism*	Education as an anti-poverty tool: a new paradigm? *Millennium Development Goals Targeting the Poor*

Figure 3. Changing paradigms in educational development.

Despite the many criticisms the method of calculation based on rates of return has received [3], both this and the short education policy menu have been maintained throughout the 1990s as priority methodologies and policies of the World Bank. Its 1995 policy paper is a good example of this, highlighting in a very prescriptive way the orientations that should guide education investment strategies. However, in the most recent debates on educational policy for development, there are indications of change in the normative approach of the dominant paradigm. The widely documented failure of structural adjustment policies (Reimers & Tiburcio, 1993; Stewart, 1995; Chossudovsky, 1998). is at the root of the need for such changes. The incapability shown by the adjustment programmes to reduce poverty explains the relative deterioration of the explanatory and normative frameworks for educational policies for development. How can the same policy recipes be maintained when they are shown to be incapable of improving education in poor countries? How can the priority of reducing poverty be maintained when, in practice, the policies are incapable of reducing it? Despite the use of counterfactual arguments ('without these policies things would have been much worse'), in the last few years it appears to be possible to discern greater flexibility in the normative judgements intended to guide education for development. The leading roles taken on by the struggle against poverty at global level seem to have also moved some of the causes of underdevelopment into the area of globalisation, including the recognition of the effects of globalisation on education in poor countries. It is no coincidence that an example of this movement toward global explanatory frameworks should have coincided with the search for global consensus in the area of policies in the struggle against poverty, a search which culminated in the signing of the Millennium Development Goals in 2000. However, the normative frameworks of the dominant education and development paradigm have not been modified as a result of this. Global recipes continue to predominate and, among them, the struggle against poverty by targeting specific programmes aimed at the most vulnerable sectors has taken on particular importance. In this scenario, education maintains a central leading role, through transfer programmes conditional on school attendance and interventions focused on schools where poor students are taught.

The political agenda for developing countries ultimately shows us some particular uses of the concept of globalisation, both concerning explanatory frames of reference and normative ones concerning education and development paradigms. In the name of globalisation, certain changes in the political agenda have been consolidated and managed to become 'globalised' as the best practices to follow. The results of this are prescriptions for the right form of governance and for measures which southern countries should follow if they are to become incorporated into the global network.

Educational Globalisation in a Northern World Region: education and social cohesion in the European Union

Without any pretensions to being exhaustive, this section attempts to evaluate the possibilities offered by Gore's pattern for observing turning points in the combination of the national and global frames of reference for European Education Policy. Although the majority of European Union countries have not been subject to the worldwide controversies about development, it can be seen that the definition of education policy in this world region has moved in the same direction as indicated in Figure 1. Many studies of southern countries have also discussed their semi-peripheral or semi-developed nature; whereas Eastern European countries have clearly received the message of the Washington Consensus following the fall of the Berlin Wall. There are clearly differences, both in the content and form, that have characterised the debates about education and development between Europe and the countries of the south. In fact, the relationship between education and development has changed a great deal more in the north than in the south. In the southern hemisphere, the lower level of development has clearly limited the social and economic functions that educational institutions have to carry out. In Europe or in other northern regions, by contrast, successes in economic development since the War have generated spaces for new definitions and conceptualisations of the social functions of education for development. For example, the functions assigned to schooling in the post-war period (democratisation and aid for reconstruction of nations devastated by war) have little to do with the predominant role today assigned to education as a driving force for international competitiveness and social cohesion based on the Lisbon Agenda.

Figure 4 can be read alongside Figure 3, although it is not possible to fill in all its cells. So, while in the 1970s Human Capital Theory and educational planning emphasised endogenous mechanisms of educational development, in the main European countries there were also political debates and conflicts about the integration of the different social classes into the school system. The Maastricht Treaty of 1992 meant a significant extension of the normative framework to a supra-state level, as it encoded the Union's education action in a 'European dimension', with respect to which the actual situation in each member country had to be measured. Perhaps it did not manage to generate such a sophisticated apparatus as the World Bank's rates of return, but it is undeniable that it opened up the possibility that the governments of Member States, without giving up sovereignty, should see themselves as subject to aligning their educational policy with the guidelines of a higher body.

In addition, a certain analogy can initially be seen concerning the meaning of education in the context of the United Nations' Millennium Development Objectives and the European Union's Open Method of Coordination. However, within this initial similarity important differences must also be pointed out in the sense in which the same concept of education has been adopted in the two contexts. Part of these differences is probably due to the different average level of human development in the countries referred to in each case. However, another part has revealed different implications during the political disputes that have emerged in the European Commission.

In the decades before the 1990s, the educational policy of the countries which are today members of the Union corresponded to a diagnosis focused on endogenous factors entrusting the leading role in terms of action to Member States and the final judgement to their governments. Moreover, the democratisation of the south made it clear that this final judgement also corresponded to popular sovereignty, given the educational demands of the

151

movements fighting against dictatorships. For its part, in Eastern Europe, educational expansion had taken off in the nineteenth century under the German and Austrian empires, and the socialist governments put in place in 1945 strongly accelerated the expansion of the school system.

		Normative Framework	
		National	Global
Explanatory Framework	National	Debates on comprehensive education in Britain, France and Germany Vocational education and training-driven reaction to 1970s recession	The Maastricht Treaty (1992) fostered the European educational dimension 'by encouraging cooperation between Member States'
	Global		The Lisbon Strategy (2000): The Open Method of Coordination and educational benchmarks

Figure 4. Normative and explanatory frameworks
in EU educational policy (1970s-2000s).

If we focus on the west of the continent, where the European Economic Community was at that time exercising its influence, the historical pattern of educational policies clearly reflects this state-based approach. In the 1960s and 70s, France, Great Britain and the Federal Republic of Germany underwent strong controversies about the appropriateness of integrating academic and vocational curricula into secondary education, which resulted in their effective integration, first in Great Britain, later in France and finally in some German *Länder* (Weiler, 1989). These processes unleashed a mechanism of initial expansion, followed by restriction and new pressures in favour of expansion (Levin, 1978), which was an internal driving force in their social structures and political systems.

Because of all this, when the crisis of the 1970s also eroded this confidence in wider schooling, the Community's response was limited to the output of the education system and a very indirect advisory role. This very response concentrated its attention on vocational education and on the passage from education to employment, in order to attack one of the flanks of the overwhelming social problem of the period, youth unemployment. Literally, Community strategy noted that 'the planning of programmes to ease transition from education to working life is an important local and regional concern, as well as a question of national policy' (European

Communities, 1976) and only reserved for itself the power to encourage some pilot tests and experiments that could give governments some ideas.

When Greece, Portugal and Spain joined the Community during the 1980s, their educational systems were undergoing a pattern of expansion that, in a way, came to be the last wave of the endogenous Continental processes that went before. At least in the Iberian Peninsula, the expansionist reforms adopted the same philosophy of integration at secondary level, although they gave these initiatives fewer resources than their European neighbours and very mechanically borrowed the formulas of the Community pilot experiments reacting against the crisis (Bonal & Rambla, 1996).

The very establishment of a European Union by means of the 1992 Maastricht Treaty involved an expansion of the normative sphere of education policy in all Member States. The foundation text explicitly respected Member State sovereignty on this point, but, at the same time, it declared that: 'the Community shall contribute to the development of quality education by encouraging cooperation between Member States and, if necessary, by supporting and supplementing their action' (European Union, 1992). Consequently, the Treaty sanctioned a certain displacement between the political levels that transferred some areas of evaluation from the Member States to the Union.

It must be remembered that key political competencies were transferred from the state-level to the EU scale by emphasizing 'development of quality education'. Firstly, the Union gave itself the right to estimate the quality of what the Member States were doing and even to act to direct education policy by encouraging cooperation (as the Open Method of Coordination would later do) and by promoting the complementary actions it thought necessary. Secondly, the measurement with which the situation in each country had to be compared ended up being expressed with the term that was becoming the catchword for the assessment of education policies: quality. The Treaty did not itself define the meaning of this concept, in the same way that many official documents it has used since then have also shied away from defining it. However, it is notable that 'educational quality' was achieving a new legal validity in being introduced into a text of this legal standing. Since the 1980s, the Organisation for Economic Co-operation and Development (1991) had been proclaiming the importance of quality in directing and evaluating educational policy, but, with the Treaty, this changed from being a mere recommendation of an advisory body to becoming a notion incorporated into an international treaty. What had been only a piece of advice, working guidelines or an opportunity for organisational innovation was now at the level of a principle forming part of the legal organisation of 15 democratic countries that were very powerful in the world.

The Open Method of Coordination has driven the latest movement between Gore's cells, as it has also taken the explanatory framework beyond the sphere of Member State activity. This method consists of fixing common measurable objectives (benchmarks) which each Member State must achieve by itself, something which ends up giving explanatory priority to global factors at the same time as it gives meaning to the aforementioned principle of educational quality. In fact, it consecrates the expectation that, when the Open Method is systematically applied, good practices essential for achieving the expected advances will be found. The parallels between the definition of the Lisbon Agenda and the establishment of the Open Method of Coordination not only seem to define the purposes of educational and economic development which need to be achieved; the Lisbon Agenda and the Open Method of Coordination also involve maximisation of the means available for intervention by an organisation that does not have direct sovereignty over Europe's education policies and systems.

The constant setting and resetting of benchmarks provided by the Open Method of Coordination firstly provides the EU, as a body overseeing competitiveness and social cohesion, with dynamism. At the same time, it is an open door for the participation of Member States in collectively defining the best practices for achieving the benchmarks. Along the same lines, we could consider what the introduction of the OECD's Programme for International Student Assessment (PISA) has contributed to globalising the explanatory and normative frameworks for education and development in Europe. The publication of rankings in the PISA report has an interesting effect on the 'convergence of the means' the countries are planning to use to improve the quality of their education systems. There is no space here either to explore the creation of the European Higher Education Area, the result of the Bologna Process, and the trends in European convergence in this field. However, it is worth highlighting that this is also a process resulting from globalisation and, in the name of globalisation, it is once again another example of the displacement of the frames of reference for policies.

It seems clear, therefore, that there are sufficient empirical indicators that the development of agendas around education and development has been moved from national frames of reference to global explanations and standards. Both in the south and in the European case, processes of giving up educational sovereignty can be seen. However, the differences in priorities and strategies in education policy for development that have been established in different regions of the world are just as clear. These differences illustrate different conceptions of the effects of globalisation on education processes and also give rise to different political agendas. We will concern ourselves with these differences in the final section of this chapter.

Conclusion: in the name of which globalisation?

It is commonplace in different social science approaches to highlight the irreversible nature of globalisation. In effect, regardless of the multiple positions for or against neoliberal globalisation, if the different political and ideological positions seem to coincide on anything in recent years it is the impossibility of 'turning the clock back', understood as seeking autarchic development strategies through the isolation of the nation state from international financial flows, world trade or supranational political areas. However, the same type of consensus is far from being achieved either concerning the specific ways in which globalisation affects the different areas of social life or, above all, concerning the type of political strategies that should be developed at a national or supranational level to get countries successfully incorporated into the global economy.

This work has made clear an unequal development of the agenda on education and development in the south and in the north. In both areas, there is no doubt that such evolution has developed both as a consequence of globalisation and 'in the name of' globalisation'. In effect, globalisation has consequences for the displacement of explanatory and normative frames of reference at a national or global level, but it also has consequences through legitimising, in the name of globalisation, particular types of political strategy and models of governance which are defined as necessary and appropriate.

And it is precisely in the area of these differences where the existence of different mechanisms through which globalisation affects the orientation of national education policy is clearest (Dale, 1999). The different mechanisms reflect unequal positions in international power relationships and their consequences for different countries' possibilities both of intervening in the 'form' adopted by globalisation and in their possibilities of following or not following particular agendas. In our case, there is no doubt that these mechanisms become clearly visible in the specific forms taken on by the 'global education agenda' in different parts of the world and in the capacity shown by the different nations to follow or adulterate it. The impact the Washington Consensus has had on education agendas in the southern countries, with the adoption of the 'short education policy menu', is not the same as that in the Maastricht Treaty concerning the orientation of educational policies in European countries. Neither has the new priority for the social function of education to fight poverty defined in the Millennium Development Goals had the same consequences for education policy as the Lisbon process has had for competitiveness and social cohesion. In both areas, the need to seek strategies going beyond the national scale converges, and in both cases it can be seen that the process of globalisation directs discourses, agendas and even instruments. However, the impact and the political consequences of these agendas are different.

At the risk of oversimplifying, it is easy to identify imposition as the mechanism one that best defines the ways in which the global education agenda has been installed in the education policies of the south. Dependency and conditional loans have ensured a very high level of compliance with the priorities and strategies defined by the World Bank and other international development bodies and have had an effect on educational reform trends towards decentralisation, an increase in the range of private education and policies of recovering costs. Although each country's capacity for negotiation has been different, there has been great convergence of practices. But this has not been so in terms of effects, as the application of the same agendas in different contexts is a long way from achieving the same results.

In the Union there are indirect and less explicit mechanisms ensuring that Member States take part in the convergence of political objectives. However, the criterion of free will, ensured through the right of veto, formally grants the Member States a different voice and position. In this way, the mechanisms that have predominated in the processes of convergence towards a global education agenda for European development have been those of policy harmonisation and standardisation, the latter particularly strengthened in recent years thanks to the Open Method of Coordination and to educational assessment instruments such as PISA. Dealing with globalisation in the European area, as in dependent countries, means converging towards common targets and means, but the content of these targets and, especially, the means of achieving them, differ notably from the prescriptions put out by the Washington Consensus.

The analysis carried out illustrates not only the polycentric and multidimensional nature of the concept of globalisation, but also its different and unequal uses in different areas of power in the process of establishing educational agendas. Recognising the change in the explanatory and normative frames of reference takes note both of the transformations in educational development discourses and instruments and of the power relationships underlying a particular direction in the changes. It is a type of analysis that can be used both for uncovering what is being done in the name of globalisation and for having a map available in order to navigate other discourses and practices.

Notes

[1] This piece of research is an outcome of the following project: 'Beyond 'targeting the poor': education, development and poverty alleviation in the Southern Cone. An analysis of the new political agenda in the region'. It has been funded by the Ministry of Education and Science (Government of Spain: reference SEJ2005-04235).

[2] See Heyneman (2003) or Bonal (2004) for an analysis of the external and internal factors favouring the predominance of the method of calculation of rates of return to establish educational investment priorities.

[3] See, for example, the excellent critique by Bennell (1996).

References

Bennell, P. (1996) Using and Abusing Rates of Return, *International Journal of Educational Development*, 16, 235-248.
http://dx.doi.org/10.1016/0738-0593(96)00016-8

Bonal, X. (2004) Is the World Bank Education Policy Adequate for Fighting Poverty? Some Evidence from Latin America, *International Journal of Educational Development*, 24(6), 649-666. http://dx.doi.org/10.1016/j.ijedudev.2004.03.002

Bonal, X. & Rambla, X. (1996) Is There a Semi-peripheral Type of Schooling? Education, the State and Social Movements in Spain, 1970-1994, *Mediterranean Journal of Educational Studies*, 1(1), 13-27.

Bowles, S. & Gintis, H. (1983) El problema de la teoría del capital humano: una crítica marxista, *Educación y Sociedad*, 1.

Carnoy, M. (1974) *Education as Cultural Imperialism*. New York: David McKay.

Chossudovsky, M. (1998) *The Globalisation of Poverty. Impacts of IMF and World Bank Reforms*. London: Zed Books.

Dale, R. (1999) Specifying Globalisation Effects on National Policy: focus on the Mechanisms, *Journal of Education Policy*, 14, 1-17. http://dx.doi.org/10.1080/026809399286468

European Communities (1976) From Education to Working Life, *Bulletin of European Communities Supplement*, 12/76. http://aei.pitt.edu/archive

European Union (1992) Maastricht Treaty: Treaty of the European Union, Article 126. http://europa.eu.int/en/record/mt/top.html

Gore, C. (2000) The Rise and Fall of the Washington Consensus as a Paradigm for Developing Countries, *World Development*, 28, 789-804. http://dx.doi.org/10.1016/S0305-750X(99)00160-6

Heyneman, S.P. (2003) The History and Problems in the Making of Education Policy at the World Bank 1960-2000, *International Journal of Educational Development*, 23, 315-337. http://dx.doi.org/10.1016/S0738-0593(02)00053-6

Kuhn, T. (1971) *La estructura de las revoluciones científicas*. Mexico City: Fondo de Cultura Económica.

Levin, Henry (1978) The Dilemma of Comprehensive Secondary School Reforms in Western Europe, *Comparative Education Review*, 22(3), 434-451. http://dx.doi.org/10.1086/445997

Mundy, K. (2002) Retrospect and Prospect: education in a reforming World Bank, *International Journal of Educational Development*, 22, 483-508. http://dx.doi.org/10.1016/S0738-0593(02)00008-1

Organisation for Economic Cooperation and Development (1991) *Escuelas y calidad de la enseñanza*. Barcelona: Paidós.

Reimers, F. & Tiburcio, L. (1993) *Education, Adjustment and Reconstruction: options for change*. Paris: UNESCO.

Stewart, F. (1995) *Adjustment and Poverty*. London: Routledge.

Weiler, Hans (1989) Why Reforms Fail: the politics of education in France and the Federal Republic of Germany, *Journal of Curriculum Studies*, 21(4), 291-305. http://dx.doi.org/10.1080/0022027890210401

World Bank (1980) *Education Sector Policy Paper*. Washington: World Bank.

World Bank (1995) *Policies and Strategies for Education: a World Bank review*. Washington: World Bank.

CHAPTER 8

Education, Equality and the European Social Model

PALLE RASMUSSEN, KATHLEEN LYNCH, JACKY BRINE, PEPKA BOYADJIEVA, MICHAEL A. PETERS & HEINZ SÜNKER[1]

SUMMARY Social welfare and education have been themes in European collaboration since the early days of the Treaty of Rome. Especially after the establishment in 2000 of the Lisbon agenda the EU has stepped up its efforts in these two areas and has integrated both of them in a strategy for growth and employment. The importance of education is often mentioned in EU documents on social welfare. However, European policies in the areas of welfare and education are marked by a fundamental tension between the pursuit of capitalist growth on one hand, the pursuit of social justice and equality on the other. This often leads to an impoverished conceptualisation of education as just another service to be delivered on the market. A more holistic approach to education policy is necessary, an approach which takes account of the broader conditions of equality and includes not only the economic, but also the political, cultural and affective dimensions of educational equality.

Introduction

The concept of 'Social Europe' is an ambiguous and contested one. In a recent contribution Anthony Giddens defines the European Social Model in the following way:

> A developed and interventionist state, funded by relatively high
> levels of taxation; a robust welfare system, which provides effective
> social protection, to some considerable degree for all citizens, but
> especially for those most in need; the limitation, or containment,
> of economic and other forms of inequality. (Giddens, 2007, p. 2)

He adds that this model gives a key role to the social partners.

This definition is in fact a blend of several meanings that the concept has acquired in current public and scientific discourse. We can distinguish at least three distinct meanings.

Firstly, 'Social Europe' designates an area of European Union policies. Some main issues in this area are employment, quality of work, gender equality, social cohesion, social inclusion and the quality of social policy. These policies are mainly the responsibility of the European Commissions' Directorate General for Employment, Social Affairs and Equal Opportunities, but they are linked with many other areas of EU activity, including education.

Secondly, in a broader sense 'Social Europe' (and more recently the 'European Social Model') is used to designate qualities of social life and welfare that characterise Europe in contrast to other parts of the world, not least the United States. The character of these qualities is often not clear because the systems and traditions of welfare in the European nations differ widely.

Thirdly, the term is used by certain actors, not least socialist parties and trade unions, to indicate the qualities they strive to realise in the European Union. These actors emphasise social equality and solidarity as part of their vision for Europe, and as alternatives to neoliberalism. It is telling that 'Social Europe' has been chosen as title for a journal published by a group of socialist politicians and intellectuals, and that a book published in connection with the journal has the subtitle 'a continent's answer to market fundamentalism' (Albers et al, 2006).

Educational practices, institutions and policies are not an explicit theme in the EU social policy agenda, nor are they mentioned in Giddens' definition of the European Social Model. Nevertheless post-Lisbon social policy has increasingly linked issues of education and lifelong learning, and these issues feature strongly in Giddens' discussion of the prospects for the 'model'.

In this chapter we discuss some crucial aspects of the roles education is assigned or can have in policies for a Social Europe.

Social Policy Agenda and Education

Social welfare has been a theme in European Union policy since the early days of the Treaty of Rome. Until recent years this area was most often called the *social dimension*, and it could be seen as an attempt to partially compensate the overwhelming focus on coordination of economic policy and removal of trade barriers. Thus it was logical that the push to realise the European internal market marked by the European Single Act of 1987 was accompanied by attempts to revitalise the social dimension. Parallel with the space of the market, a 'social space' was supposed to respond to two types of fears associated with the free movement of capital, goods and persons. One fear was that the internal market would undermine working conditions, employee security and the capacity of national trade unions to protect employee interests; the response to this was dialogue with the social partners and attempts to formalise fundamental rights in areas like employment, working conditions and safety at work, equal treatment for men and women, and protection for children. Such rights were contained in the Social Charter adopted by the Commission in 1989, but not ratified by all Member States. Given this and the very general nature of the suggested rights, the impact of the Charter was limited. The second fear was that 'social dumping' would increase economic and social inequalities between and within the countries of Europe. The response to this was a strengthening of the structural funds that had earlier been established to support the funding of regional development schemes. Funds were increased, the division of responsibilities between EU and national authorities was clarified and more specific targets were formulated, for instance in the form of criteria for deprived regions.

One of the structural funds was and is the Social Fund, aimed at redistributing resources to matchfund national unemployment-related training programmes. However, its impact in terms of employment related to training seems to have been limited, at least until recently (Brine, 2001). An analysis of discourses associated with the Fund up to 2000 concluded that despite its name, and despite its explicit relationship to (un)employment, training and the labour market, expressed through the discourse of economic growth, the dominant discourse of the Social Fund was that of political stability, both within and across the Member States, during periods of Union expansion and consolidation (Brine, 2002, 2004).

During the 1990s the continuing attempts to define the EU as a political union rather than just a coordinated market had considerable impact in the area of social policy. An important step was the Treaty of Amsterdam (1997), which strengthened the involvement in social (and environmental) concerns, increased the emphasis on education and refocused the concern with social cohesion. As important as the increased competency in social policies was the new Treaty objective on employment which subsequently led to a shift from passive to active employability measures and the equally influential European Employment Strategy (1999) with its demand for Member State national plans regularly agreed with the Commission. In the run-up to this, the Luxembourg Council (1997) recommended a key shift from passive to active employability measures that signal the very close interplay between employment/economic policies and social ones. It recommended that these active measures be linked to state *welfare benefit* and training systems, whereby the 'benefit and training systems ... must be reviewed and adapted to ensure that they actively support employability and provide real incentives for the unemployed to seek and take up work or training opportunities' (European Council, 1997, item 53), and for young people especially, within six months of unemployment, 'to be offered a new start in the form of training, retraining, work practice, a job or other employability measure' (European Council, 1997, item 51).

With the Lisbon Strategy of 2000 the EU heads of state set up two general aims to be realised within 10 years. The EU should be developed into the most competitive and dynamic knowledge-based economy in the world, and growth should be sustainable, creating new and better jobs and social cohesion. In order to realise these aims the heads of state called for ambitious reforms in many policy areas, including areas that had previously been the responsibility of the national authorities. The method of 'open coordination' was introduced to enable the formulation of common policy targets at the EU level while keeping policy implementation at the national level.

In the area of social welfare the Lisbon Strategy manifested itself in a European Social Policy based on three elements: 1. a common social agenda and set of objectives to be pursued by all Member States; 2. national action plans through which individual Member States implement the social agenda; and 3. a common set of social indicators as a basis for monitoring implementation. The core objectives, which were laid out in the *Social Policy Agenda* (European Commission, 2000), focus on two broad areas: employment and work, and quality of social policy. The main themes of the agenda (quoted from headlines in the document) were:

- *Full employment and quality of work*, including the sub-themes of working towards more and better jobs; anticipating and managing change and adapting to the new working environment; exploiting the opportunities of the knowledge-based economy; promoting mobility.
- *Quality of social policy*, including the sub-themes of modernising and improving social protection; promoting social inclusion; promoting gender equality; reinforcing fundamental rights and combating discrimination.

Following the Mid Term Review of the Lisbon Strategy, the Commission brought out a new communication on the social agenda (European Commission, 2005). The themes were more or less the same, but the focus on growth and employment was strengthened while the question of fundamental rights seems to have been played down. This probably reflects the general difficulties that the Lisbon Strategy has encountered; European growth rates have been falling behind and it is improbable that the strategic targets for 2010 will be met. And while the Member States have generally agreed on the Strategy, the larger members have not always been willing to give it priority in negotiations on the EU budget.

Although the success of the Lisbon Strategy remains to be seen, it has substantially changed the character of EU welfare policy. Earlier its aims were mainly compensatory, in the shape of discourses and funds to reduce and redress social problems produced by economic policy and the internal market. The Lisbon Strategy, however, depends on integrating welfare policy and other sector policies in a coordinated, comprehensive policy for economic and social development. Welfare policies become more directly involved with creating the conditions for competitiveness and growth, for instance retraining employees in threatened trades or companies or through providing public childcare and thus allowing women full participation in the labour market.

The Lisbon Strategy has also made education and training a much more important element in EU policy. The celebration of 'knowledge' as a key component in the future dynamic Europe is in itself a confirmation of the importance of education and educational institutions like universities. The conceptualisation of knowledge and skills as 'key competences' emphasises the contribution of education to employability and thus to growth; the grouping of different educational programmes under the umbrella of lifelong learning signals the importance of adult education and training.

From the Treaty of Rome to that of Maastricht the EU/Commission only had legal competency in the field of vocational education and although this was extended somewhat in Maastricht, it remains limited to the 'European dimension' and improving educational 'quality' through the 'cooperation' of Member States. However, the Commission has consistently pushed at the boundaries of this vocational competency, most noticeably into higher education, adult education and more recently into the 14-19 age range of vocational/early school leaver interventions.

The Lisbon Strategy thus links both the social agenda and educational issues to growth and employment. This also means that new links are established between the areas of welfare and education. The importance of education is often mentioned in EU documents on social welfare. Examples are the 'skills gap' (skills requirements in the EU not matched by existing supply), the 'upgrading of skills and extending lifelong learning' (as a crucial element of the knowledge-based economy), the need to 'strengthen the lifelong learning theme' (in employment policy), 'enhancing the participation of women in relevant education and training', strengthening social inclusion by 'providing basic skills' through education and training, and so on (European Commission, 2000, 2005).

The version of 'Social Europe' emerging since the turn of the century can be seen as an example of what has been called a 'new egalitarianism'. According to Giddens this way of thinking is 'concerned not just with social justice but with economic dynamism. We know that the two can be closely reconciled, although there are trade-offs'. Some implications of the reconciliation are that 'progressive taxation is still highly important, but is altered where known to compromise economic needs and job creation'; 'policies that benefit more affluent groups are important if they have the effect of consolidating commitment to the welfare system' and there is 'emphasis upon activating labour market strategies' (Giddens, 2007, p. 91).

Despite all the varied and subtle discourse, the reports from expert groups and the documentation of benchmarks, European policies in the areas of welfare and education are still marked by a fundamental tension between two poles:

- The pursuit of capitalist growth, with priority given to deregulation and other ways of removing barriers to the movement of goods, persons and capital. This is the project of the internal market and has much in common with neoliberal ideology.
- The pursuit of social welfare, with social equality as a crucial element. This project is more in line with the concepts of social justice contained in social democratic philosophies and political programmes.

We do not claim that these two are irreconcilable. But we find it evident that in spite of some good intentions they have not been reconciled in the European Union's post-Lisbon policies, and we worry that some basic concepts of justice in society, not least the notion of equality, are being eroded in the process of reconciling social justice with 'economic dynamism'.

Market Values and Democratic Values

In the area of education, the pursuit of capitalist growth manifests itself in a trend to define and to shape education through the logic of the market. An important example is the current pressure in the General Agreement on Tariffs and Trade (GATS) negotiations to move education from a public service to a tradable service. In response to GATS the European Union has declined opening up sectors like health and education to such trading; but at the same time it has taken steps to open the European *internal* market more fully to trade in all types of services. The instrument is the so-called services directive. The aim of this was to abolish the service industry regulations of individual EU Member States, because they pose unnecessary barriers to service providers wanting to provide services in other Member States in addition to their own. Regulations that are objectively justified on the grounds of public interest can be upheld. The directive met considerable criticism and was modified before being passed in December 2006.

In the present western world, the conceptualisation of 'economic dynamism' and its links with education are shaped by the current hegemony of neoliberal ideology (Lynch, 2006). Neoliberalism offers a market view of citizenship, in which the citizen is defined as an economic maximiser, governed by self-interest. There is a glorification of the 'consumer citizen' constructed as willing, resourceful and capable of making market-led choices. In such a market state, the individual is held responsible for her or his own well-being and the state's role is one of facilitator. This neoliberal position is generally antithetical to rights, especially to state-guaranteed rights in education, welfare, health and other public goods (Peters, 2004).

This model of citizenship treats education as just another service to be delivered on the market to those who can afford to buy it. The rationalisation that is offered is that it provides people with choice and shifts control from the school or university to the sovereign consumer. Yet the evidence is overwhelming that in economically unequal societies, only those with sufficient resources can make choices and those who are poor have no choices at all. What is ignored is the fact that what people may want is not a choice of schools or other public services but access to an affordable, accessible and available education of high standard. For those with limited resources, choice is a secondary rather than a primary value, taking its place behind quality, affordability and access (Lynch, 2006).

The Lisbon Strategy draws on and attempts to reconcile different European traditions of citizenship, including some with an emphasis on state responsibility for welfare (Wind, 2003; Rasmussen, 2006; Peters, 2007). Nevertheless, influence from the neoliberal model of citizenship and its idea of education can be felt. Education is conceptualised as the learning of cognitive knowledge and employable competences. Although the benefits of education are seen as rich and multiple, these benefits flow from the citizen's use of knowledge and competencies in the labour market; education itself and the process of learning is a means to this end.

Against this impoverished concept of education we find it necessary to emphasise the democratic and critical aspects of education and learning. The potential for personal autonomy, critical reflection and democratic mobilisation present in processes of education and learning has been demonstrated by many educators and theorists during the history of education. We mention just one example, the German educator Heinz-Joachim Heydorn, who conceptualised education as a process of the human subject reflecting on and entering its own history (Heydorn, 1970; cf. Sünker, 1989). In his fundamental works, in which he connects social history with education history, Heydorn analysed the requirements and perspectives of these topics. Here the question of general education, as education for everyone, forms the anchor for its historical and systematic constitutions and for its social-political as well as individual meaning. At the same time it refers to the importance of an education theory founded on social theory and proceeding in a critical way. In this way, at the same time the challenge is presented of determining and deciphering the relations between social structures, the structuring of social relationships between the members of a society and the constitutional conditions of subjectivity, as Heydorn does in his earlier writings when he refers to connections between the priority of capitalist utilisation logics, the market shaping of social relationships and a reduction of social existence to bare efficiency. The functionalism existing in this social constitution based on inequality and social injustice leads to the question of an education that ensures the maximum efficiency of people in a technological society; a society that is based on adaptation, change and mobility in largely determined social borders. Here, according to Heydorn, education, as always in history, should ensure ideology and power to an existing society; it must omit the reflection by which the demythologising of power takes place. Thereby, it finds itself in an obvious contradiction. If the

165

production of a socially compliant worldview stands in the centre of hegemonic strategies and ideologies that secure power, then the question of resistance and the alternatives arises as a question of actors, movements and freedom-securing ideas; Heydorn (1970) draws this out as a central theme of the institutionalisation of education with the perspective of education as everybody's responsibility; beyond its class-historically founded disunity.

Heydorn's theory of education, as well as many other contributions, reminds us that education is much more than the acquisition of knowledge and competences for use in the labour market; it is a process of becoming competent in all aspects of life, of becoming an independent and responsible person and citizen (Sünker, 2006). And the process of learning itself can contribute substantially to the life quality of learners.

Education and Equality

The ambiguous discourses of post-Lisbon social policy and the 'new egalitarianism' as well as the equivocal attitude of the EU to neoliberalism signal that the principles of welfare being pursued in European Social Policy are by no means clear, and need to be restated. One such principle is social equality.

The theme of equality has limited visibility in EU policy documents on education. For instance, in a recent communication on modernisation of universities, equality is not mentioned at all, and modernisation is viewed as improvement of performance and 'full institutional accountability' in universities (European Commission, 2006a). Where the theme is mentioned, equality is most often seen merely as a question of access. However, another recent document does explicitly discuss equality and its relation to other aspects and policy objectives in education. In this communication (European Commission, 2006b) on equity and efficiency there are indications of a broadening of perspective from both the dominant market-based approach with its emphasis on efficiency and accountability and the narrow understanding of equality which limits it to equality of access opportunities. The communication is among the few European policy documents to acknowledge that: 'It is too often the case that existing education and training systems reproduce or even compound existing inequities' (European Commission, 2006b, p. 2). In the document 'equity is viewed as the extent to which individuals can take advantage of education and training in terms of opportunities, access, treatment and outcomes' (p. 2). The Communication further argues for 'cross-sectoral approaches ... to link education and training policies with those related to employment, the economy, social inclusion, youth, health, justice, housing and social services' (p. 4). It links accountability with equality and states that 'accountability systems should be designed to ensure a full commitment to equality' (p. 6).

The communication on equity and efficiency may signal a welcome increase in commitment to educational equality in EU policy, but the visibility of the theme as well as the conceptualisation of equality is still limited. To take the discussion further we outline in the following sections an understanding of equality that emphasises the social aspect, which we find relevant to assessing and developing education, not least in the European context.

Equality can be defined simply as the belief that people should be as equal as possible in relation to the central conditions of their lives. It is not a question of trying to make inequalities fairer, or giving people a more equal opportunity to become unequal, but about ensuring that everyone has roughly equal prospects for a good life. It is about equalising what might be called people's 'real options', which involves the *equal enabling and empowerment* of individuals. Lynch & Baker (2005) call this an 'equality of condition' which involves several dimensions. Drawing on their analysis we indicate here four dimensions we find especially relevant for policies and practices for educational equality in Europe. These dimensions are resources, respect and recognition, power, and finally love, care and solidarity.

The generative sources of inequality and exclusion are not the same for all groups and consequently the strategic policy responses are not all the same. At the very least there are four major sets of structural relations that generate inequality in education: economic relations, sociocultural relations, power relations and affective relations. The policy response to each of these needs to be different, and there needs to be recognition as to how the structural relations interact to create multiple inequalities for some groups.

An equality of condition perspective requires us to take a holistic approach to educational policy, one that recognises in particular the integrated links that exist between economic, cultural, political and affective inequalities in education. We discuss these inequalities in the two following sections, dealing first with economic and cultural relations, then with political and affective relations.

Resources and Respect

Economic inequalities are generated through economic relations and the resulting inequalities in income, wealth and welfare. Economic equality is promoted by equalising resources. By equality of resources we mean not just equality in obvious economic forms of capital such as income and wealth, but also in forms of social capital developed through social networks and affiliations, and in forms of cultural capital such as educational credentials. Other important resources are time itself, and health and environmental resources, such as high-quality healthcare, good housing, accessible and available public transport, and a clean environment.

There are multiple studies over the last 50 years showing how people cannot participate and progress equally in education if they have very diverging economic resources (Shavit & Blossfeld, 1993; Gamoran, 2001; Mayer, 2001; Green, 2003). There are two interrelated reasons for this.

First, education is resource intensive and competitive; those with greater access to resources tend to perform better in education by virtue of this (there are a range of studies about access to higher education demonstrating this, see e.g. Raftery & Hout, 1993; Clancy, 2001). Even in equitably funded educational systems private resources will be used by parents outside the state sector to give their children an advantage. Education has become a marketable commodity, and in many European countries there is a burgeoning of private markets in education which better-off parents use (Ball, 2003; Lynch & Moran, 2006). The middle classes and upper middle classes use their economic and related capital advantages to out-compete and exclude lesser resourced groups. If European policy is to be effectively as opposed to nominally inclusive, it must recognise the role that privileged groups will play in countering attempts by policymakers to combat injustice and exclusion. Addressing injustices and exclusion in education means reducing the capabilities of the relatively advantaged to undermine the impact of equality and social inclusion policies.

The groups who are most affected by economic inequalities in education are those who are living on low wages and/or who are welfare dependent. As the former category overlaps with migrant status in many cases, there is a need to recognise that for the children of certain migrant workers, their educational problems may be as much financial as cultural, especially if they have to participate in an educational system where the norms of participation are set by a majority who are well off.

The policy message for Europe is that if it allows economic inequalities to persist through the unequal distribution of wealth and incomes, it will inevitably perpetuate educational inequalities for some groups even if the identity of the groups keeps changing. The skin colour, the ethnic or cultural identity of those at the top or the bottom may change, however inequality in access to and benefit from education will persist. Attempts by states to improve the educational prospects of disadvantaged groups are generally neutralised by the efforts of economically advantaged households to increase their private investment in their own children. While there is evidence however that investing in high-quality childcare and related educational and welfare support for children, as well as providing high-quality universalised welfare provision for adults, offsets negative class effects on educational attainment (Sweden being a case in point, see Shavit & Blossfeld, 1993), there is no comprehensive 'internal settlement' to the problem of class-related inequality in education, as the defining source of class inequality lies outside the educational system. Eliminating income and wealth inequalities outside of school is essential if we are to ensure that excess resources cannot be used to undermine more egalitarian policies within schools. Europe must develop some concept of equality of resources between its citizens if it is to address the fundamental economically generated inequalities in education.

The second set of relations where inequality is generated in education is in social and cultural relations. It is in the cultural sphere that our statuses are determined in terms of what is or is not culturally valued. Schools and colleges do not just transmit and create knowledge, they legitimate certain knowledge forms and invalidate others through what they include and exclude on the curriculum. For the children of migrant workers this is a key issue both in respect to their language, values and beliefs and culture. It is also a key issue for groups such as deaf children whose sign language is not recognised in education, or for young people who are gay or lesbian whose sexuality is not granted respect and recognition within school education programmes. Equal respect and recognition is not just about the liberal idea that every individual is entitled to equal rights and the privileges of citizenship in the country in which they live, it is about appreciating or accepting differences rather than merely tolerating them. Having said that, it is important to note that this does not mean that we have an obligation to refrain from criticising other points of view. None of us has to give up the belief that some ideas and practices are unacceptable. What we do need is to engage in a critical dialogue with others. This approach has been called 'critical interculturalism' (Baker et al, 2004). In contrast to the problem of unequal resources, the task of resolving inequalities of respect and recognition within schools and colleges is much more amenable to action within education itself. Research on effective pedagogical practices has shown how education can play a major role in developing the kind of critical thinking and inclusive ethical perspective that underpins respect for differences (Adams et al, 1997, pp. 30-43).

Educating people to respect the values, beliefs and lifestyles of others is not a simple matter for which one can provide a blueprint in one paper. It is possible, however, to outline one of the key principles that would guide such education: the principle of inclusion.

If students and teachers are to learn to respect and recognise diversity, they need to experience it; they need to live with differences, rather than merely learning about them in the abstract. Respect is internalised not only through the development of a critical and empathetic perspective, but also through the experience of dealing with diversity on a daily basis. And in many societies, schools are the only places where such learning can safely take place, although this is sometimes impossible due to severe hostility, conflict or separation between groups. The first principle that must guide us in respecting difference in education, therefore, is that of inclusion and promoting diversity in the intake of all schools, not just in schools where migrant workers or new ethnic communities happen to live.

Language remains a major barrier to educational inclusion for migrant workers and their children. If inclusion is to be meaningful it needs to be integrated with language policy. There is a need for substantial financial investment in second language acquisition and social integration in Europe. Such a policy development needs to be preceded by research and planning.

A second principle that is needed to educate for mutual respect is that of critical interculturalism, not only in relation to the personal values and cultures of others, but also in relation to curriculum, pedagogy and assessment systems. Examples of how such a critical perspective can be developed are outlined by Freire (1972), King & Kitchener (1994) and Shor (1992).

To promote egalitarian ways of seeing the world, students as well as teachers and educational decision makers must be educated about the subject of equality, inclusion and other cognate concepts such as human rights and social justice. In particular, schools and colleges need to educate their staff and students about the equality-specific issues that arise in relation to migration, language differences, social class, gender, colour, nationality, ethnicity, ability, religion and other differences. Education about equality could become part of the formal curriculum of subjects dealing with social issues (such as civil, social and political education, geography, history and politics) as well as being mainstreamed into other subjects including literature, art, music, engineering, mathematics and science.

An essential part of any initiative to educate people about inequality is to include members of marginalised groups in the design of educational programmes. Without such engagement there is a danger of privileged experts colonising the experience of subordinate groups or misrepresenting or misunderstanding new communities whose life-world they do not know. On the positive side, a cooperative practice of educational planning can help create alliances for social change between those with experiential knowledge of inequality and those with professional knowledge. Such alliances would also be mutually beneficial educationally. This principle of partnership has operated successfully in the education of minorities in a number of EU countries.

By promoting the principle of inclusion through formal study, and the practice of inclusion through the adoption of procedures and processes respectful of difference, schools and colleges can help challenge inequalities of respect and recognition. However, while education is a very powerful cultural institution it is by no means the only one and its work needs to be complemented by wider educational initiatives in the media, workplace, law and politics if it is to be fully effective.

There is a need for a cross-European language education policy that addresses the issues of migration. At the moment the private sector reaps the benefits and the public sector manages the costs of integrating into schools children who know neither the language nor the culture of their country of destination.

Power and Solidarity

When educators have addressed the issue of power and authority, it has frequently been from a managerial perspective: how to manage schools more effectively, how to 'keep discipline' (Ball, 1989). In new managerial discourse schools have been increasingly defined within a management science framework, as hierarchical bureaucracies (Packwood, 1988; Bennett & Lecompte, 1999). Hierarchical relations have been routinised in education and made unproblematic. Yet, such hierarchical relations are not only fundamentally inegalitarian; they are organisationally dysfunctional, not least because educational institutions of all kinds are highly complex organisations whose central project is education and care rather than control.

When educators think of why certain young people leave school early, fail to attend when schooling is compulsory, and generally dislike school, they often fail to examine the role that power and the abuse of power plays in the process (Lynch & Lodge, 2002). Yet, one of the major reasons why some young leave school early is because they experience school as a highly judgmental place where they exercise little autonomy, and where they are often defined as failures. They see no point in staying in a place where their sense of educational and personal self-worth is undermined on a daily basis. In many respects, leaving school early may be a positive decision, in the psychological sense, for those whom schools are failing.

Schools and colleges select, classify and stratify students in a hierarchically ordered way. In so doing, they not only exercise power over students but also assign them to positions of relative power and powerlessness. Students are increasingly aware of being treated as insignificant others in terms of how power is exercised in schools. With the emergence of more democratised relations in families and with greater participation by school-going students in part-time work, students have become less willing to accept the older hierarchical model of control that was central to the nineteenth-century model of schooling (Yoneyama, 2000; Lynch & Lodge, 2002; Devine, 2003).

While many would argue that power inequalities are endemic to the hierarchical organisation of schooling, and are inevitable given its role in examining and in operating as a tool of social selection, there are certain power inequalities that can be greatly modified and that not only make schools more inclusive, but would also forestall conflict and reduce rates of drop-out.

The relations of schooling need to be democratised not only because students expect it but because it is vital to the successful functioning of the school organisationally. Democratisation is necessary because it is intrinsically valuable educationally. If we are to educate students to engage in public life as democratic citizens, it is essential that they learn how to participate democratically in the public domain of schooling. (Dewey, 1916).

At the micro-level of teacher–student relationships, democratisation involves substituting dialogue for dominance, cooperation and collegiality for hierarchy, and active learning and problem solving for passivity (Freire, 1972). At the meso-level of school and college organisation, it involves institutionalising and resourcing democratic structures such as student and parent/community councils that exercise real authority and responsibility. Creating curriculum-specific experiences that are democratic in practice as well as in theory is also a fundamental part of the democratising project of education. In effect, it involves devolved governance requiring trust and involving education of all parties in the education process (Apple & Beane, 1999).

Democratising education is not simply about democratising schools and colleges. It is also about developing a participatory politics in which those who are affected by policy decisions have a say in all levels of educational planning and decision making. It is not just a question of consultations; these can be easily ignored when the relevant party absent leaves the table. It is about listening, engagement and accountability in a participatory democratic context.

There needs to be a review of pedagogical practice in European schools in terms of how power is exercised, and the role that inequalities in power play in excluding certain children from school, especially children whom school is failing. How do we address schoolchildren in school: do we know their names? How do we teach: is it didactically and hierarchically or dialogically and democratically? In whose language do we teach? What kinds of tests do we use to classify and group children: are they culturally and linguistically sensitive? What message do we give to schoolchildren, especially new migrants to our countries, when we ignore or trivialise their specific language learning needs in education?

Being cared for is a fundamental prerequisite for mental and emotional well-being and for human development generally (Nussbaum, 1995; Kittay, 1999). Consequently it is vital that people are enabled to provide for, and benefit from, care, love and solidarity. But to promote care, solidarity and love in life requires work, work which is variously emotional, mental and physical. While we cannot always institutionally guarantee that everyone's needs for love, care and solidarity are met, we can try to arrange societies in ways that make this more or less likely. We can ensure that people are educated about care, love and solidarity relations, that employment, transportation networks and neighbourhoods are structured in a manner that facilitates caring, and that vulnerable groups, such those who lose their care networks through migration, who are unaccompanied minors, or who are institutionalised, have adequate protection for their care needs. We can also ensure that the balance between paid and generally unpaid care, love and solidarity work is such that the latter is facilitated, and is equally distributed.

Because women do significantly more care work than men, recognising the importance of care work is a deeply gendered issue and one of the most profound ways in which women's work can be fully recognised in society and in education (Lynch, 2007).

Within European education the student is defined as an autonomous, self-determining human being. The focus is on educating for the future public life of the citizen, especially her or his future economic life.[2] The student is educated to perform, and to define herself or himself in terms of grades and performance in a narrow range of cognitive skills. An indifference to the affective domain, and an allegiance to the education of the rational autonomous subject and public citizen, is at the heart of this concept of education. The focus on Cartesian rationalism is intensifying with the glorification of performativity measured by league tables and rankings.

Four affectively related issues arise from this: first, the education of the student as a relationally engaged person is written out of the educational agenda with serious gendered implications; second, because the focus on preparing students to service the economy is deeply embedded in the practice of selecting and ordering students hierarchically for the labour market, this focuses student effort throughout formal education on self-centred individual achievement which undermines their sense of solidarity and care for others; third, the emotional and affective consequences of labelling and ordering students hierarchically in education are largely ignored, despite the fact that this in itself operates by undermining the self-worth and self-esteem of those who are not successful; fourth, the teacher's role as an affectively engaged caring person is not attributed much significance, not least because the teacher is largely seen as a midwife for delivering student performance.

To educate a student to be a carer citizen and not just a performing citizen would radically alter what we do in education, not least because of the way in which it would redefine the education persona. Education would have to address the fact that the carer citizen is relationally engaged and other-directed; she or he is not entirely self-determining (see Sevenhuijsen, 1998; Hobson, 2000 for a discussion of the carer citizen model). Within a carer citizen model, education cannot be seen as abstracted from others; students cannot be educated to act as purely autonomous entities whose lives are solely about individual performance and achievement.

Recognising the affective domain of life would also require us to assess schooling differently, not only in cognitive terms but also in terms of its emotional impact on students. A carer citizen model would require us to assess the impact of compulsory education on a student's sense of self-worth and well-being. A carer perspective would also require us to attend to the affective implications of teaching work for teachers and of the emotional demands that schooling makes on parents, particularly mothers.

Conclusion

The strategies pursued by the EU since the turn of the century have made education and training a much more important policy area and have substantially changed the character of welfare policy. Both education and welfare policies have become more directly involved with creating the conditions for competitiveness and growth. In this article we have discussed some implications of this. We have found serious absences and contradictions in the discourses and policies discussed. While the EU has rejected pressure in the GATS negotiations to open up sectors like health and education to international trading, it strives at the same time to increase trade in all types of services on the European internal market, and encourages marketisation in some sectors of education, especially higher education. The concepts of education and learning underlying the EU educational policies are limited, focusing mainly on cognitive knowledge and employable competencies.

Most of the discussion about equality in education is focused on how to equalise access to and participation within different levels of formal education for different social groups. While equalising access and participation are key equality objectives, we have argued here for a more holistic and integrated approach to the achievement of equality in education if we are to make schools truly egalitarian institutions. We argue for the need to promote equality of educational conditions. Equality of condition is not about trying to make inequalities fairer, or giving people a more equal opportunity to become unequal; it is about ensuring that everyone has roughly equal prospects for a good life and good education, and creating conditions for that life for all. Measured against a multidimensional concept of equality, post-Lisbon discourses and 'new egalitarianism' reveal a limited and employment-focused idea of social equality, in which questions of power and of love and care are almost absent.

An equality of condition perspective points to a holistic approach to educational policy, one that recognises in particular the integrated links that exist between economic, cultural, political and affective inequalities and educational inequality, and the need to focus on deep structural inequalities rather than the symptoms of injustices when they become embodied in individuals. For example, there is now a large body of evidence showing that the greater the economic inequality in a society, the greater the educational inequality and vice versa. Having positive action plans can modify this outcome but it cannot alter it in any substantive sense, a major reason being that powerful and privileged groups will use their excess resources to undermine positive actions, either through legal challenges through the courts (as is happening in the USA) or by creating alternative privileged institutions for their own members (elite schools funded privately or set up as businesses, such as has happened in many countries in recent years). If Europe is to have a more egalitarian educational system it must have a more egalitarian society; it must create equal conditions of living for its citizens, not just equal opportunities to become unequal.

Notes

[1] The authors participated in a sub-group on 'Social Europe' in the GENIE network. The task was to review and structure the topic, including key issues, concepts and contributions. The work proceeded through a number of written exchanges and several face-to-face working sessions in Joensuu, Finland, in July 2004. This article has been written by Palle Rasmussen (who

also coordinated the sub-group) on the basis of contributions from members of the group.

[2] See the Key Competences for Lifelong Learning developed by the European Commission and agreed by the European Parliament (European Parliament, 2006).

References

Adams, M., Bell, L.A. & Griffin, P. (Eds) (1997) *Teaching for Diversity and Social Justice: a source book*. New York: Routledge.

Albers, D., Haseler, S. & Meyer, H. (2006) *Social Europe: a continent's challenge to market fundamentalism*. London: European Research Forum at London Metropolitan University.

Apple, M.W. & Beane, J.A. (Eds) (1999) *Democratic Schools: lessons from the chalk face*. Buckingham: Open University Press.

Baker, J., Lynch, K., Cantillon, S. & Walsh, J. (2004) *Equality: from theory to action*. London: Palgrave Macmillan.

Ball, S.J. (1989) Micro-politics versus Management, in S. Walker & L. Barton (Eds) *Politics and the Processes of Schooling*. Milton Keynes: Open University Press.

Ball, S.J. (2003) *Class Strategies and the Education Market: the middle classes and social advantage*. London: RoutledgeFalmer.

Bennett D.K. & Lecompte, M.D. (1999) *The Way Schools Work: a sociological analysis of education*, 3rd edn. New York: Longman.

Brine, J. (2001) Education, Social Exclusion and the Supranational State, *International Journal of Inclusive Education*, 5(2/3), 119-131. http://dx.doi.org/10.1080/13603110010020589

Brine, J. (2002) *The European Social Fund and the EU: flexibility, growth, stability*. London: Continuum/Sheffield Academic Press.

Brine, J. (2004) The European Social Fund: the Commission, the Member State and levels of governance, *European Educational Research Journal*, 3(4), 777-789. http://dx.doi.org/10.2304/eerj.2004.3.4.4

Clancy, P. (2001) *College Entry in Focus: a fourth national survey of access to higher education*. Dublin: Higher Education Authority.

Devine, D. (2003) *Children, Power and Schooling: how childhood is structured in the primary school*. Stoke-on-Trent: Trentham Books.

Dewey, J. (1916) *Democracy and Education*. New York: Macmillan.

European Commission (2000) *Social Policy Agenda*. Communication. Brussels: European Commission.

European Commission (2005) *The Social Agenda*. Communication. Brussels: European Commission.

European Commission (2006a) *Delivering on the Modernisation Agenda for Universities: education, research and Innovation*. Communication. Brussels: European Commission.

European Commission (2006b) *Efficiency and Equity in European Education and Training Systems*. Communication. Brussels: European Commission.

European Council (1997) Presidency Conclusions, Luxembourg Extraordinary European Council on Employment, 20-21 November.

European Parliament (2006) Recommendation of the European Parliament and of the Council of 18 December 2006 on Key Competences for Lifelong Learning. Brussels.

Freire, P. (1972) *Pedagogy of the Oppressed*. New York: Penguin.

Gamoran, A. (2001) American Schooling and Educational Inequality: a forecast for the 21st century, *Sociology of Education*, 34, Special Issue, 135-153. http://dx.doi.org/10.2307/2673258

Giddens, A. (2007) *Europe in the Global Age*. Cambridge: Polity Press.

Green, A. (2003) Education, Equality and Social Cohesion: a comparative approach, paper presented at the first GENIE conference, Globalisation(s), Identity(s) and Europe(s) in Education in Europe, Nicosia, 10-12 July.

Heydorn, H.-J. (1970) *Über den Widerspruch von Bildung und Herrschaft*. Frankfurt am Main: Europäische Verlagsanstalt.

Hobson, Barbara (Ed.) (2000) *Gender and Citizenship in Transition*. London: Macmillan.

King, P.M. & Kitchener, K.S. (1994) *Developing Reflective Judgement: understanding and promoting intellectual growth and critical thinking in adolescents and adults*. San Francisco: Jossey-Bass.

Kittay, E.F. (1999) *Love's Labor: essays on women, equality, and dependency*. New York: Routledge.

Lynch, K. (2006) Neo-liberalism and Marketisation: the implications for higher education, *European Educational Research Journal*, 5(1), 1-17. http://dx.doi.org/10.2304/eerj.2006.5.1.1

Lynch, K. (2007) Love Labour as a Distinct and Non-commodifiable Form of Care Labour, *Sociological Review*, 55(3), 550–570. http://dx.doi.org/10.1111/j.1467-954X.2007.00714.x

Lynch, K. & Baker, J. (2005) Equality in Education: the importance of equality of condition, *Theory and Research in Education*, 3(2), 131-164. http://dx.doi.org/10.1177/1477878505053298

Lynch, K. & Lodge, A. (2002) *Equality and Power in Schools: redistribution, recognition and representation*. London: RoutledgeFalmer.

Lynch, K. & Moran, M. (2006) Markets, Schools and the Convertibility of Economic Capital: the complex dynamics of class choice, *British Journal of Sociology of Education*, 27(2), 221-235. http://dx.doi.org/10.1080/01425690600556362

Mayer, S.E. (2001) How did the Increase in Economic Inequality between 1970 and 1990 Affect Children's Educational Attainment? *American Journal of Sociology*, 107(1), 1-32. http://dx.doi.org/10.1086/323149

Nussbaum, M.C. (1995) Emotions and Women's Capabilities, in M. Nussbaum & J. Glover (Eds) *Women, Culture and Development*, 360-395. Oxford: Oxford University Press.

Packwood, T. (1988) The School as a Hierarchy, in A. Westoby (Ed.) *Culture and Power in Educational Organisations*. Milton Keynes: Open University Press.

Peters, M.A. (2003) Rethinking Citizenship and Identity within a Context of Globalisation: Europeanisation or Americanisation? Paper presented at GENIE Conference, Cyprus, July.

Peters, M.A. (2004) Rights to Education and the Learning Citizen in European Democracy, *Kwartalnik Pedagogiczny*, 4(194), 93-102.

Peters, M.A. (2007) Europa, Europeanization, Europe: constituting new Europeans, in M. Kuhn (Ed.) *Who is the European? – a new global player?* New York: Peter Lang.

Raftery, A.E. & Hout, M. (1993) Maximally Maintained Inequality: expansion, reform, and opportunity in Irish education, 1921-1975, *Sociology of Education*, 66, 22-39. http://dx.doi.org/10.2307/2112784

Rasmussen, P. (2006) Danish Learning Traditions in the Context of the European Union, in M. Kuhn & R. Sultana, *Homo Sapiens Europæus? Creating the European Learning Citizen*, 47-68. New York: Peter Lang.

Sevenhuijsen, S. (1998) *Citizenship and the Ethics of Care: feminist considerations on justice, morality and politics*. London: Routledge.

Shavit, Y. & Blossfeld, H.P. (Eds) (1993) *Persistent Inequality: changing educational attainment in thirteen countries*. Boulder: Westview Press.

Shor, I. (1992) *Empowering Education: critical teaching for social change*. Chicago: Chicago University Press.

Sünker, H. (1989) Bildungstheorie als Gesellschaftskritik, in O. Hansmann & W. Marotzki (Eds) *Diskurs Bildungstheorie II*, 447-470. Weinheim: Deutscher Stidienverlag.

Sünker, H. (2006) *Politics, Bildung and Social Justice*. Rotterdam: Sense Publishers.

Wind, M. (2003) The European Union as a Polycentric Polity: returning to a neo-medieval Europe?, in J.H.H. Weiler & M. Wind, *European Constitutionalism beyond the State*. Cambridge: Cambridge University Press.

Yoneyama, S. (2000) Student Discourse on Tokokyohi (School Phobia/Refusal) in Japan: burnout or empowerment? *British Journal of Sociology of Education*, 21, 77-94. http://dx.doi.org/10.1080/01425690095171

CHAPTER 9

Languages, Education and Europeanisation

JANET ENEVER

SUMMARY Adopting a specifically European focus, this chapter reviews and accounts for the patterns of language shift and change in Europe as a defining feature in the formation of national states. Within an increasingly interconnected world today, the consequence of escalating economic migration and the virtual world of multimodal digital technologies, it is argued that the continuing shifts in the balance of economic and political power are precipitating a global trend in the re-shaping of educational policies in an attempt to equip future generations with the cultural capital preceived to be necessary. This chapter focuses on a European pattern of policy formation whereby currently English is seen as a near-essential tool of a flexible, mobile labour force.

Introduction

This chapter provides a broad introduction to the topic of languages in Europe today. It will aim to contextualise current trends, debates and implications for education within a broader picture of a pattern of shift and change in language choice across many domains of use over time. It will be argued that such shift and change is an inevitable and necessary response to shifts in the balance of power within and between nations in recognition of the economic and political benefits for speakers of particular languages, rather than an expansion of the language purely for the intrinsic worth it might offer its speakers, or for the express purposes of maintaining elements of a culture embedded in the language. In problematising the contemporary role of state and regional legislation in support of minority and plurilingual language agendas through education policies in Europe, the real impact on both schooled and unschooled learning of languages will be interrogated and the dimensions of power in such policymaking further explored.

New Ways of Thinking about Languages Today

Reflecting on the relatively recent period of European expansion (fifteenth to nineteenth centuries) when representatives of some of the more powerful European rulers 'set sail to conquer the world', these European adventurers/conquerors/exploiters (depending on the reader's perspective) took their languages with them, initially resulting in a mix of the local and European language being used for trading purposes and later an imposition of both language and rule on the local population. So, empires were formed – in which (theoretically) the language of the more powerful ruler was employed, at least in the public domain. The power relations, particularly in the imperial period, were relatively clear-cut, ruler and subject. The language of the ruler was imposed and the subject had little choice but to use it within the public domain. In varying degrees these European languages gained a cultural prestige as a consequence of such power relations, a prestige which in some instances outlived the imperialist reign of power (Ostler, 2005, p. 259).

Today, within a context of globalisation, there appear to be new forms of power in action – not just an extension of the old forms. Thus, the old imperialist model and discussion about language rights is inadequate as a construct for analysing the new local realities in ways similar to those of previous times. Neither, though, do claims of neutrality for the position of specific languages work either. Examples such as the African country of Tanzania illustrate the problematics of this concept all too clearly. Since independence in 1964 debates on the most appropriate choice of language for delivery of the primary school curriculum in Tanzania have gone back and forth. There exist a number of local languages of which the regional language of Kiswahili is the most widely spoken. Whilst the use of Kiswahili might appear to make best sense, others argue that delivery of the curriculum from Grade 1 in English would offer the possibility of neutrality on the language front, whilst also equipping the next generation with fluency in a global language (Eliphas, 2003). However, this proposal is challenged by those who perceive English as a language of external, dominant powers. In truth, it is not the language that is/is not neutral – it is the power position of the language *users* that is the key.

In seeking ways to talk about the impact of globalisation, then, we meet the challenge of a complex, multilayered discussion. The discussion is about real people moving in real places. In relation to the question of language, it is important to observe that when people move, they move through different hierarchies of different value systems in which language is operating differently. In talking about the question of language in Europe today we need now to consider how to address this phenomenon. Clearly, we need to rethink what language is, how we use it, why and when we use it.

As a starting point to the proposal for a re-viewing of language and its role, I will put forward some ideas here that can be returned to later in the discussion. Considerable data now available from the historical linguists trace the migration of peoples across continents, together with their subsequent language changes. From this we can identify a continuous process of shift and change in response to new circumstances or as a consequence of the shift in power relationships between neighbouring languages. Relating this history to a discussion of language today, operating within a very different climate of interconnectedness through globalisation, we now need to consider a quite new discourse about language in this quite different era. It could be proposed that we should be talking less about *communication* with 'the other' across borders/nationalities and more about *interaction* between peoples (Bakhtin, 1986).

This question of *viewing language differently* and focusing on *interaction* rather than *communication* essentially aims to foreground the *human* condition of a social being. Within a global climate of supra-powers competing for dominance this proposal can be perceived as both naive and untenable, yet I will argue that through the potential offered by multimodal digital technologies today, this is already being achieved (Lo Bianco, 2005, p. 129). Further, that we need urgently to reconsider our perceptions of language to refocus our education systems in acknowledgement of the role of these unmonitored networks in forming our linguistic and cultural identities today. To more fully grasp the scale of the currently emerging shift in the nature of how we are beginning to use language, I will first set out a brief summary of the conceptualising of language over the past few centuries in Europe, followed by an outline of contemporary debates over domains of use for particular languages in Europe. These sections will aim to provide a backdrop for returning to the question of perceptions of language and of how our education systems might be employed as catalysts of change.

A Brief Historical Summary of Language Shift in Europe

Historically, languages have always been associated with ethnic groupings. When a more powerful group subjugated a less powerful one, the language of the more powerful would become dominant – at least in the public domain. This process of 'learning languages "upwards", from the small to the large language, ... from the poor to the rich language group, from the subjugated to the dominant nation' (de Swaan, 2001, p. 25) has always been a feature of language shift (as suggested by the example of Tanzania above).

Shift in language choice over the past 500 years or so across Europe can be substantially accounted for by the establishment of the nation state and the importance attached to defining its borders. From the seventeenth century onwards as dominant power groupings in Europe sought to consolidate their lands, increasingly language was employed as a means both of identifying and uniting the population. Prior to this phase, languages spoken in the different regions of Europe were diverse, yet increasingly as unification took shape, so those languages associated with the less powerful groupings were discarded (at least in the public domain) in preference for the languages of wider currency and greater prestige. The eighteenth century brought a period of increased expansionism, together with greater wealth and opportunities to consolidate kingdoms and the subsequent emergence of the first (French) republic. Since this time, language increasingly has served as a vehicle for unification, a defining marker of boundaries, a vehicle for nurturing a sense of national identity and for maintaining national cohesion. Lo Bianco (2005, p. 112) proposes that: 'Many national states in Europe ... deployed the discourse of a distinctive and exclusive national tongue to mobilise and make congruent a self-conscious nation aspiring to autonomous statehood'. He further suggests that whilst 'this sense of language-defined nationalism ... is not exclusively European, ... [it] has taken on a very public and recognisable form in various European nationalisms'.

Returning again to the question of exactly how language contributed to the process of nation formation, varying accounts describe this political and economic process in different parts of the world. One such account of the process in Europe is that outlined by de Swaan (2001, p. 147). In summary, he suggests that in France and the United Kingdom (UK), for example, national language unification has occurred through a process whereby:

> A central language, surrounded by a number of more or less
> peripheral ones, gradually comes to predominate, as it becomes
> the second language of almost all citizens and the mother tongue
> of a growing majority, and finally succeeds in driving out the
> peripheral languages from practically all domains.

It appears that this process of defining and redefining borders through language can today be viewed as a continuing one, with very recent evidence in Europe itself. The process of partition in the former Czechoslovakia offers a contemporary illustrative example of what has become known as linguistic Balkanisation. Here, the Czechoslovakian language (apparently) ceased to exist and the two distinct languages of Czech and Slovak emerged (or, perhaps, re-emerged). In this instance languages were used to distinctively mark a newly formed political and geographical entity. Over time, it might be assumed that the formerly close mutual intelligibility of these languages across the borders would be further differentiated as a result of either less contact, or language intervention activities to demarcate the differences more clearly (previous examples of this practice include the official changes made to Polish spelling in the 1960s to confirm a newly defined border position between Poland and Germany and the introduction of new vocabulary into the French language in efforts to prevent the further Anglicisation of French).

Whilst de Swaan's analysis of the role of language in the formation of the nation state does not fully reflect the pattern of all European states, nonetheless it serves as a useful illustration of one of the processes by which some (perceived) less prestigious languages spoken in Europe may have lost in value and fallen out of use as a process of homogenisation helped to confirm national borders through the vehicle of one national language (in many instances). It is further evident that official policies in recognition of societal multilingualism have been a relative rarity in Europe until recently, although they can be found more commonly outside Europe (Hroch, 1996, p. 55).

By the early twentieth century in Europe the provision of state education for six years of elementary schooling was to further consolidate national languages in almost all parts of Europe (de Swaan, 2001, p. 148). In summary, over a period of up to 200 years national languages have established a robust role in the cultural identity of most nation states of Europe – one which appears unlikely to radically shift in the immediate future, despite the occasional expressions of alarm raised by some commentators and political figures from time to time.

Contemporary Language Debates and Dilemmas

Given the robust nature of national languages in Europe today, changes in the official national language are rare. Those mentioned above can be identified as the result of newly drawn geographical and political boundaries. Mainly though, in Europe debates concern domains of use for specific languages rather than disputes over national languages. These debates have become increasingly high profile and appear likely to escalate further as membership of the EU continues to expand. At national and sub-national levels both local and minority languages (in addition to the national language) operate effectively within the private domain and increasingly are recognised within the domain of education at elementary level, in part due to the support given by European policies for maintenance of minority languages by the centralised European state. Most commonly, the national language(s) continue to be used for communication within the public national domain.

It is these minority languages, combined with the languages of small states (for example Sweden, Malta), that may be most affected by economic globalisation and may, in the future, be at risk. Lo Bianco (2005, p. 118) proposes that here, 'exclusion [of the language] from economic modernity' may cause 'a declining vitality'. It is to halt the progress of such 'declining vitality' (in both linguistic and cultural terms) that current European policy is ostensibly designed to achieve. The question of whether such social engineering is possible or indeed desirable is a much-debated issue in Europe today.

It is beyond the national level, in the forum of the European public domain, where concerns about language are increasingly evident as the number of official EU languages continues to expand (an increase from 12 to 20 in 2003). Here, we can identify a new phenomenon emerging as languages are positioned in competition with one another for both political and economic gain. Whilst national (or official) languages continue to be employed in the most public of European public domains, by politicians for ceremonial or televised appearances, in other less public domains within the European institutions there is an increasing tendency to use one or other of the more widely spoken languages for debate and daily working purposes. Many examples are quoted in the literature (de Swaan, 2001, pp. 144-175; van Els, 2001; Phillipson, 2003, pp. 105-138; Truchot, 2003) indicating the extent to which the daily workings tend increasingly to be carried out in French or German, but most often in English. Opinions on the likely outcome of this trend all too often polarise around concerns for the possible decline of some European languages (and their related cultures), juxtaposed with the enormous expense of translation facilities and publications in 20 languages (at present).

More urgently – and of central concern in this languages section – the question of *real interaction* taking place as yet has not been fully addressed in discussions regarding language choices in the European public space. Whilst van Els (2001) touches on this briefly, Streetly (2005) has elaborated on this challenge more fully. As a senior conference interpreter for the United Nations (UN), EU and other similar international organisations she reports on the unique practical difficulties of working with so many languages (EU interpreters work with 20 languages, whilst UN interpreters work with a mere 12). A single meeting might require up to 60 interpreters. Streetly notes that increasingly many delegates prefer to give a prepared speech in English, since they (apparently) view themselves as sufficiently proficient to do this. The problematics arising may include pronunciation problems, misunderstandings as a result of the linguistic phenomenon of 'false friends' (a lexical item in one language with a very different meaning in another), or simply the low level of idiomatic speech that results in a simplification or 'dumbing down' of the speech. Streetly suggests there currently exists a quite high tolerance of inaccuracies in such exchanges but highlights the difficulties for delegates with lower levels of English who are unable to participate in the subsequent debates and may in effect be silenced as a consequence of their lower language competency.

Across the European business world the choice of language in supranational industries is increasingly towards major regional languages and away from the national language of the country of operation. The need for political sensitivity (as evident in EU institutions) is less vital here and a pragmatic choice of English is often made by such organisations. This choice has now become almost the norm for middle management and above. An interesting and perhaps unexpected example of the extent to which this trend has become widespread is that of the European Central Bank. Whilst this institution operates fully on behalf of the regional European institutions of governance, its business is substantially conducted on a global level. The linguistic consequence of this is a decision for the institution to function principally in English, despite its geographical location in Frankfurt, Germany (Truchot, 2003, p. 105).

In addition to the above contexts of centralised European state institutions and supranational European industries, there exists one further important dimension of language dilemma in Europe today: that of the shifting position and perceptions of some minority languages in some of the nation states of Europe. There is now clear evidence of a number that appear to be developing expansionist tendencies (for example Welsh, Catalan), whilst others are stabilising and consolidating their roles (for example Friesian, Basque). This shift may in part be accounted for by the support given by EU policy statements, particularly since the early 1990s. Such support has consisted of EU centralised encouragement to nation states to give official recognition, funding support from the EU for national policies that facilitate minority language programmes and similar initiatives.

It appears today that whilst the internal power relationships between specific minority/majority languages may reflect a tension, their regional (EU) relationship may be perceived quite differently and more positively. For example, the recent EU accession states of Hungary and Slovakia found difficulty in acknowledging and respecting minority language speakers at the borderlands between their countries as a consequence of long histories of disputed territories. Ambitions of gaining early entry to the EU were substantially responsible for a rapid change of official attitude here (although a true cultural change may actually take longer) (personal communication, J. Sarosdy, 1999). This centralised EU emphasis on the importance of acknowledging minority languages reflects a policy of emphasising both diversity and plurilingualism in Europe on the premise that a more equal and thus stable balance of power can thereby be achieved across the region. Such a policy may work in opposition to a pattern of power relations at national and sub-national level that has existed for some centuries. It appears then that agenda setting may rest in the hands of those more powerful groupings which have most to gain economically from such an agenda, operating beyond and possibly against the interests of individual nation states.

Drawing together the strands of this section, I have attempted to highlight here the essential language dilemmas for European politicians today. Maurais & Morris (2003, p. 5) summarise the global language challenge in these words: 'ongoing competition between languages within and across regions is by its essence dynamic in nature'. On the one hand the use of English continues to grow in supranational interactions across Europe, whilst on the other centralised EU policy seeks to nurture an environment of plurilingualism and improved minority language status. The question of the extent to which a minority language status is sustainable will depend on the factors that promote an upward spiral in the domains for use of the language (Mackey, 2003, p. 78). Much of this will depend on the power relations of specific minority languages and of their perceived prestige status. Linked to this argument, it is important also to seek possible evidence of covert agenda setting in this supranational policy, by those power groupings which will gain most from the loosening of language management from the ties of national

185

legislation. Lo Bianco (2005, p. 117), for example, proposes that 'international communities of communication' now exist which increasingly 'add instrumental power to language forms'. Such power groupings may impact on the 'scope and range of national languages' as a consequence of their increasing communities of communication. For a review of such potential the following section will explore trends in language-in-education policy and practice across Europe today.

Language in European Education

The preceding sections of this chapter have outlined a history of substantial shift in languages in Europe and a contemporary picture of new language demands and dilemmas. Positioning school language teaching within this picture, it should be noted firstly that rarely has educational provision been at the forefront of innovation and certainly on the matter of language teaching the tendency has been towards a conservatism which somewhat lags behind current needs.

Nonetheless, over the past 25 years in Europe both policy and practice have altered substantially in perspective. Taking the year of 1980 as a useful barometer by which to measure that change, it could be said that at that period the main objectives of school language provision in the nation states of Europe were for their brighter students to achieve an intermediate-level fluency in at least one other European language – most often that of their nearest and most prestigious neighbours. Hence, students in Spain might learn French, students in Germany English or French and students in Poland mainly German, though also some French. In addition, those countries where another language held a high minority status or where the country retained links with a currently/previously dominant external power, they might additionally make extensive school provision for this second language (for example, Russian in Czechoslovakia, English in Cyprus, Swedish in Finland). The extent of provision varied from country to country. In some, one second/foreign language was compulsory for all secondary-aged children, in others provision was made only for those considered to be of higher intelligence.

In school contexts where a foreign language was taught it was assumed that much of the population would have little or no future need to *speak* the language; the teaching emphasis was thus mainly on the two skills of reading and writing. Where a second language was taught, there might be a greater emphasis on gaining some competency in the skills of speaking and listening also. In addition to the above, Latin also was commonly taught in the more academic schools across Europe – viewed as providing an underpinning to how languages operate and perceived as a valuable root source of the most prestigious European languages. Hence, adolescents in these elite schools (perhaps some 10% of the population) might find themselves studying three, or even four, classical/contemporary European languages for periods of up to five or six years in secondary education.

Today, patterns of school language provision have substantially refocused with the aim of responding to the contemporary and future needs of *all* learners. In many countries the experience of curriculum overload is a familiar concern contributing to decisions of making compulsory provision only for those languages of key value to the next generation. Latin is hence unlikely to be found as a compulsory requirement today anywhere but in Italy (where it continues to be provided in at least one school in each town throughout the country).

The recent publication of a first edition of the Eurydice (European Commission, 2005) collection of data on school language provision in Europe is indicative of the increased importance that the centralised state is placing on this element of cultural capital. Published every two years, it will provide an invaluable future source of data from which to analyse changing provision. It should be noted then that Eurydice statistics quoted here are taken from the Eurostat, New Cronos database (source years are given in relation to each statistic). Selecting from the wealth of data now available, a brief summary of language choices made and the extent of provision available will suffice to indicate the pan-European position in the first few years of the twenty-first century. Firstly, it appears that whilst diverse languages are available in many countries, only five languages (English, French, German, Russian and Spanish) represent 95% of all languages learnt (European Commission, 2005, 11, data year 2001-02). The data further indicate that English is the most taught language in virtually all countries and that approximately 90% of all pupils in upper secondary education learn English, regardless of whether or not it is compulsory (European Commission, 2005, 11, data year 2001-02). Whilst German is the second most taught language in northern and central Europe, French occupies this position in southern Europe (European Commission, 2005, 50, data year 2001-02). It appears also that the increasing tendency to learn English is especially marked in Central Europe (European Commission, 2005, 54, data year 2001-02). This dominance of English occurs despite the fact that most countries aim to offer a wide range of other language possibilities. Currently, these are more likely to be taken up only as second or third languages (Westlau-Schlüter, 2005, p. 1).

The data indicating the dominance of English are sometimes the consequence of choices made by school authorities, parents and children, rather than politicians, in individual nation states. Only in some 50% of European states is English the required first choice at secondary level. English as a voluntary choice is particularly evident at state primary level and within the private language school sector of Europe, where more often there are a range of other alternatives available. The consequence of such choice appears to be an overwhelming preference for English throughout the age ranges, from 7-19 years.

187

However, this provision and selection reflects only one part of the contemporary picture, a picture which suggests a political and economic agenda for future cultural capital which may offer advantage to the learner and hence economic gain for the nation state. Current data provide no information on *what* is being taught and what is being *learnt* as a consequence of this provision. Such qualitative data require complex methods of collection if they are to hold any degree of validity for interpretation. Importantly, aims and objectives of national curriculum programmes currently differ quite widely from country to country across Europe, as do teacher qualifications and number of hours spent weekly on teaching provision. Insufficient agreement exists at present as to what measures of achievement are most valid as markers of relevant cultural capital at each stage of competency. Elements such as grammar accuracy, vocabulary knowledge, assessment at sentence level, translation skills, oral competency in prepared and unprepared simulated situations, reading comprehension and various extended written tasks all compete for a central role in national testing systems. Such systems often reflect a specific cultural history of testing approaches across the whole curriculum which may no longer be relevant or appropriate for today's changed needs of language users.

In this outline review of recent language choice and provision in Europe there are some indications that it is becoming increasingly possible to be able to discuss the European region as a whole. Whilst this should in no way be taken as indicative of a cohesive pan-European policy, substantial attempts have been made to move in this direction. For example, a recent policy agreement of a European Action Plan (European Commission, 2003) has proposed that all citizens should become competent in their mother tongue plus two other languages (interestingly, there is, for the first time, some acknowledgement that these may include non-European languages). All European nation states are politically committed to move towards this achievement (although some more so than others). At a recent language research seminar (2005) Lid King (Director, UK National Languages Strategy, Department for Education and Skills) proposed that embedded within this overarching policy three underlying policy assumptions could be identified:

1. Language diversity can be regarded as a problem, therefore a policy is needed to overcome this possibility.
2. Multilingualism is a 'right'. Hence, citizens have a right of access to acquiring it.
3. Language can be regarded as a resource: intellectually, economically, culturally and socially.

In discussion of these points, King proposed that whilst viewing access to language learning as a right has some merit, this perspective can also be identified as limiting. He argued that we should not ignore the rights, but that we need to move beyond this perspective. In this analysis there is some recognition of the pragmatic difficulties of quality provision for all and the reality of insufficient interest (and perceived gain) in learning more than one language in some regions of Europe today. Working with this perspective, it could be proposed that approaches to providing 'right of access' should be mindful of these factors. King highlighted the concept of 'language as a resource' as of particular importance. He argued that high-level competency should not necessarily be perceived as the goal but that language learning should be regarded as a resource that offers inclusion, with opportunities for achieving higher levels, where necessary, for future economic mobility, inclusion and social engagement.

In this discussion of both policy and current language provision at school level in Europe little is mentioned with regard to the question of student motivation. Throughout all the documentation it is notable that there appears to be an assumption that school students will be keen and willing learners. Little if any mention is made of the uniquely different nature of languages as school subjects and of the consequent necessity for learners to be willing to *engage*, if they are to make progress towards competency. Language is not simply a body of knowledge that can be learnt and reproduced for examination purposes; an ability to transform this knowledge through a process of shaping new identities is required in order to be at ease with interacting through this newly acquired means of self-expression. In recognition of the complexity of this process, researchers in the field of applied linguistics have, in recent years, increasingly acknowledged the central importance of student motivation and the challenge of sustaining it if learners are to engage in the complex process of establishing multiple identities through which they are empowered to *appropriate* the language for their own purposes (Dörnyei, 2001). In no other school subject is this appropriation so necessary *as a measure of learning having taken place*. In confirmation of the central importance of motivation we need only turn to the recent evidence of Russian as previously taught throughout the former Soviet Bloc countries of Central and Eastern Europe. Whilst taught as a school subject for some 10+ years, a substantial majority of these school students claim to have learnt little or nothing of the language. The curriculum time and energy expended proved to be excessively unproductive.

As many school students will testify, the rich and essential element of motivation is not always to be found in classrooms. Classrooms offer a quite challenging environment in which to learn languages, since essentially language is about interaction – engaging in sharing and exchanging ideas on matters of mutual interest. This kind of engagement may well be easier to achieve outside the classroom than inside. Certainly, with the rapid development of digital technologies over the past 20-30 years, evidence of language learning for social purposes has now emerged as a major motivating factor, particularly for the adolescent learner. Two recent European studies confirm this situation in relation to the learning of English. Firstly, in 1992 Hasebrink et al (1997) investigated the influences for learning English on over 200 German school students (aged 15-16 years) in Hamburg. They found substantial opportunities for contact with English both in and out of school and that much of this out-of-school contact was through the media, popular music and computers. It was particularly noted that neither the school type nor the students' socio-economic background appeared as a significant variable in these findings. A later linked study by Berns & de Bot (2005, p. 194) reports on in-school and out-of-school influences for similar-aged groups in Germany, the Netherlands, Belgium and France – a total of 2000 15-year-olds. Here, there was very substantial evidence of music and computer use as a social activity *in English*. Students identified this as a major source of English learning and claimed that little of their learning took place in the classroom. Nonetheless, student perceptions of their own abilities in learning English and their self-evaluations of personal 'liking for English' correlated closely with their achievements in school tests. It appeared that those who considered themselves good at learning English and perceived the English language positively were actually high achievers in school-based assessments (p. 204). Further studies are now needed in other regions of Europe, particularly in the more rural regions, to provide a more comprehensive picture of current patterns of learning.

Conclusion

This study began by proposing that we need to find new ways of viewing and talking about language today. It was suggested that the potential offered by multimodal digital technologies brings us closer to that possibility and invites us to reconsider our perceptions of language and to refocus our language education in acknowledgement of these unmonitored networks of interconnectedness. In setting out the past history of shift and change in language patterns across Europe and recording the contemporary provision of languages in education, the data have highlighted recent change in language choices and indicated something of the extent to which this is supplemented by out-of-school practices for social purposes. In this, we confront the rationality of European policy (an agenda for a trilingual citizenry) with the subjective realities: the inclusion/exclusion characteristic of urban/rural populations; the choice of global cultural capital above local/regional cultural capital; and the power of unmonitored networks of global digital communities for language learning.

It appears that the project for interconnectedness has been launched so successfully via the Internet and other multimodal digital technologies that it is unlikely to be willingly set in reverse by today's youth culture. European centralised state concerns to promote language diversity essentially appear to reflect Tomkin's interpretation that 'the advent of globalisation has highlighted a tension between expansion, on the one hand, and interconnectedness on the other' (Tomkin, 2003, p. 322). The project for diversity aims to limit the dominance of English across Europe, at least. At the same time English is perceived as a primary tool of cultural capital for the vast majority of language learners in Europe. The consequence of such interconnectedness offers unprecedented opportunities for the formation of supranational identities where language operates to offer 'new boundaries of inclusion and belonging' (Lo Bianco, 2005, p. 129) amongst users.

Future gazing in the world of language planning has been notoriously unsuccessful in the past. Thus, planning for school provision is an unsatisfactory business. The challenge for curriculum planning is the long-term nature of the project, requiring investment in the training of teachers, language courses for teachers, development of appropriate teaching materials and staged implementation of the programme. A current example of this lengthy process is the pilot phase for the introduction of foreign language teaching at primary level in England, which indicates that at least a 10-year period will be necessary before any degree of national provision can be claimed (let alone consistency of quality in such provision). Given the long-term nature of such a project it seems hardly surprising that some nation states in Europe appear not to be investing in a strong model of plurilingualism as keenly as they might. It may well be that in another 10 years opinions on language learning will have changed again and there will be new priorities in response to new circumstances.

However, the words of Chiti-Batelli (2003, p. 138) seem to sum up the evidence presented in this study – for the interim at least:

> The bilingual/plurilingual solution is likely to be unattainable for the great majority [of the population], since most people are either insufficiently motivated or do not have the necessary aptitude.

References

Bakhtin, M. (1986) *Speech Genres and Other Late Essays.* Austin: University of Texas Press.

Berns, M. & de Bot, K. (2005) English Language Proficiency at the Secondary Level: a comparative study of four European countries, in C. Gnutzmann & F. Intemann (Eds) *The Globalisation of English and the English Language Classroom,* 194-213. Tübingen: Gunter Narr.

Chiti-Batelli, A. (2003) Can Anything Be Done about the 'Glottophagy' of English? A Bibliographical Survey with a Political Conclusion, *Language Problems and Language Planning,* 27(2), 137-154. http://dx.doi.org/10.1075/lplp.27.2.03chi

Dörnyei, Z. (2001) *Motivational Strategies in the Language Classroom.* Cambridge: Cambridge University Press

Eliphas, F. (2003) Language Policy in Tanzania. Unpublished MA dissertation, London Metropolitan University.

European Commission (2003) *Promoting Language Learning and Linguistic Diversity: an action plan 2004-2006.* Brussels: Commission of the European Communities.

European Commission (2005) Eurydice: key data on teaching languages at schools in Europe – 2005 edition. http://www.eurydice.org

Hasebrink, U., Berns, M. & Skinner, E. (1997) The English Language within the Media Worlds of European Youth, in P. Winterhoff-Spurk & T.H.A. Van der Voordt (Eds) *New Horizons in Media Psychology*, 154-174. Opladen: Westdeutscher Verlag.

Hroch, M. (1996) From National Movement to the Fully Formed Nation: the nation-building process in Europe, in G. Balakrishnan (Ed.) *Mapping the Nation*, 49-81. New York: Verso.

King, L. (2005) Issues for Language Learning in a Multilingual Europe, conference plenary: Multilingual Europe: Building Policy from Successful Practice, University of London Goldsmiths College, 12 November.

Lo Bianco, J. (2005) Globalisation and National Communities of Communication, *Language Problems and Language Planning*, 29(2), 102-233. http://dx.doi.org/10.1075/lplp.29.2.02lob

Mackey, F. (2003) Forecasting the Fate of Languages, in J. Maurais & M. Morris (Eds) *Languages in a Globalising World*, 64-81. Cambridge: Cambridge University Press.

Maurais, J. & Morris, M. (Eds) (2003) *Languages in a Globalising World*. Cambridge: Cambridge University Press.

Ostler, N. (2005) *Empires of the Word: a language history of the world*. New York: Harper Collins.

Phillipson, R. (2003) *English-Only Europe? Challenging Language Policy*. London: Routledge.

Streetly, J. (2005) Conference Interpreting: meeting challenges in an era of global English, International Association of Conference Interpreters Seminar, London Metropolitan University, 16 June.

Swaan, A. de (2001) *Words of the World: the global language system*. Cambridge: Polity Press.

Tomkin, H. (2003) The Search for a Global Linguistic Strategy, in J. Maurais & M. Morris (Eds) *Languages in a Globalising World*, 319-323. Cambridge: Cambridge University Press.

Truchot, C. (2003) Languages and Supranationality in Europe: the linguistic influence of the European Union, in J. Maurais & M. Morris (Eds) *Languages in a Globalising World*, 99-110. Cambridge: Cambridge University Press.

Van Els, T. (2001) The European Union, its Institutions and its Languages – some language political observations, *Current Issues in Language Planning*, 4(2), 311-360.

Westlau-Schlüter, P. (Ed.) (2005) Eurydice in Brief. http://www.eurydice.org

CHAPTER 10

Globalisation and Europeanisation: unicentricity and polycentricity and the role of intellectuals

M'HAMMED SABOUR

SUMMARY The European Union has enlarged in space, population, and cultural and linguistic diversity. Its integration has been strengthened on levels of law regulation, harmonisation of environment policy, standardisation of educational diplomas and accreditation, and establishment of single currency, among others. This integration has been seen by 'europhile' scholars and policymakers as a reinforcement of Europe identity in international fields of economy and technology. From their part eurosceptics criticize it because they see in it a threat to national identities, regional particularities and cultural diversities. However, it is the economic policy inspired by a neoliberalist philosophy which is perceived as weakening the role of the welfare state that has raised most scepticism and critique. This chapter analyses theoretically and thematically the process of europeanisation and its historical affinities with westernisation, when it is question of power division and relations among nations and cultures. In this ongoing process of 'higher' European integration there are implicit and explicit symbolic and political struggles for dominance and hegemony. The mainstream (core) large states like Germany, France and the United Kingdom, thanks to their economic might, cultural influence and technical prominence, try to impose their will and vision of integration on other member states, especially small and peripheral countries. The chapter seeks to describe the role of intellectuals in raising consciousness, awareness and vigilance in defending a polycentric perception of Europe against this politically unicentric, economically-driven and technically-inspired process of integration.

The Modern World System has been structured around a core area, Europe, and its core values. Civilization and Modernization (and other such concepts, like Growth and Development) have been thinly disguised synonyms for Europeanization (Westernization). The growth of world-level structures has gone

hand in hand with the growth of the European, and then Western, (and/or Northern) centrality, and the peripheralization (marginalization) of other areas and cultures.
(Strassoldo, 1992, p. 47

Europeanization ... contributes to the process of de-politicization, indifference, and popular disengagement. (Radaelli, 1999, p. 768)

All political institutions are manifestations and materializations of power (Arendt, 1970, p. 140)

Background

During the last two decades or so the process of Europeanisation has known significant quantitative and qualitative evolution. In other words, the European Union has enlarged in space, population, cultural and linguistic diversity, on the one hand, and, on the other, its integration has been strengthened on levels of law regulation, harmonisation of environment policy, standardisation of educational diplomas and accreditation (e.g. ECTS), establishment of a single currency, among others. This integration, which has seen important achievements in the political and institutional fields, has not obtained unanimous approval or gain approbation from all. While 'Europhiles' (scholars, politicians and policymakers) see in this process a reinforcement for Europe in the international fields of economy, trade, culture and technology ahead of American and Japanese rivals and competitors, the 'Eurosceptics' are critical because they consider it as a threat to national identity, regional autonomy and cultural diversity (Morin, 1990).

One of the main theses of those who defend Europeanisation is the economic pressure caused by globalisation (Fligstein & Merand, 2002). Anchored in a neoliberal ideology, their discourse gives more room to the market economy and reduces or weakens state action. This discourse has been monopolised by economists and the tendencies of some of the intelligentsia with liberal leanings. It goes without saying that a close rapprochement between the EU's Member States has been beneficial, for example, in domains of security, scientific research, environment protection, human rights, to cite only a few. However, these 'successes' cannot hide the latent conflicts and rivalries of distinction, influence, hegemony, identification or leadership caused mainly by the *rapport de force* existing between the Member States by reason of their economic, political and cultural weight, and their position as mainstream (core) or peripheral countries in the European space.

To begin with, globalisation has been at the centre of extensive and intensive debates in academia and in the political field as well. Various interpretations and conclusions have been reached depending on the respective position of debaters, on the one hand, and the dimension(s) of globalisation in question (e.g. economic, political, technical, cultural), on the other. Whatever is the case, the phenomenon of globalisation has been prominent for at least the last two decades in many disciplines in political and social sciences. If some consider that globalisation has marked the dismantling of the unicentric domination of Europe and the west in general (e.g. Morgan, 2005), others (e.g. Mazrui, 1990; Amin, 2003) argue just the opposite. In their assessment, globalisation, as a cultural phenomenon and western-centric ideology, has universal hegemony in fields of economy and politics but is anti-universalist in matters of value and culture. Its driving forces are embedded in a capitalist culture which has fashioned the world according to its own image and expects to be considered as a model and a reference. In this regard, it is seen as self-promoting and self-praising at the expense of other cultures, societies and civilisations. It has, states Mazrui (1990), hegemonic and homogenic aims and outcomes. In spite of the beneficial contributions made by globalisation in terms of communication, interconnectedness and universal awareness, it is often seen as tantamount to unicentric hegemony. As an alternative and in order to soften its impact and loosen its grip, Mazrui and Amin propose a polycentric form of globalisation where there is a multiplicity of cultural, political or economic centres. In other words, a diverse, diversified, plural, and heterogeneous perception of culture, power, knowledge and space will replace a unilateral, uniform, unicentric, egocentric and logocentric model of the world.

Building on Pierre Bourdieu's (1992) conception, Europe is seen as a large space where various national interests and particularities struggle for distinction, recognition, domination, equality, prominence and/or leadership. This chapter aims at examining the problematic of European integration as an endogenous and exogenous process of Europeanisation, and how it was one of the creating forces and simultaneously the outcome of globalisation. In addition to a short account of the dominant discourse on globalisation, this chapter sketches an analysis of the role of intellectuals in this discourse as guardians and watchdogs of polycentric Europeanisation and globalisation against any homogenising and hegemonising policy coming from the European Union (Brussels).

About Globalisation

Among many other designations, globalisation refers to a process of active change in different social, economic, cultural and political domains. This change is characterised, as Pieterse (1999, p. 5) portrays, by an 'interactive set of processes [that] includes *informatization* in technology, *flexibilization* in production, consumption and labour markets, and as regards political reorganization *refiguration* of the state and *regionalization*' (italics in original).

If there is a relative understanding about its historical genesis and evolution there is no agreement about its definition, content, impact and ontology. In this regard Scholte (2002) argues that all existing definitions are flawed. He outlines what he names 'several analytical cul-de-sacs [in] definitions that generate redundant and in some respects also unhelpful knowledge' (p. 3). After depicting the shortcomings and weaknesses in the definition of globalisation he singles out four analytical cul-de-sacs: globalisation as tantamount to internationalisation; globalisation as tantamount to liberalisation; globalisation as tantamount to universalisation; and globalisation as tantamount to westernisation. According to Scholte the linkage with these approaches and understanding of globalisation from these perspectives prevent us from recognising its 'novelty and transformative potential' in contemporary history. Scholte rejects the assumption of globalisation-as-internationalisation that perceives 'contemporary trends ... replaying earlier historical scenarios' (p. 9) and conceives globality as another form of internationality. The second flawed analytical approach, states Scholte, is the one which conceives of globalisation-as-liberalisation. This is seen as denoting 'a process of removing officially imposed restrictions on movements of resources between countries in order to form an "open" and "borderless" world economy' (p. 10). The author recognises that neoliberal macroeconomic policy has facilitated the spread of contemporary globalisation but he rejects the amalgamation of neoliberalism and globalisation. Thirdly, he criticises the perception of globalisation-as-universalisation. This 'is assumed to entail homogenization with worldwide cultural, economic, legal and political convergence' (p. 11). The fourth cul-de-sac outlined by Scholte is the one which defines globalisation-as-westernisation. This trend, argues the author, regards globalisation as a certain kind of universalisation 'in which the social structures of modernity (capitalism, industrialism, rationalism, urbanism, etc.) are spread over destroying pre-existent cultures and local self-determination in the process' (p. 12). He adds that, conceived in this way, globalisation 'is often interpreted as colonization and Americanization, as "westoxification" and an imperialism of McDonald's and CNN' (p. 12). As for the previous trends Scholte questions the plausibility of universalisation. Although the debates about universalism, neoliberalism, cultural diversity and imperialism are important, in his view they are not helpful when they are defined as synonymous with globalisation. And in so doing they fail to grasp the far-reaching change brought by globalisation in this phase of late modernity, or second modernity as stated by Beck (1999).

As an alternative Scholte (2002) argues that, due to the change in the meaning of space and the 'spread of transplanetary ... connections between people' (p. 13), globalisation 'involves reductions in barriers to transworld contacts. People become able – physically, legally, culturally, and psychologically – to engage with each other in "one world"'. In other words, claims Scholte, 'globality resonates of spatiality' (p. 133). It is a shift in the nature of social space. In fact, according to Scholte, the significance of space in social relations is crucial because space matters and it is a core feature of social life.

Scholte emphasises the centrality of social space and supraterritoriality in the analysis and the understanding of globalisation. For 'the supraterritorial aspects of contemporary globalization have far-reaching transformative potentials' (2002, p. 22).

In the same vein, he argues that there are plausible reasons for abandoning the ontological and methodological territorialism that has been used so far in defining globalisation, since, contrary to current methodological territorialism, the spread of 'supraterritoriality requires a major reorientation of approach' (p. 23). This is because:

> Methodological territorialism refers to the practice of understanding and investigating social relations through the lens of territorial geography. Territorialist method means formulating concepts and questions, constructing hypotheses, gathering and interpreting evidence, and drawing conclusions in a spatial framework that is wholly territorial. (Scholte, 2002, p. 23)

It is not difficult to agree with Scholte about the novelty of the sociohistorical character of globalisation and its transplanetary and supraterritorial dimensions. But if globalisation cannot be conceived as equivalent to internationalisation, liberalisation, universalisation, or westernisation, it is undeniably partly or totally an outcome of them (Said, 1993; Leclerc, 2000). In addition to this causal relationship there is in some historical contexts a circularity and/or interdependence of effect between globalisation and these four elements. Moreover, in agreement with Shaw (2001) I think that Scholte's arguments are sometimes mixing sociology with geography and are tainted by a confusion of 'shift in the *content* of social relations for changes in their spatial *forms*' (Shaw, 2001, p. 1, emphasis in original). Shaw adds that Scholte

> misses the maximum sense of the global: the recognition of human commonality on a worldwide scale, in the double sense that the world framework is increasingly constitutive of society, and of emergent common values. It is not that supraterritorial spaces are growing more important, but that both territorial and supraterritorial spaces – more fundamentally national-international as well as supranational-transnational *relations* – are *both* globalised in this double sense. (Shaw, 2001, p. 3, emphasis in original)

Contrary to Scholte there are many scholars, such as Latouche (1996), who see globalisation as equivalent to westernisation and in specific instances to Americanisation (Amin, 2001). In this regard, Latouche argues that westernisation represents the spread and dominance of western values, symbols, gadgets, ideologies, technology, way of life and consumption. These have been and are propagated through the process of secularisation, industrialisation, capitalism and patterns of political culture. In other words, according to Latouche, westernisation is the explicit or implicit imposition of western cultural, economic, political and moral patterns.[1]

Between Westernisation and Europeanisation

Like westernisation, Europeanisation has symbolic, cultural, spatial, political, institutional, informational, educational and economic dimensions and meanings. As for the policy, philosophy and project of Europeanisation, this is also a dynamic and active process. It is driven by the aim to disseminate values, ideals, symbols, laws and images that represent the common identity of Europe and which most citizens can identify with. Here the question is raised, what do we understand by Europeanisation?

Radaelli (2001, p. 110) defines Europeanisation in the following terms:

> Processes of (a) construction (b) diffusion and (c)
> institutionalization of formal and informal rules, procedures,
> policy paradigms, styles, 'ways of doing things' and shared beliefs
> and norms which are first defined and consolidated in the making
> of EU public policy and politics and then incorporated in the logic
> of domestic discourses, identities, political structures and public
> policies.

Dividing Europeanisation between process and outcome, Radaelli (2001) argues that 'it extends beyond the outgrowth of European integration, which can be studied in terms of convergence or divergence' (p. 11). Besides this distinction Radaelli characterises more precisely the mechanisms of Europeanisation:

> Basically, there are two types of mechanisms that is, 'vertical' and
> 'horizontal' Europeanisation. 'Vertical' mechanisms seem to
> demarcate clearly the EU level (where policy is defined) and the
> domestic level, where policy has to be metabolized. By contrast,
> 'horizontal' mechanisms look at Europeanisation as a process
> where there is no pressure to conform to EU policy models. ...
> More precisely, the 'vertical' mechanisms are based on
> adaptational pressure; the 'horizontal' mechanisms involve
> regulatory competition and different forms of framing. (p. 124)

Adding another nuance to the analysis, Lawton (1999) introduces for his part the concept of 'Europeification'. While 'Europeanization is the *de jure* transfer of sovereignty to the EU level', 'Europeification' is '*de facto* sharing of power between national governments and the EU. Thus, Europeanization and "Europeification" are identified with the emergence of EU competencies and the pooling of power (Lawson, 1999). In this perspective Börzel (1999, p. 574) defines Europeanization as a 'process by which domestic policy areas become increasingly subject to European policy-making' or, to phrase it differently, it is the 'penetration of the European dimension in national arenas of politics and policy'.

As mentioned above westernisation has meant an active spread, domination and influence of western culture, symbols, values and ideologies. If westernisation designates a global space of this culture, Europe still represents its heart and wellspring. The Crusades, imperialism and colonialism propagated European culture in different historical stages until the Second World War. With the coming into play of the United States as a major player on the international scene, the spectrum of Europeanisation broadened in its meaning for designating mainly westernisation. While Europeanisation did mean the spread of values that originated in the European space, these values were driven mainly by some countries (e.g. Portugal, Spain, the Netherlands, United Kingdom, France).[2] Now although the process of Europeanisation is based in principle on equality between EU's members, there exists an implicit or explicit form of centralised endogenous Europeanisation under the auspices of economically strong and politically influential members.

The ideal would be that this process of Europeanisation reflects the values common to the majority of its members. But the European space has been divided into centres and peripheries in the field of political decision making, cultural influence and technocratic power (Pierson, 1996; Moravcsck, 1998).

The cultural values of Europe reflect a space composed of economic, religious, political, and symbolic fields. Fields are understood in Bourdieu's framework. In other words, they are 'as structured spaces of positions (or posts) whose properties depend on their position within these spaces and which can be analysed independently of the characteristics of their occupants' (Bourdieu, 1984, p. 233); a field is defined by 'specific issues and interests, which cannot be reduced to the specific issues and interests of other fields' (ibid). Power and domination will be exercised in each field by deploying the capital specific to that field. It can be argued that the mechanisms of these fields apply to some forms of capital that are specific to the welfare universe, 'the specific logic of each field determines [which properties] are valid in the market, relevant and efficient in the game concerned, which, in relation to that field, function as specific capital and, hence as an explanatory factor of practices' (Bourdieu, 1989, p. 113).[3]

Many European think-tanks have praised the American neoliberal (or ultraliberal) economic policy and appropriated it as a *prêt-à-porter* doctrine. Hailed and marketed as the *pensée unique* it is defended as compatible with and answers efficiently the exigencies required for strengthening the position of Europe at the present stage of economic globalisation (Fligstein & Merand, 2002). During the last decade or so they have been actively trying to recruit followers and disciples among political and economic decision makers. This econocentric vision is backed by technocrats and bureaucrats in Brussels who are often perceived as a new European elite, who are 'merely an international "civil service" who, with the passing of time, increasingly alienate themselves [*sic*] from the people whose interests it is meant to serve' (Karlsson, 1999, p. 64).

It goes without saying that there are as many prognoses and configurations of future Europe as there are states and thinkers and observers. But in these passionate debates and discourses about the becoming and shaping of Europe, intellectuals are expected to be the watchdogs for maintaining a certain degree of vigilance and scrutiny against any form of hegemonic and unicentric Europeanisation and subsequently globalisation. We will now turn to the analysis of the role of intellectuals.

Intellectuals[4] and Europeanisation

A vision of Europe dominated by economic and political forces has been often perceived with scepticism and critique from left-wing and conservative intellectuals as well. Though one of the more fervent supporters of Europeanisation, Edgar Morin (1990, p. 215) deplores, nevertheless, the fact that the discourse and issues of European problems have been monopolised by the Euro-techno-economists. In other words, the conceptualisation of this integration lies almost exclusively in the hands of political establishments and financial magnates. To balance this situation, intellectuals are considered by their vocation to be the best agents for intervening in the process (Sabour, 2004). In this connection, over five decades ago, T.S. Eliot (1945), in sketching the future of Europe and of its culture, argued that the intellectual

> is not concerned with the political or economic map of Europe;
> but he should be very much concerned with its cultural map. This
> problem, involving the relations of different cultures and
> languages in Europe, must have presented itself first, to the man
> of letters, as a domestic problem: in this context, foreign affairs are
> merely an extension of domestic affairs. (p. 334)

He presented the responsibility of the intellectual as follows:

> he should be vigilantly watching the conduct of the politicians and
> economists, for the purpose of criticizing and warning, when the
> decision and action of politicians and economists are likely to have
> cultural consequences. Of these consequences the man of letters
> should prepare himself to judge. Of the possible cultural
> consequences of their activities, politicians and economists are
> usually oblivious; the man of letters is better qualified to foresee
> them, and to perceive their seriousness. (p. 336)

In the same vein Morin (1990, p. 215) contends that 'it is the European intellectuals who could and should express an awareness of a common destiny and a common identity in order to permit the common need to be advanced'. Therefore, he suggests, 'intellectuals have, as their irrevocable function to tackle publicly the fundamental problems of culture and society, and of ethics' (Morin, 1990, p. 217). For his part, Bourdieu (1992) endorses relatively the same point of view. But contrary to Eliot and more than Morin he claims for the intelligentsia, in addition to its cultural work, a more active and prominent role in social and political discourse. He is especially worried by the 'hijacking' of the fields of culture and the intellect by external forces from the spheres of business, politics and the media. These forces are, according to him, corrupting, since they marginalise the genuine historical endeavours of the intellectuals.

Hence, as the carriers of competence in the fields of the arts and sciences, intellectuals are expected to play a prominent role in this integration process, especially when Europe is probably moving towards a more unicentric, techno-bureaucratic and political unification of management. In particular, intellectuals have a crucial mission to maintain a high degree of vigilance in defending the continuation of Europe as a polycultural diversity in a polycentric space against any tendency of unicentricity. Unicentricity is aptly and multidimensionally defined by Davies (1999, p. 96) as:

> *One-centeredness*, a logic which demands a single center
> (intellectual, economic, political, cultural, geographical) from
> which all emanates. In unicentricity the logic of core and
> periphery, even in the 'world systems' sense, functions to center
> some experiences, marginalize others. Further, it assumes a
> unidimensional movement outwards from this constructed source.
> Thus, unicentricity turns the idea of a certain essential meaning,
> beginning, parentage, ancestry, origin. Unicentricity thus cannot
> imagine multiple and equal centers but instead has to operate with
> one constantly expanding center. Unicentricity, then, legitimizes
> its gains, seeking and expanding the set of peripheries that it
> gradually pulls into its orbit and thus inevitably can become a
> colonialist project. The single center logic, then, is the basis of
> dominance and control, for it functions with other communities in
> terms of competition, hierarchy, and subordination. What is
> centered becomes the most important, the proper, the politically
> appropriate. Rather than an interactive logic of multiple, relational
> spheres of interests, in unicentricity, something has to be centered.
> Thus something attains dominance and becomes the central star
> around which all others orbit. [emphasis in original]

In contradistinction to this unilateral, uniform, unicentric, egocentric and logocentric model of the world, polycentricity defends a diverse, polyvalent, plural, and heterogeneous perception of culture, power, knowledge and space. But the notion of polycentricity means different things to different people. For example:

> urban planners use the concepts as a strategic spatial planning
> tool; economic and human geographers use it to explain the

> changing spatial structure of cities; the European Union
> Commissioners and their counterparts in member states often
> promote the concept as socio-economic policy goal aimed at
> achieving a balanced regional development; and civic leaders use
> the term for 'place-marketing', presenting the notion of
> polycentricity as synonymous with pluralism, multiculturalism and
> dynamism, as well as symbol of the 'post-modern' life style. It has
> become part of the new vocabularies of inclusive politics.
> (Davoudi, 2003, pp. 979-980)

Whatever the case, polycentricity removes the hierarchical and centralised conception of power, decision making, influence and pattern, be it in culture, politics, economy, education or knowledge.

In late modern technophile, econocentric, European society, socio-humanistic intellectuals are coming under increasingly subversive pressures set up by technocracy and professionalism (Sabour, 1996, 2001). Nevertheless, according to Morin (1990), the technical-specific intellectual is seldom ready to exceed the limits of his specialty. 'The scientist is unable to think not only of society but also of his own science'. Hence, 'the nullification of society's important problems produces an intellectual invalidation. The merit of intellectuals, even in their extreme incompetence, is at least to recognize the existence of important problems' (p. 218). Therefore, instead of the intelligentsia possessing specialised competence, society needs more non-specialised, non-technical intellectuals, that is, the cultural actors in the public sphere, whose main concern is with the generic and general problems of society.

Bourdieu (1995) in turn sees no major inconvenience in the specialisation of the intelligentsia and its simultaneous orientation toward social and political issues. He argues that each intellectual must excel in his (or her) scientific field and on the basis of the respectability and recognition he acquires in this field he can intervene actively and effectively in the political and social fields with authority and credibility.

Nevertheless, even if Europeanisation can be beneficial to the countries of Europe the problems linked to its power structures and to the centralisation of decision making are a source of anxiety and the subject of controversy, especially for the smaller states. For economic, political and historical reasons those countries which have been asked to become members in this European integration do not acquire the same status and weight. In this regard, there is a well-justified concern that the members with a strong currency, prestigious culture and influential political position may directly or indirectly impose their will and worldview on the others. As the members who have this position represent the mainstream culture (e.g. France, the United Kingdom, Germany), we may ask what will be the fate of small countries and especially those whose language, culture and geographical position place them on the boundary, the interface or periphery of Europe.[5] Some scholars (Muzil, 1994; pp. 3-7; Joenniemi, 1993, pp. 17-48) seem to be enthusiastic about the increasing process of Europeanisation and consider it as a source of cultural energy that will enhance the small states' (e.g. Finland) self-confidence and galvanise their self-esteem. Others who originate from the mainstream culture are cautious in endorsing uncritically this perception. In this regard, Bourdieu (1996) states that the process of integration

> is a progress towards a higher degree of universalism, and it is a step forwards toward a world society. To be European is a little less particular, a little less nationalist than to be French or Finnish. But there could be another form of nationalism, another way to universalize ... However, there is a danger that integration will be carried out according to a pattern which is favourable to certain countries, that is those who dominate economically and culturally. In order to prevent this, there is a necessity to set up a critical intelligentsia belonging to various and different national traditions. This intelligentsia can defend different traditions from outside particular nationalisms ... a sort of pluralist internationalism. There is the danger that unification (integration) will be accompanied by monopolization. One should, therefore, be extremely vigilant about trends towards economic monopolization; but the most dangerous is, in my view, cultural monopolization, because it will destroy identities and important particularities. (p. 250)

The national diversity in the European space makes *ipso facto* the application of the same approach to all countries inconceivable. Because, according to Todd (1998), Europe's different cultures do not enable them to apply the same economic policies. In addition to the differences in their financial and social cultures their demographic rates evolve differently, which eventually confronts them with dissimilar problems. In this respect, argues Demorgon (2000, p. 87), Europe ought to be aware of its diversity instead of focusing mainly on the economic structures. This diversity, he adds, represents the source of a longstanding creativity and welfare.

Cultural Diversity in the European Space

Characteristic of the ongoing integration of Europe are large movements of people, ideas and knowledge. When cultures and peoples encounter each other, via work, study, leisure or business, there is, more than ever, an interpenetration and hybridisation of cultures and symbols (Pieterse, 2001). This encounter, in spite of its enrichment and fertilisation of culture and knowledge, involves latent or visible, conscious or unconscious, relations of power, prestige and domination. People whose culture, language and way of life have, for historical, politico-economic, technological or intellectual reasons, gained a prominent status, also seem to have acquired either a recognised or tacit influential position in such spheres as communications, the arts, international politics, and pattern shaping and decision making in various fields.[6] This prominence has often given rise to the formation of dominant mainstreams around a few main centres (Amin, 1985, 1989). Hence, the existence of cultural and intellectual centres logically implies the explicit or implicit existence of concomitant boundary (marginal) cultures.

Every society, according to its history and its cultural and social structures, creates and develops a set of abilities (e.g. technical, mental, moral, juridical, and artistic) essential for maintaining the vitality of its existence and the prosperity of its citizens. These competences, which may be developed out of a society's intrinsic forces or/and inspired by extrinsic resources, constitute the basis of equilibrium and survival of this society as a separate entity. But since the world is formed of many entities which are linked by convergent and divergent interests, these entities are therefore obliged to find the skills necessary for securing their vital interests in this global interaction and for protecting their identity. Eisenstadt (1989, pp. 44-45) has argued that there are many requirements placed on small countries:

> in the educational sphere small countries are under cross-
> pressures which may endanger their self-identity and make it
> necessary for them to emphasise their own tradition, history and
> internal problems, as opposed to sharing the more universal
> traditions of the large societies. In the cultural sphere, one of the
> problems of small countries is how to absorb cultural 'floods' (in
> terms of quantity) from prestigious international culture and still
> maintain their own identity and obtain international recognition.

Despite the common historical plinth which has characterised the European space there exists, as mentioned above, a variety of different fields where symbols, identities and cultures are striving for recognition, survival, influence and even domination. The coexistence of different cultural and social values is based, therefore, on a 'fluctuating harmony'. Hence, the status and prestige of each component in the European field is practically dependent on its own degree of competence and creativity, and its own ability to maintain its position, to provide solutions to problems and to secure recognition for its difference in that field. But maintaining and empowering national cultures and identities often remains, as mentioned above, a task which is mainly incumbent upon those who represent them, that is, the intelligentsia. But is the intelligentsia (humanist, technical, social scientific, artistic, juridical, managerial, etc.) from small states and boundary cultures (e.g. Slovenia, Finland, Portugal, Malta) aware of the ongoing historical process of Europeanisation and its implications for national identity? It seems that an important change is occurring in the academic and intellectual fields in favour of the technocratic and economic groups and this has alienated and weakened intellectuals' capacity to influence efficiently and convincingly the policy and process of Europeanisation and globalisation (Posner, 2001).

The factor linked to the process of Europeanisation and to the opening of the European market and the 'free' movement of goods and people from one country to another will inevitably cause tremendous change in the cultural and social landscapes of Europe for the coming decades. Among its positive features is the possibility of facilitating human contacts and hybridising cultures and values. But it could also have negative aspects. The more economically, scientifically and intellectually attractive regions may become the poles where the best and most creative human capital is attracted and concentrated. In other words, the important and influential cores may form centres of gravity which may cause a serious brain drain and a cultural and intellectual 'desertification' in some areas of Europe.[7] This phenomenon is already visible in Eastern Europe, where people with advanced skills are finding refuge in countries like Germany, France, the United Kingdom, Israel, and the USA. In the space of a very short period, this has become the most unprecedented and profound movement of scientific and cultural capital from one region to another since the Second World War (Sabour, 1995, pp. 32-39; Horvat, 2004, pp. 76-93).

By Way of Conclusion

Academic as well as political discourses about globalisation have been characterised by various trends and tenets. The 'globophiles' enthusiastically praise the benefits and opportunities brought by globalisation in the field of economic growth, technical development, human interactions, communicational accessibility, and movement of goods, people and capital. Among this trend there is an economically driven tendency of 'globapologists' that focuses mainly on the 'bright' sides of globalisation. It is largely influenced by a neoliberal perception that perceives Europe as mainly an economic field which should be made efficient, competitive and productive (Bourdieu, 1998). Their insensitivity to the harm caused to the powerless and the vulnerable is partly sustained by their conceptual short-sightedness in recognising some hegemonic and homogenic features of globalisation. Some see in the economic globalisation another disguised way of capitalist or western dominance (Mazrui, 2001). Many attributes have been given to this disguised process in the form of liberalisation, Americanisation, 'Coca-Colanisation', 'McDonaldisation' and so on, of division of labour, popular culture and production. In response to this conception of westernisation there is a reaction from groups who are sceptical about the benefits of globalisation and take every opportunity to emphasise its dark sides in terms of reduced human welfare, environmental degradation, workforce exploitation and uneven wealth distribution.

As an economic phenomenon globalisation is seen as having a simultaneous effect of diversification and unification on present societies

(Featherstone, 1993). In this regard, Spybey (1996, p. 45) argues that if globalisation has economically stimulated wealth and growth in some countries it has simultaneously created marginalisation and poverty in others. Besides the economic aspect there is the cultural aspect of globalisation. This is manifested in the process of homogenisation (e.g. consumption, music, fashion) and heterogenisation (e.g. fragmentation and emergence of different and multiple modes of expression).

This change entails therefore a transformation in the conception and perception of the velocity of information, the division of labour, people's mobility, interactions and communications, time and space, boundaries and territoriality. As such it is expected to have a major impact in altering the centrality, concentration and monopoly of economic and political powers in some parts of the globe. But many factual indicators indicate the existence of this unicentricity that is situated unsurprisingly in the west. This unicentricity is mainly driven by a market economy and propelled by the United States (Yoshikazu, 2000, pp. 98-116). This unicentric American hegemony, together with Japan, has put Europe under an economic strain in the field of competition and performance in the international market. It is well known that one of the driving forces behind European integration is the improvement of the position of the Member States in this world market compared with Japan, the United States, and the rising Asian economic 'tigers' such as China (Gu, 2005). In this euphoria of improving and increasing performance and competitiveness, the fate and future of Europe has been mainly designed and constructed by economists and politicians. If not explicitly hailed and praised by some European countries, the American neoliberal pattern in the fields of economy, technology, education and welfare is implicitly and indirectly admired and highlighted as a reference for justifying reform, reorganisation, regulation and 'rationalisation' in European societies. All these reforms are often justified by the imperatives of economic globalisation. Therefore, in order to face this globalisation European countries have to submit to a process of 'harmonisation' of their educational system, to limit the state's interference and subvention of the public sector, and to open their market to private competition. To achieve that they have to accept various directives and harmonising rules and restrictions on their national policy. In other words, they have accepted a sort of 'endogenous Europeanisation'. In contrast to 'exogenous Europeanisation', which was directed towards external countries, cultures and continents, endogenous Europeanisation, which is often driven by mainstream countries, and corresponds in general to their interests, targets the rest of Europe, especially small, economically dependent and peripheral states. Brussels represents the epicentre of the bureaucratic and decision-making structure of Europe. It has been commonly argued that the European Commission lacks credibility in the eyes of its common citizens and its decisions do not genuinely reflect the will of the majority (Karlsson, 1999). In this context what is the position of small states who defend their interests against the unicentric power of

Brussels, which is largely conditioned by the interest of the core countries? The bulk of Brussels' 'Eurocrats', technocrats and political actors, seem to respond in their policy planning and economic development to the expectations of market forces and economic agents. One of the groups that can play a counterbalancing role in this process is the intelligentsia for defending a polycentric vision of Europe with its national particularities and regional differences.

Europe has been, and to some extent still is, the source of various dimensions of westernisation, though much of this has been appropriated by other countries, be it in culture (e.g. USA, Canada, Australia) or technology (e.g. Japan), where it has been transformed and developed either as a commodity (gadget) or as a system (capitalism). Western culture was at the source of westernisation that, economically and technically speaking, was the leading motor of globalisation. Now, Europe is still one of the main spaces that generates westernisation, but it is being economically stifled and strained by the same process in its competition with Japan and the USA, and eventually with China.

In the process of facing the impact of globalisation Europe is experiencing a shift from an exogenous Europeanisation to an endogenous Europeanisation. The former was directed towards the dissemination of European values, culture, technology, know-how, market, zone of influence, spreading of the Gospel and building up of empires, colonies or trading posts overseas. The motivation mainly was the increase of zone of influence and acquisition of raw materials. The process of this spread was mainly built on military might, invasion and domination of spaces, and indoctrination of minds through education.

On the other hand, endogenous Europeanisation is directed towards the European space and aims at integrating, emancipating, regulating, harmonising and standardising various features in European societies. This process of Europeanisation is based on consensual decision making, persuasion and awareness raising about the objectives of the integration. Endogenous Europeanisation, though its apparent equalitarian formulation and implementation remains largely dictated and conditioned by the will of the mainstream (core) countries (e.g. France, Germany).

Maybe one of the important aspects that has not been sufficiently explored by the bulk of studies, comments and discourses produced on globalisation and Europeanisation is power (Ifversen, 2002). Power encompasses, among other things, elements of coercion, influence, symbolic violence, hegemony, domination, subjugation, privilege and legitimacy. When we see globalisation as equivalent with westernisation it becomes evident that those driving forces and agencies behind the latter hold a formidable power where all or a part of the above-mentioned elements are inherent. The hypothesis defended by Samir Amin (2001) and Mazrui (2001) strongly sustains this assumption. In fact, globalisation is in many domains the outcome and result of the universalisation of values, symbols, ideologies, philosophies, fashions, ways of life, scripts, social movements and technologies produced, used and spread in and from the west. Through various processes of colonisation, indoctrination, education, industrialisation, mass communication, and consumption, to cite only a few, endorsed and propelled by capitalist mechanisms, western culture and civilisation have become prominent all over the globe. Their propagation, export, promotion and vulgarisation can be translated into an explicit and/or implicit action of westernisation (Latouche, 1996; Mazrui, 2001). Westernisation represents an extension and enlarged version of Europeanisation. In fact, the source and departure of the former is mainly tied to Europe. So, it is quite common to find that globalisation is tantamount to westernisation and that the latter is depicted as an evolved twin of Europeanisation and by the same token a driving force of globalisation (Mazrui, 1990, pp. 39-55).

As underlined above, if the process and ideology of Europeanisation were, in the past, directed towards external cultures, societies, markets and continents, the present is endogenously oriented towards the European space. The endogenous process of Europeanisation has been strengthened by the enlargement of the European Union. This process has taken economic, institutional, political, cultural, educational and military dimensions. It is equivalent to homogenisation of rules and laws, and standardisation of actions and policies in the European space. Except for a few domains of national prerogatives, there is an active attempt and intention to harmonise the various fields in European societies. If some of these measures or directives seem to be inevitable and even indispensable for a smooth functioning of the Union and interaction of its Member States, others are perceived with suspicion and anxiety, especially when they infringe on sensitive matters such as national identity, social welfare, delocalisation of means of production, national customs and way of life. It is evident that the Europeanisation process is the outcome of consensual decision making. However, due to variations in strength, and economic and political weight, some decisions reflect more the interests and the perceptions of the core countries at the expense of others, namely small countries. In fact, the position of the core countries is so prominent in various fields such as economy, language and foreign policy that they become de facto bearers of a unicentric power. Often, in the name of equality and reciprocity among the Member States, the manifestation of this power is not apparent but latently disguised, or even made invisible, under various forms of historical taken-for-grantedness and privileges embedded in the logics of size or budget contribution. This unicentricity is exemplified, for instance, in the prominence of the English language, in the division of power inside the Commission, and in the imposition, interpretation and respect of directives related to the budget, environment or immigration. This unicentric perception of the European space by core countries has been lately questioned in the name of a more comprehensive polycentric vision of Europe.

Bourdieu was a strong defender of European culture, its scientific achievements and its welfare state. But he was also a vehement critic of the neoliberal turn which the social policy of some of its members took at the end of the 1990s. For him American-inspired neoliberalism, justified by the imperatives of economic globalisation, represented a project of Europeanisation that hides a neoliberal programme. This programme

> draws its social power from the political and economic power of those whose interests it expresses: stockholders, financial operators, industrialists, conservative or social-democratic politicians who have been converted to the reassuring layoffs of laissez-faire, high-level financial officials eager to impose policies advocating their own extinction because, unlike the managers of firms, they run no risk of having eventually to pay the consequences. Neoliberalism tends on the whole to favour severing the economy from social realities and thereby constructing, in reality, an economic system conforming to its description in pure theory that is a sort of logical machine that presents itself as a chain of constraints regulating economic agents. (Bourdieu, 1998, December)

With the same tone and acerbity Bourdieu has been at the forefront of those critics of the econocentric orientation of the process of Europeanisation. He argues that, under the capitalist globalisation inspired by the USA, the social policy defended by Brussels' Europe carries a clear risk of undermining the welfare state and the basic social rights of European citizens (Bourdieu, 1999). In a way, he is performing the role which is incumbent upon committed intellectuals [8] and which he has always claimed to be his vocation (Bourdieu, 1992).

Notes

[1] If this imposition has been introduced into most societies in the world through various international institutions (e.g. World Bank, UNESCO, International Monetary Fund), in some societies westernisation has faced stiff resistance and rejection. It has even provoked a phenomenon of indigenisation and the emergence of various anti-western local movements (e.g. the Iranian revolution). Seen from a local perspective globalisation can be perceived as a source of opportunity and development when westernisation provides technical and scientific problem solving and welfare. However, when it is felt as a threat, for example, to the composition and structure of social (e.g. gender relations), cultural (e.g. identity), economic (e.g. delocalisation of means of production) and political power (e.g. demand for democracy) it can be judged as detrimental and harmful to national interests. This represents to some extent dialectic and contradictory elements in the attitude towards globalisation in its western or European aspect. Its hardware (e.g. technology)

is admired and wanted by its software (e.g. democracy, human rights) is feared, criticised and/or rejected.

[2] Spain and Portugal were the superpowers of the sixteenth and seventeenth centuries. Their influence on the world was very significant. But by the end of the nineteenth century they had lost their universal power.

[3] In the large European space there are national fields with particularities and distinctions that push some countries to claim prominence, exceptionality, and specific considerations. For instance, when it comes to culinary culture and gastronomy France expects to be given special treatment; when it comes to technical matters Germany focuses on its savoir-faire; the Nordic countries defend proudly their welfare model and status of women and do not expect any challenge from Southern European countries; Germany and France are the champion defenders of Europe, and so on. These are fields where every country rightly or wrongly pretends to have excellence and leadership and therefore arrogates the right to prominence and privilege in this field.

[4] The intellectuals and the intelligentsia are defined in various ways and according to different schools of thought. For the purpose of this study the concept of 'intellectuals' designates all those who are mainly involved in the creation, the evaluation and the dissemination of ideas, symbols, culture and knowledge, and whose work implies particularly non-material activities. The concept of the 'intelligentsia' names those highly educated people in society whose domains of activity may be situated in the spheres of science, culture, politics, business, bureaucracy and technology. Because of the European sociocultural context the concepts 'intellectuals' and 'intelligentsia' are often used interchangeably.

[5] Language is a sensitive matter in the functioning of the European Union. For national considerations around 19 languages are in principle used. But in practice two main languages are dominant: English and French. According to Karlsson (1999, p. 67) 'the problem of interpreting is becoming insurmountable. Over 40% of the European Union administrative budget is already spent on language services'. Nineteen languages make more than 400 combinations possible in the interpreting booths. 'Some form of functional differentiation will therefore be necessary, making some languages more equal than others. Although this would have a negative effect on European public opinion in the small member nations. At present, an average 66% of European Union citizens are monolingual while 10% speak at least two foreign languages. Ireland is at one extreme with 80% and 3% respectively, while only 1% of the population in Luxembourg is monolingual and no less than 80% speak at least two foreign languages'.

[6] In the field of literature and mass media (e.g. films, TV programmes, novels) Finland consumes and imports more foreign productions and publications than it exports. The impact of this state of affairs on the autonomy and the authenticity of Finnish culture for the next generation remain to be seen and studied. Nevertheless, this could go beyond the stage of 'fertilisation' to that of 'suffocating' the national cultural creativity.

[7] Many studies show the increasing migration of highly skilled people from economically poor and peripheral European areas to the core countries (see Hönekopp, 1996; Mahroum, 2001).

[8] It is said that with the death of Bourdieu at the beginning of 2002, opponents of neoliberal and unicentric globalisation and Europeanisation lost their most prestigious mouthpiece and influential intellectual (Wacquant, 2002; Wolfreys, 2002; Swartz, 2003).

References

Amin, S. (1985) *Towards a Polycentric World*. London: Zed Books.

Amin, S. (1989) *Eurocentrism*. New York: Monthly Review Press.

Amin, S. (2001) Imperialism and Globalization, World Forum Meeting in Porto Alegre, January. http://www.nycsocialforum.org/about_wsf_speech2.html

Arendt, H. (1972) On Violence, in *Crisis of the Republic*. New York: Harcourt Brace.

Beck, U. (1999) *What is Globalization?* Cambridge: Polity Press.

Börzel, T.A. (1999) Towards Convergence in Europe? Institutional Adaptation to Europeanization in Germany and Spain, *Journal of Common Market Studies*, 39(4), 573-596. http://dx.doi.org/10.1111/1468-5965.00197

Bourdieu, P. (1979) *La distinction. Critique sociale du jugement*. Paris: Les Editions de Minuit.

Bourdieu, P. (1984) *Distinction: a social critique of the judgement of taste*. Cambridge, MA: Harvard University Press.

Bourdieu, P. (1992) *Réponses*. Paris: Seuil.

Bourdieu, P. (1992) Pour une Internationale des intellectuels, *Politis*, 1, 9-15.

Bourdieu, P. (1995) Intellectuals and the Internationalization of Ideas (An interview with M'hammed Sabour), *International Journal of Contemporary Sociology*, 32(2), 237-253.

Bourdieu, P. (1998) The Essence of Neoliberalism, *Le Monde Diplomatique*, December. http://www.analitica.com/bitblioteca/bourdieu/neoliberalism.asp

Bourdieu, P. (1999) *Acts of Resistance: against the tyranny of the market*. New York: New Press.

Davies, C.B. (1999) Beyond Unicentricity: transcultural black presences, *Research in Africa Literatures*, 30(2), 96-109. http://dx.doi.org/10.2979/RAL.1999.30.2.96

Davoudi, S. (2003) Polycentricity in European Spatial Planning: from an analytical tool to a normative agenda, *European Planning Studies*, 11(8), 979-999. http://dx.doi.org/10.1080/0965431032000146169

Demorgon, J. (2000) *L'interculturation du monde*. Paris: Anthropos.

Eliot, T.S. (1945) The Man of Letters and the Future of Europe, *Sewanee Review*, 53, 335-346.

Fligstein, N. & Merand, F. (2002) Globalisation or Europeanisation? Evidence on the European Economy since 1980, *Acta Sociologica*, 45, 7-22. http://dx.doi.org/10.1080/00016990252885762

Gu, Z. (2005) *China's Global Reach: markets, multinationals, globalization, lessons, & trends.* Binghamton: Haworth Press.

Hönekopp, E. (1996) Old and New Labour Migration to Germany from Eastern Europe, in D. Corry (Ed.) *Economics and European Union migration policy.* London: IPPR.

Horvat, V. (2004) Brain Drain: threat to successful transition in South East Europe?, *Southeast European Politics,* 5(1), 76-93.

Ifversen, J. (2002) Europe and European Culture – a conceptual analysis, *European Societies,* 4(1), 1-26. http://dx.doi.org/10.1080/14616690220130973

Joenniemi, P. (1993) Euro-Suomi. Rajalla, rajojen välissä vai rajaton?, in Suonmesta Euro-Suomeen & P. Joenniemi (Eds) *Rauhan- ja Konfliktintutkimuslaitos, Tutkimustiedote,* 53, 17-47.

Karlsson, I. (1999) Reflections on European Identity, in T. Jansen (Ed.) *European Commission, Forward Studies Unit.* Working Paper. Brussels: European Commission.

Latouche, S. (1996) *Westernization of the World: the significance, scope and limits of the drive towards global uniformity.* London: Polity Press.

Lawton, T. (1999) Governing the Skies: conditions for the Europeanisation of airline policy, *Journal of Public Policy,* 19(1), 91-112. http://dx.doi.org/10.1017/S0143814X99000197

Leclerc, G. (2000) *La mondialisation culturelle: Les civilisations à l'épreuve.* Paris: Presses Universitaires de France.

Mahroum, S. (2001) Europe and the Immigration of Highly Skilled Labour, *International Migration,* 39(5), Special Issue, 27-43.

Mazrui, A.A. (1990) *Cultural Forces in World Politics.* London: James Currey.

Mazrui, A.A. (2001) Globalization Between the Market and the Military: a Third World perspective. http://igcs.binghamton.edu/igcs_site/dirton7.html

Morgan, G. (2005) The Idea of a European Superstate: public justification and European integration. Princeton, NJ: Princeton University Press.

Morin, E. (1990) *Penser l'Europe.* Paris: Gallimard.

Musil, J. (1994) Europe Between Integration and Disintegration, *Czech Sociological Review,* 2(1), 5-19.

Pieterse, J. N. (1994) Globalisation as Hybridisation, *International Sociology,* 9(2), 161-184. http://dx.doi.org/10.1177/026858094009002003

Pieterse, J.N. (1999) Europe, Traveling Light: Europeanization and globalization, *The European Legacy,* 4(3), 3-17. http://dx.doi.org/10.1080/10848779908579968

Posner, R.A. (2001) *Public Intellectuals: a study of decline.* London: Harvard University Press.

Radaelli, C. (2001) The Domestic Impact of European Union Public Policy: notes on concepts, methods, and the challenge of empirical research, *Politique européenne,* 5, 107-142.

Sabour, M. (1995) The Position of the Finnish Intelligentsia in the European Cultural Mainstream: education, knowledge and the integration of Europe, in *L & EIF (Life and Education in Finland),* No. 3, 32-39.

Sabour, M. (1996) Between Patronage and Autonomy: the position of intellectuals in modern society, in P.K. Lawrence & M. Döbler (Eds) *Knowledge and Power*. Sydney: Avebury.

Sabour, M. (2001) *The Ontology and Status of Intellectuals in Arab Academia and Society*. Aldershot: Ashgate.

Sabour, M. (2004) The Genesis of Arab Intellectual Movements and the Aims of their Discourses on Socio-Political Changes, *International Journal of Contemporary Sociology*, 41(1), 103-124.

Said, E. (1993) *Culture and Imperialism*. New York: Vintage Books.

Scholte, J.A. (2002) What is Globalization? The Definitional Issue – again, Working Paper No. 109/02, Centre for the Study of Globalisation and Regionalisation, University of Warwick, December.

Shaw, M. (2001) Review : Jan Aart Scholte. Globalization: a critical introduction, *Milleneum: a journal of international studies*.
http://www.sussex.ac.uk/Users/hafa3/scholte.htm

Spybey, T. (1996) *Globalization and World Society*. Cambridge: Polity Press

Swartz, D.L. (2003) From Critical Sociology to Public Intellectual: Pierre Bourdieu and politics, *Theory and Society*, 32, 791-823.
http://dx.doi.org/10.1023/B:RYSO.0000004956.34253.fb

Todd, E. (1998) *L'illusion économique. Essai sur la stagnation des sociétés développées*. Paris: Gallimard.

Wacquant, L. (2002) The Sociological Life of Pierre Bourdieu, *International Sociology*, 17(4), 549-556. http://dx.doi.org/10.1177/0268580902017004005

Wolfreys, J. (2002) Pierre Bourdieu: voice of resistance, *International Socialism Journal*, 94, Spring.

Yoshikazu, S. (2000) An Alternative to Global Marketization, in J.N. Pieterse (Ed.) *Global Futures: shaping globalisation*. New York: Zed Books.

CHAPTER 11

What is Language Europe?

KIRK SULLIVAN & JANET ENEVER

SUMMARY In Europe today the domain of education operates as a prime mechanism in laying the foundations of a plurilingual citizenry, equipped with the cultural capital now identified as a pre-requisite for engagement in an increasingly globalised world economy. This chapter reviews current language policy and trends relating to the sectors of tertiary and primary education in Europe. It reveals evidence of the difficulty in achieving the desired gains in quality set by Bologna and argues that quality goals are currently being undermined by the strong focus on perceived linguistic gains. In a critical examination of policy it is proposed that a deeper, more nuanced understanding of the notion of quality in language education is required if Europe is to have any possibility of meeting the goals of Bologna.

Introduction

This chapter explores two recently emerged trends in language choices across education in Europe and seeks to interpret them in the light of global, regional and local pressures that currently drive them forward. In selecting evidence of language curricula from the contrastive contexts of higher education and the early primary years it will be proposed that these strands may represent a supranational layering for creating a new flexible, mobile elite with fluency in at least one regional or global language in addition to their local/national language, rather than an initial framework for achieving the oft-stated goal of creating a whole population with this potential ability. We might identify this new elite as a technocratic elite, equipped with the cultural capital of 'technical' skills (i.e. language/intercultural skills) necessary to facilitate business deals in a global economic and political world today.

In substantiating this claim the chapter will consider the educational realities of inclusion and exclusion for membership of this elite, highlighting an increasing urban/rural divide in some regions of Europe, contrasting real and perceived differences in resourcing and expertise at both primary and tertiary levels of education. As both linguists and educators we will draw on understandings of how young children learn languages and evidence of lowered expectations for second/foreign language users at tertiary level to critique national policy and the rhetoric of 'Bologna', 'quality' and 'the market'. We will argue against the likelihood of Europe forming a cohesive unit of a bi/trilingually educated population and propose a more likely outcome of an increasing dominance of English in specific work-related domains.

Language Trends in Higher Education

Fler kurser på engelska ett av målen för ny rector.
(More courses in English is one of the new vice-chancellor's priorities.) (Lindblom, 2005, p. 11)

This quote reflects the importance placed on increasing the use of English as a language of instruction in Sweden. This trend is one of the impacts of the internationalisation of higher education. Moreover it is a trend that has received impetus from the establishment of the European Higher Education Area (EHEA); universities across Europe where the language of instruction has traditionally not been English now perceive a need to make courses more easily available to students from other EHEA countries. This often means university modules being offered in English. This trend is not restricted to countries where the societal language is a minor European language; the same trend can be observed (if to a lesser degree) in, for example, Germany.

In this section, we consider the validity of the claims made by policymakers that internationalisation is a method of assuring quality and as such can be viewed as a quality marker. We will further consider the impact on the quality of teaching, learning and outcomes when English (or another language that is not the societal language) is used as the language of instruction in higher education.

One university that views internationalisation as a method of assuring quality is Umeå University, Sweden; in a current policy document the university states: 'Internationellt samarbete uppfattas numera med rätta som en kvalitetsmarkör [international cooperation is nowadays perceived, and correctly so, as a mark of quality]' (Program för internationalisering vid Umeå universitet 2003-2008, 2002). Policy statements, such as Umeå University's, relate to all aspects of internationalisation. This section, however, focuses on a feature that impacts upon all the other elements of internationalisation: language. Language is identified here as a central feature of delivery, learning, outcome and ultimately the quality of the student's tertiary education experience.

216

In relation to the issue of language, it is interesting to look at the conclusions and recommendations of the Conference on Master-level Degrees held in Helsinki, Finland in March 2003:

> Many European higher educational institutions offer degree
> programmes designed for and marketed to international students.
> To serve this purpose, many institutions have chosen to develop
> education through widely-used foreign languages. This approach
> is understandable and welcome, as it increases the global
> attractiveness and competitiveness of higher education institutions
> in smaller linguistic areas. Development of the EHEA must not,
> however, lead to a mono-linguistic world of higher education.
> Within the EHEA governments and higher education institutions
> should make every effort to ensure teaching of the national
> languages to foreign students, even if the degree programme itself
> is in another language and proficiency in the language of the host
> country is not a prerequisite for admission. Multiculturalism,
> pluralism and linguistic skills are to remain the intrinsic values of
> European higher education. ... Europe's offer of this type
> [internationally attractive programmes taught in a major world
> language] must be considerably stepped up, beyond its present
> modest level.[1]

We see these statements feeding into Swedish policy: undergraduate and postgraduate degrees being offered in English and an increasing number of modules at all levels being taught in English aimed at EHEA exchange students. Simultaneously in the Swedish government bill 2005/06:2 on language policy (Swedish Government, 2005), there is evidence of the government wishing to see a parallel use of Swedish and English in the academy. A viewpoint supported by Leif Pagrotsky, the Swedish Minister for Education, Research and Culture, who was recently quoted as having said:

> Vi behöver en tvåspråkighet i akademin. Vi i Sverige är så vana vid
> att vara enspråkiga att vi har svårt för den tanken men finns plats
> för båda språken på våra universitet. De måste finnas parallellt.
> Det är en falsk motsättning med antingen eller.
>
> (We need a bilingual policy in the academy. We, in Sweden, are
> so used to being monolingual that we are having difficulty
> thinking that there is a place for two languages at our universities.
> They must exist in parallel. It is incorrect to think in terms of
> either/or.) (Eliasson, 2005, p. 5)

Pertinently, in the same article, Pagrotsky is reported avoiding the question as to whether there is a risk that if Swedish lecturers lecture Swedish students in English that there would be a lowering of the intellectual standard, by answering that: 'Det finns ingen anledning att på grundutbildning föreläsa på engelska i en helsvensk grupp [There is no reason for undergraduate lectures to be held in English for a completely Swedish group]' (Eliasson, 2005, p. 4) and continuing 'in almost the next breath' (own translation, p. 4) by saying that the number of foreign students was increasing. A comment that Eliasson (2005) interpreted as indicating that Pagrotsky believes that lectures in English are in many cases a necessity.

Pagrotsky's apparent inability to perceive that there are potential problems for educational standards if lectures are held in English in the Swedish academy and that these problems ought to be considered to assure educational quality is a cause for concern. This assumption reflects the received wisdom within the Swedish academy and at the centre of national educational policy 'that in most cases changing the language of instruction to English adds value whilst having few negative side effects. Put simply, the more English the better' (Airey, 2004, p. 97).

The preceding perspectives strongly indicate that if the Bologna Process leads, as it aims to, to increased student mobility within the EHEA (Bologna Declaration, 1999), the question of whether delivery in English does indeed add value or whether it may, in reality, lead to an undermining of the quality-raising aims of the Bologna Process, needs to be problematised. The Swedish government bill 2005/06:2 states that:

> Ett uttalat syfte med [Bologna] processen är att främja
> studenternas rörlighet mellan de europeiska utbildningssystemen,
> bl.a. eftersom ett ökat utbyte såväl studenter som lärare i olika
> länder bidrar till ökad kvalitet i utbildningen.

> (A stated goal of the [Bologna] process is to promote student
> mobility between European education systems, because, among
> other things, an increased exchange between students and
> lecturers in different countries leads to increases in the quality of
> education.) (Swedish Government, 2005, p. 45)

The questions can therefore be posed: does teaching and learning in English have an impact upon the quality of education? If such impact is negative will it undermine the quality-raising goal of Bologna?

If we first ignore the language aspect of Bologna and consider how the Bologna Process can lead to improved educational quality, we can create a baseline process against which to consider how language may, or may not, undermine the quality-raising aspect. For the individual student the quality of their education may be improved as Umeå's programme for internationalisation suggests since the courses offered at foreign universities may be selected by the student to complement and extend the range of course modules available to the student at Umeå University. Hence, the individual student is able to gain both general and specialist education and training that would otherwise not have been available to them. The same, of course, applies to students from any European university who undertake a study exchange programme at another university in order to complement the possibilities available at their home university.

These individual exchanges would have the potential to further generate reflection among staff members at both institutions (the home and the host): the home would receive feedback from the exchange student about course content, structure and perceived quality and be able to assess their own courses in light of this; the host would be able to gain insights into how their course content, structure and quality related to the exchange student's home university's courses. These aspects together ought to lead to a spiral of improved quality. As Zgaga (2005) discussed, superimposed upon these implicit actions for quality control and routes for improvement, is the explicit goal of the 'establishment of an agreed set of common standards, procedures and guidelines for quality assurance' (Berlin Communiqué, 2003, p. 3). It is thus apparent that the educational systems that form the EHEA will, at least in theory, operate with both explicit and implicit quality assurance mechanisms that, if functioning well, ought to lead to quality improvements in the teaching and learning in higher education.

Within the EHEA there is a growing demand from university management for courses to be delivered in one of the major European languages (most frequently English) in order to stimulate student and staff exchange. This can then be linked with the opportunity to take an introductory course in the national language of the host country. Together this use of a major language for the academic course delivery and the opportunity to learn the basics of the language of the host country aim to equip students and academic staff with democratic ideals, and linguistic and cultural skills. We argue here that such aims will be undermined along with a lowering of course and learning outcome quality if the language of delivery impacts upon the processes of teaching and student learning.

A case study conducted in 2000 by Schrader & Sullivan (2001) provides an illustration of how such undermining might happen. They reported on an interview with a Swedish lecturer teaching an introductory Swedish history class in English. Schrader & Sullivan judged the lecturer as having advanced-level academic English. They found 'a frustration on the part of the lecturer who felt limited in the quality of the job he was able to do due to the language of teaching' (p. 117):

> It's frustrating isn't it, to know that I could do this much better
> but I can't … the frustration with which I walk away from a lecture
> when I feel this was no good, I can't stop thinking about this, it
> stays for a long time. (p. 117)

Yet, as Airey (2003, 2004) pointed out, lecturers in Sweden are often asked by their heads of department 'Can you teach this course in English?', often with the expectation that the answer will be 'yes' and that this will not create staffing problems. However, as illustrated by Schrader & Sullivan (2001), this assumption is one worthy of review. If the situation found in the

Schrader & Sullivan case study (as suggested by Airey [2003, 2004]) can be generalised to the wider academic population, the use of the non-national language by non-native speakers of the non-national language of instruction can lead to, in the worse case, incorrect information being learned by the students; in an average context, to a lower quality of delivery that may or may not impact upon the quality of the learning outcomes; or in the rare case, to no difference in either quality of delivery or learning outcomes.

These three possible outcomes omit the question of the student's language competence and its possible impact upon the learning outcomes. In reality, the student's language competence may introduce another variable into the teaching and learning context. In individual instances, then, it is possible either that learning in higher education is not impacted upon by the learner's language competence (this outcome may be safeguarded by the fact that university entrance has appropriate language requirements), or that the student's lower language competence does impact upon learning outcomes.

Before turning to the cognitive load aspects of processing information in a second/foreign language and how these influence learning outcomes, it is useful to know that Sweden's young foreign language English users are, according to Erickson (2004), currently among the best in Europe. Yet, as Hincks (2005) pointed out:

> The Swedish facility with English can be deceptive. Behind the
> fluent speech produced with few intrusive segmental errors can be
> a limited vocabulary and an uncertainty as to the usage of words
> more familiar in writing than in speech. This is only to be
> expected from situations where the oral models often are, on the
> one hand, derived from the scripts of Hollywood screenwriters,
> and on the other hand, from the production of teachers who are
> themselves second language users and not always infallible. The
> result is a functional vocabulary and syntax that is more restricted
> than that of a native speaker, though this is not always evident on
> the surface. (p. 54)

Cognitive processing load when dealing with complex information presented in lecture form in a second/foreign language is a factor that can influence learning outcomes. Research from high school on content and language integrated learning (CLIL) in Sweden (known as Sprint in Sweden) has highlighted a number of problems for the learning of content through a non-societal language (most frequently English). Before elaborating on these problems a brief reference to the European Commission definition of CLIL might help clarify this perspective (European Commission, 2003, p. 8). Here, it is defined simply as a class in which 'pupils learn a subject through the medium of a foreign language'. The document claims that: 'It provides exposure to the language without requiring extra time in the curriculum' and that 'it can provide effective opportunities for pupils to use their new language skills now, rather than learn them now for use later'. The research undertaken in Sweden by Hyltenstam (2004) failed to perceive CLIL in this positive light and concluded:

> I stället för sprint behöver en engelskundervisning utvecklas som inte riskerar att bidra till försämrade ämneskunskaper hos eleverna och som inte kan misstänkas påverka deras modersmålsutveckling.
>
> (In place of CLIL, a method of teaching in English that does not risk contributing to lower subject knowledge among the pupils and that cannot be suspected of affecting their mother language development needs to be developed.) (p. 101)

If we now place these observations and findings relating to course delivery and student learning in the EHEA quality improvement cycle, the cycle becomes substantially less stable. The democracy and cultural skill gain will remain, but, it becomes apparent that the likely result of teaching using the non-societal language is that the standard of teaching and the standard of the outcomes will fall. We need to ask: 'How can this fall be avoided, or reversed?'

Paralleling the situation in the early language learning (ELL) area, there is a large body of competencies available in the academy (across the European space) with the expertise to identify how the lecturer and the student can be supported. The academies of the EHEA will need to recognise the issue and fully support and train, both lecturer and student, in order to be able to achieve student outcome levels comparable to those achieved in mother-tongue taught classes. This will demand more than is currently being undertaken in the academy and more than the Swedish Government (2005) mention in Swedish government bill 2005/06:2.

The current situation in many European universities needs substantial improvement. Not only should students not have to be personally proactive and look for this support, but lecturers should automatically be provided with support from the first time they are to teach in the non-societal language. Further, the current policy at some European universities, which assumes that an Erasmus, or other exchange, student who has passed high school English in their home country, will have English competency appropriate for university-level study (J. Ahlinder, personal communication, 8 November 2005), needs to be reconsidered. The current situation feeds into a quality-lowering loop since it cannot be assumed, and it is inaccurate to claim, that 'high school English' competency is of the same level throughout Europe. We view a Europe-wide language skill test as desirable. Such a test would permit the host university to place students in academic courses and revise expectations based upon each student's linguistic ability. This will assist in defining expectations, and together with a planned programme of support for the student and the lecturer in the academy, the quality assurance and improvement loop of Bologna will become an impetus for improvement rather than an unstable cycle with a language deficit.

As tertiary-level education across Europe shifts to increased use of English as a language of instruction, globally changes in provision and starting age are occurring at primary school level (defined here as from 5/6 years to 10/11 years) that might be expected to have an impact on university provision and student mobility in 10 to 15 years' time. The second part of this paper explores the extent to which these global trends may be influencing changes in Europe and considers what part European Union (EU) language education recommendations may also play in these changes.

Language Trends at Primary School Level

Current EU recommendations propose that all children should have the opportunity to learn their first foreign language within the primary phase of schooling. This is generally understood to mean no later than 11 years of age. This policy recommendation to nation states is not a statutory requirement, but all governments are signed up to an Action Plan, whereby there is a current requirement to report back on progress towards lowering the start age by 2006 – and no doubt future reporting goals will be set on the basis of such reports (European Commission, 2003, p. 7).

The above recommendations represent an attempt at the supranational level to consolidate a global trend for early language learning (ELL), which has rapidly gained pace since the collapse of the Soviet Bloc countries in the late 1980s. The move away from Soviet socialism has precipitated a substantial change in world order which continues to be worked out at all levels in our communities today. Coincidentally, economies have been challenged to harness the rapid advances of digital technology which are transforming our understandings of the interconnectivity of world markets. These unprecedented changes appear also to have prompted a re-viewing of the role of language as a necessary tool of cultural capital for engaging in all spheres of global exchange today.

At primary level, some of the former Soviet satellite countries of Central and Eastern Europe were among the first to seize the opportunity for teaching a Western European language to their young children. Previously Russian had been required learning for all primary school children – perceived as a uniting feature for the great Soviet family. As a result of the political changes in the late 1980s and early 1990s this was rapidly rejected by many and societies enthusiastically grasped the opportunity to 'turn westwards' with the introduction of a Western European language. Here, English was most frequently the language of choice – given its newly available potential and thus symbolic status for 'everything western' (it should be recalled that German had been more accessible under Soviet dominance, with East Germany as a member country – as a consequence, German has failed to represent the same symbolic gain). At all stages of education the learning of Western European languages became identified as an important asset of cultural capital for Central/Eastern Europeans wishing to participate in pan-European and global markets. For a number of national governments this was also perceived as a first step to gaining membership of the EU. To this end, funding rapidly became available from the EU for these countries to support the development of their primary language programmes via the EU Tempus/Comenius budget for developing teacher language competency and establishing tri-national primary school link/exchange networks.

The renewed interest in language learning outlined above was further encouraged by the enthusiasm of parents. This societal grouping perceived bilingual and multilingual acquisition as an invaluable asset of cultural capital for their children's later advancement in the workplace, seeking opportunities in private language schools in addition to the state schooling system, for their children to make a start on becoming competent bilinguals as early as possible. In this new climate of parentocracy (Brown, 1990, p. 66; Enever, 2005, p. 190) little attention appears to have been paid to the earlier research of linguists, psychologists and educationalists regarding the optimum age for beginning foreign language learning (Lenneberg, 1967; Scovel, 1988, p. 2). Instead, as the decade of the 1990s progressed, availability and developments in the field of new technologies rather changed perceptions of the concept of 'foreign' languages, prioritising a reappraisal of the impact of motivation on the acquisition of high-status regional/global languages in preference to optimum age debates, in this new era of intensive language learning.

Whilst those former Soviet Bloc countries with an interest in rapid EU accession led the way for introducing ELL in the 1990s, by the late 1990s a similar pattern could be observed in South-East Asia and elsewhere. In this region of the world there seems to have been little question of 'which' language to learn. With the perceived opportunities for global – and particularly North American – business, English became the only desirable language asset. This asset was held to represent 'westernisation' and entry into the 'global space', particularly in the economic domain – but also to those of world-class education and of the (perceived) interconnected global community. Since the turn of the twenty-first century this trend has continued to develop, a number of these countries having now introduced national requirements for the introduction of English teaching from the very early phases of schooling, for example: Malaysia from 7 years (grade 1), South Korea from 8-9 years (grade 3), Taiwan from 8 years (grade 2), China from 9 years (grade 3), with smaller regional pilot projects beginning from age 6 (grade 1).

During the first few years of the twenty-first century the economic potential of East/South-East and Southern Asia has increasingly been acknowledged worldwide. The potential linguistic impact has not so far precipitated a rush for Europeans to learn Chinese (though the language has received renewed interest in some western universities). In Europe instead the trend towards English has rather tended to gain pace. The current new membership of Central and Eastern Europe and those of the potential new membership (e.g. Romania, Bulgaria, Croatia, Turkey) show a marked trend towards English at primary level – often with a start age of 7-8 years. Those members of 'old Europe' display a more diverse pattern of language choices at primary level than in both the 'newer Europe' and in East/South-East and Southern Asia, but still with a strong preference for English as a first choice. Data on national policy changes in Europe between the years 1990-2005 (see Table I) provide an interesting summary of the extent to which start ages have fallen across this period.

	Number of countries with start age of:		
	6/7 years	8/9 years	10+ years
1990	1	2	24
2005	6	10	11

Table I. Mandatory foreign language start age policies in Europe, 1990-2005 (including 25 countries of European Union and two accession countries for 2007). Source: data compiled from Eurydice 2005 and updated personal communication from in-country professionals.

The above data indicate a shift from approximately 10% to 60% of countries in Europe selecting an earlier start age for the teaching of a first foreign language over the 15-year period analysed. However, marked evidence of regional trends across Europe as a whole tends to conceal the very varied patterns of detail evident in individual nation states, often the consequence of specific histories of migration, economic development, societal opinion and political decisions. The dangers of generalising the European picture cannot be overstated in a region whose alliance relies on maintaining that sensitive tension between a 'federal union of states' and yet respecting the existence of national boundaries. As an illustration of this important tool of cultural maintenance, a snapshot of just a few current national patterns of ELL provision are summarised below – intended as a sample of the richly textured variation now evident in Europe.

Latvia (pop. 2.5 million)

Policy.
Latvian – medium of instruction from start of primary schooling.
English as first foreign language from age 6 (introduced in 2005).
Russian available in ethnic minority schools (30% of population of Russian ethnic origin – a result of both voluntary and forced migration).
Policy reflects country's newly independent status (former Soviet Bloc) from 1993, including the desire to 'de-Russify' the country.

Italy (pop. 57.2 million)

Policy. All primary schools are required to introduce English from Grade 1 (with the exclusion of ethnic minority schools). This policy introduced from

2005 is proving controversial in traditionally French second-language communities (e.g. Piedmont region).

Germany (pop. 82.5 million)

Policy. Sixteen regions of Germany (*Bundeslaender*) operate autonomous education policies. Most introduce the first foreign language from grade 3 (8-9 years); two regions make an earlier start from grade 1 (with a further region planning also to do so from 2008).

Of the 16 regions, one offers only French, the others offer English, and in some cases, also French, Italian or Russian as further choices. However, despite this available diversity, 95% of all schools choose English as the first foreign language (personal communication, Professor Schmid-Schonbein, November 2005).

Poland (pop. 38.5 million)

Policy. Schools have right of language choice, 80% choose English first. Pilot project to introduce ELL from age 8 (currently 10 years at the latest).

Substantial developments in competency levels since 1995. Evident that by age 15 students who were previously at elementary-lower intermediate levels have now typically raised their levels to lower-upper intermediate levels. Key reasons relate to economically and socially driven motivation, increased social access to English, development of teacher expertise and perceptions of future economic advantage (personal communication, Marta Bujakowska, November 2005).[2]

As can be seen from the above brief summaries, individual country patterns differ widely. The realities of actual provision at community and individual school level, as might be expected, are even more widely varied. This relates often to sharp contrasts between urban and rural contexts. Particular difficulties may be experienced here in providing appropriate local teacher training and in attracting qualified teachers to such communities. In a number of European countries policies of ELL introduction have failed to address such training issues, resulting in a markedly increased urban/rural divide in the quality and availability of provision.

Further differences across Europe relate to local or national responsibility for the choice of which language should be introduced first at primary level. In some cases this is decided nationally, in others this decision is devolved to local authority or individual school level. The consequence of this variety creates much inconsistency, yet offers an important acknowledgement of local autonomy. For example, Austria offers a choice of five languages, which allows individual schools to make their own selection yet results in 97% of schools choosing English (European Commission, 2005); Italy stipulates that English should be introduced for all pupils from age 6 (Sanzo, 2004) – a policy which has brought much disagreement from regions where French has traditionally been the first choice. In contrast to this, in the Netherlands – a country where English can be identified as more of a second than a foreign language (the outcome of substantial media/digital technologies access to English outside the school system) – there is some debate about the first choice at primary level. Given this wide societal access to English, proposals have included arguments for introducing an alternative first foreign language (e.g. French/German) to support and encourage trilingual skills for the population (de Bot, 2000).

Yet another set of dilemmas is currently appearing in England as the first steps towards introducing ELL are being taken via initial pilot projects (Department for Education and Skills Pathfinder Primary FL Project 2003-05). Data from one regional study reveal that individual school language choices are mainly based on preferences for those languages that teachers themselves learned at school (most often French). However, younger teachers and pupils tend more often to indicate a preference for Spanish – a consequence perhaps of the growth in bargain holiday prices for Spain and also the popular Spanish second home market for British purchasers. Very few of those interviewed indicated a preference for Italian and almost none for German. Such a complex picture of choice reflects the dilemmas (and thus decrease in motivation) related both to language choice and to motivation for learning a foreign language for first-language speakers of English in a European and global context that currently predominantly employs English as a lingua franca (Watts & Enever, 2005, p. 33).

Interpreting the Evidence on ELL

The above data clearly indicate an increasingly strong commitment to ELL across Europe, with some signs that start ages will continue to fall in the near future. The current likely practice is one of some initial introduction of the first foreign language from the start of schooling, throughout the European state education space.

However, clarity of aims and the broader understanding of educational development in this field are not yet well understood or defined in either policy or practice. This lack of both knowledge and awareness in current practice increases the likelihood that ELL will fail to instil the vital early positive attitudes to foreign language learning necessary if this early start is to be capitalised on with the acquisition of higher level competency at a later stage. If Europe is to sustain and build on the policy trend towards an earlier start, there is a need for research into how young children learn languages in school situations, development of a shared understanding of what constitutes age-appropriate methodology, together with substantially raised language expertise amongst teachers and extensive teacher training provision throughout Europe. In addition, there is a need for substantially improved provision in many rural areas of Europe if democratic ideals are to be upheld.

Whilst such goals for ELL might offer a blueprint for a European policy in this field, it should not be assumed that state education provision is in any position to control such development, however. The increasing influence of media/digital technology offers access for young people today to global sources of language learning for social purposes through mechanisms which are only just beginning to be charted in research terms. Such networks have the potential to substantially increase exclusion of sections of the European (and global) population, whilst offering impressive language gains for others. A foreseeable consequence is one of much language learning happening outside the classroom, for social purposes, in Europe. It is conceivable that the role of language learning in schools may well have to shift to a compensatory one for those less affluent communities in some parts of Europe if we are to achieve any kind of multilingual Europe in the foreseeable future.

Exploring the Common Strands

The particular features of languages in education discussed here suggest the existence of somewhat conflicting agendas with the potential for a diverse range of consequences across Europe. In this section we will comment on two central concerns.

Commitment to a Trilingual Europe

Evidence on ELL in Europe and on trends towards more higher education courses delivered in English appear to reflect similar problematics. Both reflect a political commitment to a policy of operational fluency in at least two languages with the aim of achieving an ability to engage in world markets, yet the reality of the implementation of these policies at both phases of education is not infrequently of variable quality at micro-level. Expertise to overcome gaps in quality at teacher training level, design of support mechanisms and other relevant skills are already available in some parts of Europe. With a full commitment at national or European levels (or preferably both) such gaps could easily be overcome with priority funding – yet, this does not appear to be happening. We would question therefore the real commitment of either or both strata of governance to this ideal.

Linked to the above, we would further question whether it is realistic to propose that Europe has the economic resources to create a social Europe in linguistic terms. Such a project would require very high-level funding of resource and training provision, together with a clear consensus on the potential gains both within and between nation states. With the recent example of the failure of Russian teaching imposed on the satellite states of the former Soviet Bloc countries, such experience has taught us that supranational language projects may meet with insurmountable resistance at the micro-level of classrooms. Political or economic commitment to one language, or even three or four widely spoken languages, might well prove ineffective in achieving the desired goal. People simply do not learn languages unless they want to or have to.

Achieving Quality through a Foreign/Second Language

The trend towards the marketisation of education now appears to include the commodification of languages. At ELL level parents are selecting those schools where ELL is available for an ever-younger age group, or supplementing school provision with private language classes (for example, in Greece it is almost the norm to attend a private language class in addition to state school language lessons). At higher education level the data presented here suggest that students may be unable to achieve the same academic results in a second/foreign language as they might in their first language. Whilst hard evidence in support of either the Bologna Process or of global pressures as drivers is difficult to establish, European agendas do currently prioritise the importance of achieving a bi/tri-lingual population, perceiving English (mainly, but not exclusively) as the global language. The inherent difficulties of such implementation are, however, given insufficient space in the political discourse. In prioritising particular agendas and excluding others from reaching the point of discussion, the Bologna Process may now arguably be presented as a neoliberal movement that will create a mobile trilingual elite at the expense of the highly able monolingual. Thus, the new high-status cultural capital may be bi/tri-lingualism. Hence, it can now be proposed that language rather than academic achievement may offer the key to the future.

The impossibility of either 'world English' or 'plurilingualism' becoming a project for wholesale implementation throughout Europe is well argued by Fettes (2003, p. 40), who suggests that 'both imply radical reforms to well-entrenched bureaucracies and pedagogical cultures, requiring long-term political commitment in order to succeed'. He further argues that: 'the most likely result in the medium term [in Europe] appears to be a combination of "élite plurilingualism" with what might be termed "consumer English": active competence in several languages for the upwardly mobile, and limited, primarily passive competence in English for the rest'.

Conclusion

The evidence set out in this chapter suggests that Europe faces many dilemmas in its attempt to identify Language Europe. There currently exists neither a consensus on this, nor a clear mandate for the possible alternative of *Languages* Europe. Whilst the political agendas appear contradictory across the Union, so do the wider social agendas. The economic realities seem also to suggest the near-impossibility of achieving substantive provision for a bi/tri-lingual Europe, at present.

Future predicting for language choices is a notoriously problematic venture (see, for example, Graddol, 1997) and certainly well beyond the scope of this chapter. However, on the basis of the analysis so far presented, we can offer an initial proposal for how languages in education might more effectively be structured with some hope of achieving competent operational fluency for all citizens in Europe (though with little certainty!).

It is clear for our examination of foreign language learning and use at two points in formal education that there is a need for a commitment to language learning from ELL through compulsory schooling, to university and beyond. This commitment needs to be long term and support language development in all EU citizens; without such a commitment we perceive a danger in which in a future Europe only the linguistically most able can fulfil their potential. An indication of this danger can be found in Falk (2002). She found that it was only the brightest students that benefited from the target language communication in the CLIL classroom. This danger is also evident in our examination of impact of the use of a non-societal language on teaching and learning quality in Sweden. The use of English in the Swedish academy without support for the teacher and the learner of the types suggested by the research presented in Flowerdew (1994) and Flowerdew & Miller (2005), we feel, is hampering some students from fulfilling their full potential.

The commitment across the EU and the EHEA to language learning from YLL to higher education and beyond that we propose recognises the importance of helping all citizens achieve their full academic potential, whether this occurs in their first language alone, due to the student's low linguistic ability, or in a combination of languages. Moreover, with appropriate support to teachers and learners the situation of surface proficiency masking an underlying lack of competence as outlined by Hincks (2005) can be avoided and a lowering of academic quality across Europe for the less linguistically able student can be avoided.

Notes

[1] Conclusions and Recommendations of the Conference: Conference on Master-level Degrees held in Helsinki, 14-15 March, 2003, p. 2. http://www.bologna-bergen2005.no/EN/Bol_sem/Old/030314-15Helsinki_Results.pdf (accessed 6 November 2005).

[2] United Nations (2004) United Nations World Population Prospects: the 2004 revision, population database. http://esa.un.org/unpp/ (accessed 20 December 2005).

References

Airey, J. (2003) Teaching University Courses through the Medium of English: the current state of the art, in G. Fransson, Å. Morberg, P. Nilsson & B. Schüllerqvist (Eds) *Didaktikens mångfald, Lärarutbildningens skriftserie 1*, 11-18. Gävle: Högskolan I Gävle.

Airey, J. (2004) Can You Teach it in English? Aspects of the Language Choice Debate in Swedish Higher Education, in P. Wilkinson (Ed.) *Integrating Content and Language: meeting the challenge of a multilingual higher education*, 97-108. Maastricht: Universitaire Pers Maastricht.

Berlin Communiqué (2003) Realising the European Higher Education Area. http://www.bologna-bergen2005.no/Docs/00-Main_doc/030919B (accessed 8 November 2008).

Bologna Declaration (1999) http://www.bologna-bergen2005.no/Docs/00-Main_doc/990719BOLOGNA_DECLARATION.PDF (accessed 12 December 2005).

Brown, P. (1990) The Third Wave: education and the ideology of parentocracy, *British Journal of Sociology of Education*, 11(1), 65-85. http://dx.doi.org/10.1080/0142569900110105

de Bot, K. (2000) An Early Start for Foreign Languages (but not English) in the Netherlands, in R.D. Lambert (Ed.) *Language Policy and Pedagogy*. Philadelphia: John Benjamins.

Eliasson, P.O. (2005) Avhandlingar måste skrivas på engelska, *Universitetsäraren*, 16, 24 October, 4-5.

Enever, J. (2005) Europeanisation or Globalisation in Early Start EFL Trends across Europe? in C. Gnutzmann & F. Intemann (Eds) *The Globalisation of English and the English Language Classroom*. Tübingen: Gunter Narr.

Erickson, G. (2004) *English: here and there and everywhere. En undersökning av ungdomars kunskaper i och uppfattningar om engelska i åtta europeiska länder*. Stockholm: Skolverket.

European Commission (2003) *Promoting Language Learning and Linguistic Diversity: an action plan 2004-2006*. Brussels: Commission of the European Communities.

European Commission (2005) *Eurydice: key data on teaching languages at schools in Europe – 2005 edition*. http://www.eurydice.org (accessed 10 December 2005).

Falk, M. (2002) *Språk- och innehållsintegrerad inlärning och undervisning i praktiken: meningsfull målspråksträning? MINS 51*. Stockholm: Stockholms universitet.

Fettes, M. (2003) The Geostrategies of Interlingualism, in J. Maurais & M. Morris (Eds) *Languages in a Globalising World*. Cambridge: Cambridge University Press.

Flowerdew, J.L. (Ed.) (1994) *Academic Listening: research perspectives*. Cambridge: Cambridge University Press.

Flowerdew, J.L. & Miller, L.J. (2005) *Second Language Listening: theory and practice*. New York: Cambridge University Press.

Graddol, D. (1997) *The Future of English?* London: The British Council.

Hincks, R. (2005) Computer Support for Learners of Spoken English. PhD thesis, Royal Institute of Technology, Stockholm.

Hyltenstam, K. (2004) Engelskan, skolans språkundervisning och svensk språkpolitik, in Svenska språknämnden (Ed.) *Engelskan i sverige: språkval i utbildning, arbete och kulturliv*, 36-110. Stockholm: Norstedts ordbok.

Lenneberg, E.H. (1967) *Biological Foundations of Language*. New York: John Wiley.

Program för internationalisering vid Umeå universitet 2003-2008 (2002) http://www.umu.se/studentcentrum/regler_riktlinjer/ pdf/Policy_for_internationalisering.pdf (accessed 6 November 2005).

Sanzo, R. (2004) La Retrospettiva per la Prospettiva, presented at L'educazione linguistica nella scuola primaria, Turin, 17 December.

Schrader, J. & Sullivan, K.P.H. (2001) Academic Listening: is the confusion increased by the use of an L2? in *Proceedings of Lärares liv – vision och verklighet, Universitetspedagogisk konferens i Umeå*, 15-16 February, 110-118. Umeå: Universitetspedagogiskt centrum, Umeå universitet.

Scovel, T. (1988) *A Time to Speak: a psycholinguistic inquiry into the critical period for human speech*. New York: Newbury House/Harper & Row.

Swedish Government (2005) Swedish Government Bill 2005/06:2, Bästa språket – en samlad svensk språkpolitik. http://www.regeringen.se/content/1/c6/05/07/61/d32f62b5.pdf (accessed 6 November 2005).

Watts, C. & Enever, J. (2005) Monitoring and Evaluation Report: BHCC pathfinder primary modern language project. Brighton and Hove City Council.

Zgaga, P. (2005) Bologna and the Creation of a European Higher Education Area, presented at GENIE Summer Institute, Aalborg, 5-7 July.

CHAPTER 12

Performance, Citizenship and the Knowledge Society: a new mandate for European Education Policy

ANTÓNIO M. MAGALHÃES & STEPHEN R. STOER

SUMMARY This chapter maps out the debate concerning a new mandate for European education policy based on recent socio-economic, political and educational developments, seen from the perspective of educational researchers located on the European (semi)periphery. The first part of the chapter looks at the category 'preparation for the labour market', while the second part concerns itself with the category 'citizenship'. With regard to the former, it is argued that a new mandate for European education policy finds itself inextricably linked to the new education mandate of the new middle class, in a setting of globalisation and, closer to home, European construction. The latter attempts to conceptualise the emergence of new forms of citizenship at a time when the modern social contract suffers a process of transformation (or, what we term, reconfiguration). Based on the distinction between 'attributed citizenship' and 'demanded citizenship', the authors analyse changes taking place in state regulation as well as explore some of their implications for schooling.

Introduction

Edith Cresson's White Paper on the knowledge society (1996) constitutes an important document in the development of European Education Policy. Central to the document is the concept of competencies, which are brandished as being fundamental to success in this new knowledge, or learning, society. This society not only 'alters the funding of enterprises (firms), it also lays out new horizons for education and training' (1995, p. 8).

The concept of competencies appears as the key mediator between the world of production and the field of education: to be competent is to acquire the capacity to constantly recycle oneself, to have the ability to be permanently retrained (Bernstein, 2001). Europe takes on the task of becoming a learning society in order to be competitive with both Japan and the USA. Thus a new mandate for education policy appears to be developing directed at orienting the elaboration of policy at the nation-state level. Dale, in a recent work, refers to the 'European Social Model' and the role of social policy 'in making a fundamental and essential contribution to economic policy' (2001, p. 4), which includes the idea of the 'EU as agenda-setter in education' (p. 6). This mandate is structured around the concept of competencies, which are conceived above all as performance driven, and which tend to treat performance and learning as if they were mutually exclusive.

The concept of competencies introduces, most of the time implicitly, into discourses on social policy in general and into discourses on education policy in particular, the characteristic of 'adaptability' to permanent 'environmental change' as crucial to both individual and organisational survival. All that tries to resist the transformations that are taking place, mainly in the world of production, is condemned to perish: from professional careers to present organisational features, everything must take part in the process of transformation. In the midst of such change, education appears as a privileged field of action. This is due to the fact that 'flexibility' is being conceptualised in EU political discourse as the only way to guarantee 'employability' (to be 'employable' means to have the right – meaning flexible – competencies) and because knowledge has become a central factor of production. It is our contention that it is in this context that the emergent mandate calling for 'educational performance' should be framed.

We will argue that, when one analyses the gap that exists between pedagogy's impact on the educational process (namely the effects of the basic assumption that the main goal of education is the development of the individual independently of its social and economic relevance) and the emergent mandate calling for educational performance (both at the organisational level and at the individual level, with its emphasis on the economic and social relevance of education), one must conclude that such a dichotomy is itself induced by the very debate taking place between pedagogy and performance. Additionally, we will argue that political claims based on pedagogy alone may lead to an educational vacuum, while those based solely on performance may lead to a simplistic and unrefined reduction of education to economy.

Another important aspect of a new mandate for European Education Policy is the reconfiguration of the modern social contract as part of the reconceptualisation of citizenship as difference. Indeed, one can argue that differences have rebelled against the cultural, political and epistemological yoke of western modernity, refusing to be classified as passive objects to be known like the 'primitive' that anthropology took as its object of study or like the mythical-magical thinker, without history and without state, that received the intellectual favours of scientific thought. What characterises differences and their social relations today is precisely their heterogeneity and their inescapable resistance to any attempts at epistemological or cultural domestication. The implications of the rebellions of differences for the concept and practices of citizenship are profound. Given the cultural diversity of the European space, new forms of citizenship will be central to the project of European construction and, thus, central to a new mandate for European education.

The Rise of Performance as a Culture of Learning

After the effects of the post-Fordist mandate that began to feed into core-country education systems during the late 1970s and early 1980s became apparent, resulting from the fragmentation of work and the restructuring of professions and where 'transferable skills' began to play an increasingly important role, it can be argued that a new culture of learning based on the claim of academic excellence started to appear. Part of the new middle classes, feeling their present and future lifestyles threatened by such a change, sought to regain the upper hand in a context where 'performance' became the keyword, both at the political and pedagogical levels. Performance and transferable skills, in their proximity to the demands of the labour market, tend to require a learning context based on an explicit, 'visible' pedagogy which involves their being separated from pedagogy as a process (with its mainly implicit, or 'invisible' pedagogy) while they take on an increasingly central role in the elaboration of education policy. Hence, the emergence of a new learning culture which is a combination of: 1. the assertion of a pedagogy of teaching (transmission) in secondary education in accordance with the traditional tension associated with the new middle class, which, as Bernstein has argued (1978), promotes invisible pedagogy in primary education but as entry into the labour market gets nearer switches over to explicit transmission pedagogy, and 2. supporting even at the level of primary education a visible pedagogy either because a concern with labour market entry now occurs earlier on in schooling (particularly true in a country like Portugal where many youth leave school after the ninth year and particularly true in a socio-economic context where entry into the labour market is more problematic than it was during Fordism) or because, even at these levels of schooling, pedagogy as process is seen as undermining academic excellence (crucial to a successful economy in an epoch of globalisation).

As both Giddens (1994) and Apple (1998, 2000) have noted, emphasis on the decrease in academic standards and on the unworkable features of progressive models of teaching are central arguments of a rather *contra natura* coalition of neoliberals and neoconservatives in their attack on public schooling. The organising concept for this alliance appears to be 'performance', arguably a major plank in 'conservative modernisation' (Dale, 1989), which is set up against a concern with pedagogical processes. The concept of 'performance' has emerged as part of the legitimating discourses on post-Fordism. Knowledge in this context appears as both a central factor of production and as a medium for the functioning of market relations. Indeed, Bernstein refers to:

> A new concept both of knowledge and of its relation to those who create it ... Knowledge should flow like money to wherever it can create advantage and profit. Indeed, knowledge is not just like money: it is money. ... Knowledge, after nearly a thousand years, is divorced from inwardness and is literally dehumanised. Once knowledge is separated from inwardness, commitment and personal dedication, then people may be moved about, substituted for each other, and excluded from the market. (1990, p. 155)

Knowledge, in this sense, instead of qualifying the individual, transforms the individual into a set of cognitive-driven competencies. Knowledge no longer educates the individual and society, rather it becomes a tool for positioning individuals on (or excluding them from) the labour market. One of the results of this transformation is a process of *individualisation* where individuals are reduced to their 'performance' (similar to Castoriadis' notion of the 'privatised individual' [1998]). Market regulation only recognises individuals on whom is placed the onus for both the excesses and the deficits of the market.

As a result, pedagogy is attacked and questioned, in terms of its social and political utility, on the basis of its assumption that knowledge is part of inwardness – as it gives value to and qualifies the individual – instead of realising that such an assumption tends to make schooling inefficient, overly concerned with the individual as subject and less concerned with knowledge as a factor of production. In other words, instead of concern with the output of the educational process, and knowledge as an element of mere 'throughput', pedagogues are concerned with the effects of input on the individual and social developmental processes.

In Portugal the simultaneous crisis and consolidation of mass schooling (see Stoer & Araújo, 2000) is also inspiring the rise of 'performance culture'. The simultaneous crisis and consolidation of mass schooling involves oscillation between a preoccupation with a pedagogy of teaching based on the transmission of knowledge – in which the centrality of the knowledge to be transmitted determines the pedagogical process – and a concern with a pedagogy of learning in which the sociocultural and educational characteristics of the pupil take on a central role in the teaching–learning process. As we have argued above, the first perspective can be referred to as the performance approach to pedagogy and the latter as the pedagogical approach to pedagogy.

With regard to the former, two presuppositions are implicit and taken for granted: 1. the knowledge to be transmitted has in itself a positioning potential and, therefore, it can be separated from the pedagogical process – pedagogy and performance are seen as independent from each other; 2. the pedagogical recontextualisation of knowledge, to use Bernstein's expression (1990), in which the teacher takes an active part, is socially and culturally neutral. As a result, the educational process tends to be reduced to both the teacher's transmission performance and to the pupil's reproduction performance. There have been claims by sociologists and opinion makers that the teaching–learning process must be focused on teachers' academic and professional competencies linked to the effective transmission of knowledge (Mónica, 1997; Fernandes, 2001) and on pupils' competencies in reproducing this corpus. In many ways, similarities with the Durkheimian model of education can be found; education is the socialisation of the younger generation by their elders (Durkheim, 1978).

With regard to the latter, at the basis of the pedagogical approach to pedagogy lies the gardening metaphor: *laissez croître*. The pupils as subjects are the core of the learning process, not the knowledge to be transmitted. According to this perspective, if learning does not take place in the teaching–learning process the reasons for this must be found in the teachers' actions, in institutional structures and processes, in education policies and so on, anywhere but in the child. In this extreme perspective (for instance the experience of Summerhill comes to mind), the claim for academic excellence does not make sense (it becomes, rather, almost a dirty word), for the goal to be achieved is emancipation (*tout court*). This is also the reason why militant pedagogy is so critical of the concept of evaluation; it is seen as functioning mainly on the basis of reducing educational processes to performance indicators.

The opposition between the two approaches appears to be more than simply one of adopting a pedagogical method. Indeed, the opposition between 'performance' and pedagogy reflects a political debate based on two different conceptions of the development of mass schooling: on the one hand, the idea that the consolidation of mass schooling depends upon a participatory and emancipatory pedagogy resulting in an authentically democratic school; on the other, the idea that meritocratic schooling based on 'performance' holds the key to success in a post-Fordist labour market based on knowledge competencies. The debate appears to take place as if the consolidation of mass schooling according to the former meant continuing loss of academic excellence, the meritocratic model being the only way out.

Schooling in a Post-Fordist Environment: the debate over the relationship between 'performance' and academic excellence

In fact, there exist two further conceptions of the development of mass schooling that introduce important nuances that need to be taken into consideration. The first is a conception, still largely identified with Fordism, that sees meritocratic schooling as based on individual talent and merit. Here representative democracy and the principle of equality of opportunity are seen as the norm. The second, more identified with the post-Fordist context, sees democratic schooling also capable of developing through the consolidation of meritocratic schooling. At stake is the relationship between education and social change which, rather than being seen as domination, either in the form of social engineering or as a relationship leading necessarily to emancipation, is seen as a reflexive attempt to manage social change (see Cortesão et al, 2001). Also the process by way of which the individual becomes central in the post-Fordist context, rather than being seen as based on individualisation, is seen as a process of individuation where the reflexive individual becomes master of his/her own choices (Giddens, 1990; Beck, 1992; Beck et al, 1994).

The debate over 'performance' in schooling appears to be taking place as if pedagogy were its opposite, where 'performance' is the keyword, interpreted in its postmodern sense as the attempt to obtain maximum output on the basis of minimum input (Lyotard, 1986). However, this is only one way of focusing the issue which is incapable of portraying the whole picture, creating and perpetuating in its turn a false dichotomy between academic excellence and pedagogy. Indeed, 'performance' is a concept that can also be seen as containing a pedagogic content. For example, for progressive pedagogues, like Paulo Freire for instance, 'performance' can also be defined as that which is central to Barnett's notion (1997) of 'critical being', where the domains of knowledge, the self and the world are appropriated by critical thinking skills as a process of reaching 'critical dialogue' (1997, pp. 66-68). In both these polar positions with regard to 'performance', it is the concept in itself which is given absolute value: in the first case, with regard to the maximisation of results, and, in the second, with regard to the self-development of the subject.

Between these two polar positions, we find other nuanced positions where 'performance' takes on a different meaning, particularly when related to the consolidation of mass schooling, be it via the meritocratic route, or via emancipatory-driven democratic schooling. With regard to the latter, to the extent that a pedagogy based on learning does not negate a pedagogy based on teaching, 'performance' is not opposed to the process of the self-development of the subject. Indeed, here 'performance' is defined as incorporating pedagogy itself, that is, there is no 'performance' without pedagogy – even the most directly transmissive teaching processes require pedagogical recontextualisation, for example in the adaptation of the scientific text for the purposes of teaching. With regard to the former, the subaltern position of a pedagogy of learning with regard to a pedagogy of teaching attributes to 'performance' a predominant meaning identified with the efficient *effectiveness* of the socialisation process of younger generations. That is, it is argued that pedagogy without 'performance' leads to an educational and socio-economic vacuum. Therefore the assumption is that 'good' pedagogy is precisely that pedagogy which produces the 'best' results; in other words, meritocratic schooling is the first and foremost promoter of social mobility (Fernandes, 2001).

The issue of academic excellence is only relevant for these latter two positions (Figure 1). For the other two polar positions, a concern with academic excellence is clearly a non-issue: emancipatory-driven democratic schooling rejects a clear link, on the one hand, between labour market concerns and the competencies it requires and, on the other, the educational process; meritocratic post-Fordist schooling places all its emphasis on the competencies acquired through schooling, being totally oblivious to the individual or collective qualities of the subject. Academic excellence, in fact, only becomes an issue for those positions that aim at relating education with 'performance'.

Performance as Critical Being: *Democratic Schooling 1* – Emancipatory Pedagogy

<u>Academic Excellence based on Subject of Learning Process</u> – *Democratic Schooling 2* – Learning Pedagogy/Transmission Pedagogy – there is no 'performance' without pedagogy

<u>Academic Excellence based on Knowledge to be Transmitted</u> – *Meritocratic Schooling 1* – Transmission Pedagogy/Learning Pedagogy – pedagogy without 'performance' leads to an educational and socio-economic vacuum

Performance as Maximum Output achieved through Minimum Input – *Meritocratic Schooling 2* – 'Performance' – knowledge as money

---

Figure 1.

Schooling in a Post-Fordist Environment: the new middle class, the labour market and the recomposition of skills

One can argue that the following assumptions frame new middle-class perceptions of meritocratic schooling:

1. Mass schooling puts at risk the 'quality' of the teaching–learning process, that is, new middle-class parents are becoming increasingly aware of the fact that their children's schools have been 'invaded' not only by children coming from working-class families but also from cultural minority groups.

2. Massified secondary schooling puts at risk the 'distinction' strategy (see Bourdieu, 1986), that is, secondary schools no longer sufficiently prepare their youth for university studies. This assumption is slightly different from the previous one in that it stresses the fact that it is not sufficient to provide middle-class students only with 'good' teaching pedagogy.

Students *must* achieve 'excellent' results if they intend to enter the university's gates and, even more importantly, to be able to choose which gates they want to enter. The choice of the secondary school one wishes to attend, therefore, becomes crucial in guaranteeing preparation where one 'really' 'learns'. Thus an emphasis on 'performance' makes up for what is seen as insufficient pedagogy.

3. Mass schooling puts at risk the production of competencies relevant to post-Fordist labour market needs. As the visibility of post-Fordism increases, the new middle classes tend to elaborate strategies that will provide their children with the education needed to make a successful transition from schooling into the world of work.

Presently, the political debate on education appears to be hegemonised by discourses centred on 'performance', competencies and labour market needs. It can be argued that these discourses appear as middle-class strategies in the context of the changing nature of work and the labour market. With regard to those occupations identified with the middle classes, work was defined until recently as closely linked to the social category of profession. Work was a set of technical gestures and individual and group attitudes normally developed within the scope of an institution (business firm, corporation, etc.) within which labour activities took place. Unified under the label of a profession, work was also central to the individual's identity. Modern times under capitalism increased this tendency to identify individuals by way of their profession (for example, when asked of an individual, 'Who are you?', the response often came in the form of professional identity: 'I am a teacher'), and work was also deeply embedded within class strategies. For example, the profession of electrician is no longer conceived as a profession which implies training as socialisation in a set of attitudes, values and technical skills but rather as a set of disaggregated competencies (in the field of maintenance, in outdoor or architectural lighting, etc.), acquired directly through training, and which constitute specialisations which do not identify the individual as an electrician *tout court*. However, as is widely recognised, the nature of work is changing and work, in the sense of profession, it may be argued, is dissolving: 1. it is dissolving as a result of the increasing fragility of the wage relationship; 2. it is dissolving through the effects of the increasing 'lightness' of firms (i.e. the bigger they are the more they tend to subdivide until they melt into the air of 'offshore paradises') and 3. it is dissolving into competencies. Until recently people identified themselves with their profession, with the institution where they worked, and with the set of activities that defined their 'work'. Today, it is becoming more and more difficult for someone to identify with 'work' as it assumes a position in the increasingly volatile forms of production, distribution and consumption. That which remains appears to be definable as 'competencies'.

Braverman's thesis (1974) emphasised that the de-qualification of work in capitalist societies derived from the separation of work into its constituent elements by dividing the craft and reducing its parts. In actual fact, what was at stake was not so much a redistribution of crafts but rather a systematic subdivision of work, providing the basis for the subsequent destruction of all-round skills. At the same time, Braverman argued that the origins of management could be found in the struggle to devise the most effective means to ensure the employer's control over work.

The emergence of post-Fordist forms of production, distribution and consumption seems to impose important changes in the nature of work that apparently contradict Braverman's thesis of the long-term de-qualification of work within the framework of capitalism. It is not managerialist approaches of 'job enrichment' that we are referring to, but rather the apparent recomposition of skills and competencies that the new *learning-network-knowledge-based* economies seem to demand. To be creative, innovative, able to communicate, flexible, adaptive, and, perhaps most importantly, capable of being trained (i.e. in Bernstein's words, capable of 'responding effectively to concurrent, subsequent or intermittent pedagogies' [2000, p. 14), and so on, are the post-Fordist demands that appear to surpass the Fordist–Taylorist divide between *conception* and *execution* and the consequent deskilling of work. However, as Thompson argues:

> Widespread deskilling is often accompanied by an increased
> 'qualification' of smaller layers of workers involved in planning,
> programming and similar tasks. But the general tendency
> immediately tends to reassert itself as the enhanced skills are
> subjected to similar subspecialisation and the embodiment of skills
> in more complex machinery. Braverman's evidence of progressive
> deskilling of computer programmers is a major example of this
> type of development. (Thompson, 1989, p. 81)

According to this perspective, we are not witnessing a recomposition of work into new forms of craftsmanship in which work can be reappropriated by workers (the opposite of alienation), but, rather, an extension of the de-qualification trend. However, Thompson recognises that reality is more complex and affirms that in economic sectors with a higher proportion of investment in capital than in labour there exists a '*dual labour market* for skilled and unskilled labour within the long-term trend towards de-qualification' (1989, p. 83, emphasis in original). It is our contention that it is towards this dual labour market that middle-class education strategies are directed, and it is within this framework that the notion of 'skills', 'competencies' and 'academic excellence' should be understood. Interesting to note in this context is Castells' argument that:

> Under this new system of production, labor is redefined in its role
> as producer and sharply differentiated according to workers'
> characteristics. A major difference refers to what I call generic
> labor versus self-programmable labor. The critical quality in
> differentiating these two kinds of labour is education, and the
> capacity of accessing higher levels of education; that is, embodied

> knowledge and information. ... Education (as distinct from
> warehousing of children and students) is the process by which
> people, that is, labor, acquire the capability constantly to redefine
> the necessary skills for a given task, and to access the sources for
> learning these skills. Whoever is educated, in the proper
> organizational environment can reprogramme him/herself toward
> the endlessly changing tasks of the production process.
> (Castells, 1998, p. 361)

New middle-class strategies relate to this divide between 'education' and what we have termed competencies by promoting their children's access to a teaching/learning process based on 'performance' and a pedagogy of transmission. What appears to be paradoxical in this process is that the world of work based on self-programmable labour – here Ball's interviews with members of British industry come to mind (1990) – apparently emphasises what we have referred to as a learning pedagogy based on the subject of the teaching/learning process and not on the knowledge to be transmitted. Such an approach tends to promote a desire for innovation, a non-differentiated schooling and cooperative work in the classroom, all of which were referred to by Ball's interviewees.

The False Dichotomy: performance without pedagogy versus pedagogy without performance

Bernstein asks what happens to pedagogic modalities when their social base changes. In other words, what does the development of flexible capitalism mean for pedagogy? Bernstein's reply (1996) is that there has been a change from a pedagogic model based on competence, dominant from the 1950s, to a pedagogic model based on performance, dominant from the 1980s. The first model was important in the sense that it meant control by the learner of the selection, sequence and rhythm of the learning process and was based on implicit recognition and realisation rules (i.e. on an invisible pedagogy) in which all persons were considered inherently competent (Bernstein refers to the linguistic competence identified with Chomsky, the cognitive competence of Piaget, the cultural competence of Levi-Strauss, the practical competence of Garfinkle and the communicative competence of Dell Hymes.) The second model places the emphasis on the specific output of he/she who learns and on the capacities necessary for the production of this specific output (a text, a product).

Here it is necessary to make a distinction between 'visible pedagogy', based on explicit recognition and realisation rules (a pedagogical modality normally identified with the domination of the education system by that class which Bernstein designates as the 'old middle class'), and that which Bernstein designates 'generic performance', based on training objectives, focused on that which occurs exterior to the school and on new sites of recontextualisation – meaning that this pedagogic mode is constructed and distributed exterior to and independent from pedagogic recontextualising fields. In other words, the objectives of training inherent to 'generic performance' reconfigure the location of recontextualisation, enabling potentially the domination of the space of pedagogic recontextualisation by the official (state) recontextualising field, thus reducing the relative autonomy of schooling and assuring control – even when remote – by the state. Generic performance requires a pedagogic modality that prepares the learner for learning about 'work and life', that is, based on an identity projected towards the exterior, instead of an identity looking inward, and which conceives work and life in the short term (short-termism). In this sense, argues Bernstein, 'he/she who learns will never know enough and will never develop all the capacities required' (cited in Bonal, 2003, pp. 173-174).

The change from a model of competence to a model based on performance, argues Bernstein (1996), results from the fact that in the first model knowledge was linked to *habitus* (of the new middle class) and not necessarily to 'work and life'. In other words, in the first case, the market could only have an indirect ('invisible') impact on what and how one learns in the school.

In order to escape the pitfalls that the notion of competence appears to carry with it, we have analysed the debate on education policy in Portugal (see Magalhães & Stoer, 2002) by trying to avoid entering into the discussion on the more or less wide, or more or less restricted, character of the competencies to be produced by the schooling process. The price to be paid by entering into this discussion appears to us to be the limitation of the discussion to the dilemma of what count as 'good' competencies – which promote the integral development of the individual – and what count as 'bad' competencies – those which, based on the short term, only enable the individual to deal with situations, frequently in the context of the firm, relatively simple in nature and requiring low-level qualifications. As an alternative, we have tried to construct a heuristic *continuum* on which pedagogy and performance constitute polar opposites (see Figure 2). In placing on this continuum the different proposals for a mandate for the education system, the political nature of these proposals appears to be made more explicit. Given that one cannot be idealist with regard to the increasingly rapid selective effects of the labour market, and given that the knowledge transmitted in the education process should not aim solely at performance in a given work context, we do not oppose pedagogy to the demands of performance. If, indeed, it is true, as the most frantic neo-defenders of the meritocracy remind us, that pedagogy without performance is 'nothing', it also appears to be true that there is no performance without pedagogy, in the sense that even the most mechanically transmitted knowledge is always transmitted, meaning that it is mediated by a pedagogic process.

Thus, the assumption of the continuum not only permits one to map out the proposals of the different participants in the debate, it also suggests that, in the present context of a labour market structured by flexible capitalism, it is not compulsory that one remain confined to the radically pedagogical defence of education (as if pedagogical autonomy were independent with relation to the economy) nor to the reduction of education to performance (as if performance could exist without pedagogy).

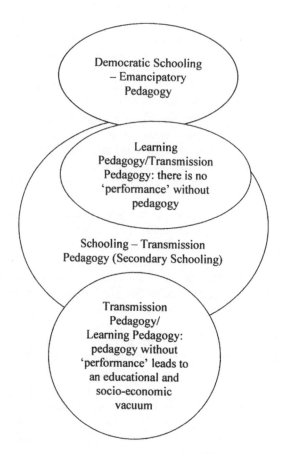

Figure 2.

Alternative paths may be found in the differences (eventually incommensurable) that structure the educational mandates and in their mutually critical analysis. This is even more the case given that the school has ceased to be perceived by families and students as 'the' source of education and, therefore, the production of competencies. Other organisations and institutions, both public and private, as well as the most diverse contexts, provide education/formation and, as such, are sources for qualification. Enterprises, associations, social, political and religious movements and even the family now present themselves explicitly as alternatives to public schooling. The school is no longer the central socialising institution and the legitimating educational narratives of the almost redeeming mission (the creation of the new human being, of the new individual-citizen) that the project of modernity attributed to it seem to live on only in some exceptional places and in the generous minds of some of the most stoical educators. The institution and the services that it provides are now increasingly integrated in the strategies which individuals are reflexively constructing.

In a totally pedagogised society, schooling appears to see much of its relevance confined to its function of accreditation, of distributing diplomas. As a consequence of growing social and individual reflexivity, it is the school that is placed on the trajectories which individuals construct for themselves, rather than the contrary, just as many modern pedagogues dreamed might happen. That is, the school provides the 'good' material with which people construct their lives. According to Beck (1992), the capacity for each one to choose, maintain and justify his or her own social relations and life options is not the same for all, it is

> as any sociologist of social classes knows, a learned capacity that
> depends on special social and family origins. The reflexive
> conduct of one's life, the planning of one's biography and social
> relations, produces a new inequality, an inequality in dealing with
> insecurity and reflexivity. (1992, p. 98)

In this context, schooling arises at the same time as a mechanism for escaping one's 'social and family origins' and as a consequence of these same origins. In the same way, we think that the appearance of a new mandate for European education is not a mere product of economic determination imposed by flexible capitalism. It coincides, rather, with cultural changes that involve phenomena that range from intimacy to the reinvention of traditions and the cult of the ephemeral to the reflexive assumption of new lifestyles. Effectively, the implications of the changes of a cultural nature lead us to an analysis not only of lifestyles but also of the rise of new forms of citizenship.

The Reconfiguration of the Modern Social Contract, New Forms of Citizenship and Education

The social contract, such as it was conceived by modernity, was based on a citizenship delimited by the nation state. This was the political architecture that guaranteed individuals and groups a series of rights and social and political protection in exchange for relinquishing identities developed at the local level. That is, loyalty was no longer based on ethnic, family, religious or other forms of traditional ties, but, rather, on that which was assumed to be common to a national culture, territory, language and so on.

The project of modernity with regard to the construction of nation states was based on the principle according to which national ties, or belonging, were as 'natural' as it was for an individual to have 'two ears and a nose' (Gellner, 1983, p. 6). Nevertheless, this 'naturalisation' of national belonging is mediated by identification processes. Modernity grounded the process of the formation of identities on three axes: 1. national identity – 'You are/I am a subject of this or that country'; 2. legal or juridical identity – 'You are/I am the holder of rights and duties'; 3. subjective identity – 'You are/I am an aware, rational and affective being'. The legitimacy of nationality-citizenship-individuality was assured by the metanarrative of modernity that localised the Self at the crossroads of its three founding axes: Reason, Humanity and the State. These three axes duplicated themselves, in turn, into mediating narratives such as science, philosophy, art, social institutions and the state (see Table I). Reason articulated the narratives of science, philosophy and art which, thus, emerge as the discursive mechanisms that, within the project of modernity, frame the development of subjectivity/individuality. In other words, modernity based its project of rationality on the fact that reason, in Cartesian fashion, was that which was best distributed throughout the world. This universality of the capacity to distinguish the real from the false made science an enterprise both of individuals as subjectivities and, even more so, of humanity. The expression of personal idiosyncrasies eventually finds more space for expression in the arts, although in the project of modernity – and it is not the objective of this work to carry this discussion further – there does not appear to be a paradigmatic contradiction between the romantic version and the eventually more rationalist Enlightenment version. History, with a capital H, developed itself as a process whose finality (in the sense of *telos*) appears as a stage on which the maximum self-consciousness of the individual as humanity, and as Reason itself, should occur in the realisation of the State. It is in Hegel that this identification (Humanity [individual/subjectivity] = Reason = State) appears to have attained both the maximum of consciousness possible and the best consciousness possible. Humanity and the individual, and this latter as subject/subjectivity, come together and realise themselves in the State, 'where liberty acquires its objectivity and lives in the fruition of itself' (Hegel, 1965, p. 11).[1]

Metanarrative of modernity	Mediating narratives	Identifiers
Reason	Science/Philosophy/Art	Consciousness
Humanity	Social Institutions	Individual
State	Nation State	Citizen

Table I.

It is in the figure of the citizen that the three identifiers – consciousness, individual and citizen – appear to intersect with most profundity, consistency and legitimacy. The universality of Reason is only realised by the organisation of Humanity in States that, in turn, give shape to individuals as citizens. Citizenship, then, is founded on a social contract as a social ontology, that is to say, the social contract constitutes the social body as *polis* and individuals as citizens.

> What man loses by the social contract is his natural liberty and an unlimited right to everything he tries to get and succeeds in getting; what he gains is civil liberty and the proprietorship of all he possesses. If we are to avoid mistake in weighing one against the other, we must clearly distinguish natural liberty, which is bounded only by the strength of the individual, from civil liberty, which is limited by the general will; and possession, which is merely the effect of force or the right of the first occupier, from property, which can be founded only on a positive title.
> (Rousseau, 1993, p. 196)

The nation states that developed during modernity found in this conception of the social contract the ultimate legitimisation of their tutelage over their subjects-citizens. Individuals gave up action on the basis of their 'inclinations' (Rousseau, 1993, p. 25) and gave up their most immediate senses of belonging (ethnic, local) and delivered themselves, as a founding act of citizenship, to the justice of the civil state; that is, they gave up their sovereignty in order to endorse the nation state. In compensation, individuals were guaranteed the maximum use of their capacities. These capacities are made up of each individual's talents, brought to fruition by the achievement obtained in the different contexts of state, community and market. Thus, the social value of individuals depends upon equality of opportunities in the exercise of their talents (concretised through schooling as both the instrument and the privileged place), upon the liberty to express entrepreneurial spirit in the market and upon fraternal participation in the community.

The citizenship at the heart of this process of legitimisation finds its concretisation in the model of representative democracy. The attribution of citizenship took place, in a first moment, above all at the formal level, due to the fact that the position of individuals in the world of work determined their inclusion in the social contract. At the beginning, this process was restricted to property owners, spreading later, after a century of political struggle around claims for the recognition of the importance of labour in capitalist development, to the working classes. In a second phase, representative democracy became, one might say, 'real', in the sense that those represented increased substantially to the extent that almost all those previously excluded were now visibly present, and, as such, represented. This consolidation of representative democracy did not take place in all western countries at the same time. The blacks resident in many states in the south of the United States saw their status as represented only achieved in the middle of the decade of the 1960s, and the women of some cantons in Switzerland only recently, in the 1970s, achieved the right to be represented.

Education in this model of representative democracy is, thus, attributed essentially to the School, conceived of as the socialising institution, par excellence, of individuals. The school is the place where their capacities both liberate themselves from the shackles of tradition and reinforce the values of the community, a community now identified with the Nation State. It is expected that the school, in addition to developing citizens, should also prepare workers apt for moving into the occupation structure. In this way, the school and the occupation structure work together, harmoniously, in the interests of society. This republican school (Touraine, 1997) attains its apogee in the post-war years as the embodiment of mass schooling.

The Reconfiguration of the Modern Social Contract

It is frequent to attribute the current questioning of the modern social contract to the end of the grand narratives, above all to the exhaustion of the metanarrative of modernity (Lyotard, 1986). In this perspective, all seems to happen as if the west had collapsed under the weight of questioning itself as a form of political, civilisational and cultural organisation. That is, the west is implicitly a form of state and a set of values and norms that were presented as a model to follow and as an aim of development. This model, above all from the middle of the twentieth century, was challenged, both internally and externally, by intellectuals and by political action that denounced it as phallocentric, ethnocentric and colonialist. This denunciation of the west as a model of development had as protagonists of political action those who were refused recognition as subjects of their own action and choices: women, other cultures, other societies (for example, indigenous peoples) and lifestyles that managed to escape from the normativity of modern societies. The western world, in the second half of the twentieth century, exhibited clear signs of disbelief in itself. This disbelief in itself does not, however, appear to explain everything, nor, perhaps, very much. First, because never, as today, has the west (the United States, the European Union and other political and economic associations which have taken on modernity as their sociocultural model) been so singular in economic, political and cultural terms and, second, because the deconstruction of the west as a model has arisen not only as a result of its own auto-critique, but also as a result of that which we termed in another work 'the rebellions of differences' (Stoer & Magalhães, 2001).

With regard to the first aspect, diverse works and research on forms of hegemonic globalisation explain sufficiently the so-called end of history (Fukuyama, 1992) as a mystification of the perpetuation of the hegemony of the economic, cultural and political forms invented by the west (e.g. Santos, 1995a; Dale, 2002). This mystification is embodied in the identification of globalisation with capitalism as a form of economic organisation and with representative democracy as a form of political organisation.

With regard to the second aspect, the assumption of voice and of action by those who during the course of modernity and of the development of nation states saw their 'sovereignty' handed over to the civil mechanisms of these latter appears to mark an important reconfiguration of the social contract and, even more logically, of citizenship itself. In this case, it is the research on counter-hegemonic forms of globalisation that has offered explication for the emergence of an active posture on the part of differences in a world where one is 'condemned' to live among them.

Effectively, individuals and groups, whose difference was, during this period, delimited, described and activated on the basis of a citizenship founded on the nation state, have increasingly assumed difference, with the assumption of their own voice. And they have done so going beyond the right of citizenship designed by modernity and beyond its morale and its politics of tolerance (who is in a position to tolerate whom?). These differences, based on ethnic group or on race, others on sexual orientation or on lifestyle, even others on religious preference, to mention only these, burst forth from the interior of western societies themselves. They are not a 'threat' that the exterior has imposed; they arise, rather, from within as a new claim to sovereignty: the right to manage individual and collective life in accordance with their own frames of reference, the right to educate their children according to their own convictions, to treat their sick according to their own understandings of medical practice, and so on. The conditions of realisation of these new sovereignty claims will be considered below.

When we speak of the rebellions of differences, we mean by this that differences have rebelled not only against the cultural and political, but also the epistemological, yoke of western modernity. They have refused to be behave as the passive 'objects' of knowledge, such as the 'primitive' that anthropology took as its object of study, such as those 'without history', or 'without state' (or 'without land') that were to be introduced into the cycle of development, such as the mythical-magical thinker that was to receive the intellectual benefits of scientific thinking, or the thinker trapped in the concrete and to whom psychology would open the riches of abstract thinking. All at the same time that they have denounced the ideal normative of what is socially and epistemologically legtimised as 'normal' (for example, the revolt of women, of sexual minorities, etc.).

Differences have taken on agency and ceased to passively accept discourses made *about* them, even the most generous. Essential to their projects has become their assumption of the role of enunciating subjects, that is, subjects of discourses *on* themselves. And, furthermore, these discourses (based on differences and not about differences) cannot be grouped under a single coherent narrative, in which all 'others' can recognise and affirm themselves as a unity. What presently characterises differences and their social relations is precisely their heterogeneity, their undeniable resistance to any process of epistemological or cultural domestication. It is for this reason that one stresses the *rebellions* of differences and not simply their rebellion, as if their differences could be united under one banner. Some postmodern positions even appear to suggest that, given the host of centres (civilisational, ethical, aesthetical, political), what is at stake can only be thought of in terms of differences. In other words, the relational character of differences is defined not in relation to a common meaning, but in relation to alterity itself. Western culture, then, surges as difference itself and not as the standard on the basis of which alterity itself is defined.

Effectively, the reconfiguration of individual and collective citizenship appears to ineluctably escape the nation state, whether seen as a territory, as a narrative construing identity, or as a source of social and physical protection. With regard to the latter, the question is to know how the nation state can deal with the promotion of a 'quality' that derives from forms of economic organisation that, paradoxically, constitute a risk for the well-being of individuals, a context in which, as Beck (1992) argues, individualisation predominates over individuation.

Sovereignty, as a power exercised by delegation to the state and in the name of individuals-citizens, finds itself mitigated in two principle ways. On the one hand, supranational bodies weaken the sovereignty of states which voluntarily cede such sovereignty in exchange for economic well-being and political stability. Such a process, in its turn, weakens the feeling of belonging of individuals to national spaces. Castells, for example, in a recent work, declares:

> So take the two countries I know best, France and Spain: 80 per
> cent of the legislation in France and Spain has to go for approval
> to the European Union. In that sense they are not sovereign states.
> (Castells, 2001, p. 121)

On the other hand, the locale, alternative modes of life and the ethnic factor appear to be emerging as important forces in the structuring of citizenship. Citizenship, thus, becomes thought of on the basis of difference, that is, on the basis of that which distinguishes and not on the basis of that which promotes common characteristics.

Above all, this last aspect leads to a re-signification of active citizenship, as if individuals and groups made new claims for a return to the individual and collective sovereignty that was renounced in exchange for the modern social contract. This transformation, as referred to above, is notable in comparison with the forms of citizenship resulting from that same contract and which were founded precisely on that which was considered common heritage. The attribution of citizenship, by the modern social contract, was a founding act of the legitimisation of the state apparatus as guardian of the nation. This latter was assumed to be a community based on language, territory and/or religion. Such an 'imaginary community' (Anderson, 1983) gave license to the state to exercise legitimate power, in the name of that which was common to all, by attributing rights and duties. In order to be a citizen, it was enough to be born in the fold of this community.[2] The implications of this new multicultural form of citizenship are only now beginning to show themselves and instigate an urgent reconceptualisation of the concept of citizenship, of the rights and duties of social actors.

The social contract of modernity that expressed the exchange referred to above (of local belonging for national loyalty) appears, indeed, to be undergoing a process of reconfiguration. This process is taking place at the site of tension between factors of an economic nature (such as the restructuration of the labour market), of a cultural nature (such as the confrontation between ways of life, for example of ethnic origin, and those based on the normative universality of the nation state) and of a political nature (such as, for example, the effects on national sovereignty of European construction).

In the European context, the emergent social contract finds itself delimited by three dimensions, which are also demands: employability (which implies having the qualities of being both flexible and 'trainable'), local identity (which implies being able to express differences) and European citizenship (which involves the construction of a new 'imagined community'). All seems to take place as if citizenship were determined and, at the same time, actively articulated with the recomposition of the global and European economic fabric and with the repositioning of the nation state in this context.

The emergent forms of citizenship are characterised by a strong touch of social reflexivity (Giddens, 1992), that is to say, citizenship is already not only of the order of that which is attributed. It does not result immediately from belonging to a national social category. It is emerging, rather, as that which is demanded. The sovereignty which individuals and groups ceded to the modern social contract is now being reclaimed, to the tune of 'I want my sovereignty back'. In other words, individuals and groups want to decide themselves, as we mentioned above, with regard to how they live, how they educate, how they care for themselves, how they reproduce, and so on.

At its heart, this demand is based on an appeal for economic redistribution that is combined, in variable arrangements, with the recognition of difference. In this sense, what is at stake is the possible uprising of a form of 'demanded' citizenship by individuals and groups against social and political institutions and their respective rationalities. Still, this form of emergent citizenship, founded mainly on cultural factors, has as its presupposition the satisfaction of the realisation of social citizenship (of the sort that T.H. Marshall theorised). We are not arguing here that the recognition of differences thus expressed is dependent on reaching a 'stage' where economic equality has been assured, but rather that, in the present context, the claim for the cultural recognition of difference is at the same time a demand for economic equality.

Marshall's social citizenship (1950) developed on the basis of a form of economic redistribution normally identified with the welfare state. Social justice depended on a proactive state with regard to the redistribution of income based on the principle of equality of opportunity, one of the pillars of representative democracy. The problem which arises today with the restructuration of the labour market is knowing to what extent it is true that inclusion in the labour contract (a basic condition of the modern social contract) signifies, in fact, access to citizenship. In other words, as Bauman (1992) has emphasised, the liberation of capital from labour, which has resulted, at least in part, from a process of re/deterritorialisation where the very territory of capital is deterritorialised (Santos [2001] gives the example of the New York Stock Exchange), appears to imply on the part of the state a reduction of its preoccupation with the carrying out of redistributive policies and, therefore, an undermining of the principle of equal opportunity which, as we mentioned earlier, is at the base of such policies.

The implications of this process can also be seen in the evolution of 'possessive individualism' towards 'an individualism of dispossession' (Santos, 1995b). As already mentioned above, in the modern social contract 'man, the individual, is seen as absolute natural proprietor of his own capacities, owing nothing to society for them. Man's essence is freedom to use his capacities in search of satisfactions' (McPherson, 1973, p. 199). McPherson argues further that

> (t)his freedom is limited properly only by some principle of utility
> or utilitarian natural law which forbids harming others. Freedom
> therefore is restricted to, and comes to be identified with,
> domination over things, not domination over men. The clearest
> form of domination over things is the relation of ownership or
> possession. Freedom is therefore possession. Everyone is free, for
> everyone possesses at least his own capacities. (1973, p. 199)

However, the erosion of the principle of equality of opportunity by the restructuration and re/deterritorialisation of the labour market produces a situation in which, according to Santos,

> The metamorphosis of a system of inequality into a system of
> exclusion takes place both at the national level and at the global
> level ... . At the national level, exclusion is even more serious due
> to the fact that no substitute for the integration of individuals
> through work has been invented ... . The result is an individualism
> of dispossession, an inexorable form of destitution and loneliness.
> The erosion of institutional protection, being a cause, is also an
> effect of a new social Darwinism. Individuals are convoked to be
> responsible for their own destiny, for their own survival and their
> own safety, individual managers of their own social trajectories
> without dependencies and without pre-determined plans. ... The
> individual is called upon to be master of its own destiny when all
> appears to be outside of its own control. Holding the individual
> accountable is a form of alienation; an alienation which, contrary
> to Marxist alienation, does not result from the exploration of

waged work, but from the very absence of such work.[3] (1995b, pp. 27-28)

In sum, one is referring to the individual dispossessed of its capacities of possession, because it finds itself in a territory undergoing decontractualisation, a process taking place both in the economic sphere and in the cultural sphere. In the economic sphere, the process of re/deterritorialisation, in its creation of new territories where labour is not present, undermines the social contract by way of the restructuring of the labour market (Magalhães & Stoer, 2002). In the cultural sphere, it is not the modern social contract that new citizenship claims desire, but rather a new contract in which difference, in the name of people themselves, is inscribed. In order to defend itself against this new situation, the individual is obliged to permanently retrain/re-educate itself for the work situation, acquiring the competencies necessary for a volatile labour market (above all at the level of what Castells terms 'generic labour' – cited in Magalhães & Stoer, 2002), based on 'short-termism', and knowing, as Bernstein has pointed out, he/she who learns will never know enough and will never develop all the necessary capacities and competencies (Bernstein, cited in Bonal, 2003, p. 173). Thus, the individual becomes vulnerable to a form of social and cognitive injustice that conditions its very status as citizen.

The main conclusion that may be drawn from this analysis is the need to rethink redistribution policies not only on the basis of 'new' territories (local, regional and supranational), but also on the basis of deterritorialised territories. That is, one can sustain on the basis of our argument that social citizenship requires the political regulation of all territories, without exception, Even deterritorialised territories (those in which, for example, as mentioned above, financial capital flows) are politically coloured and, as such, require regulation. Indeed, the fact that social citizenship requires the political regulation of territories suggests that one can also think of regulation *as* emancipation (and not just as its polar opposite). In this sense, the work of Mary Kaldor (1995) is interesting for it proposes a model of European construction based on themes (such as human rights, security, environment, economic and financial management) and not on territory. Habermas as well, in his appeal for the elaboration of a European Constitution, defends the need to 'corral markets' and to 'confront the tendency of capitalism to produce environmental chaos' (Habermas, 1999, 2001). The proposal of Sousa Santos, for a bottom-up form of globalisation on the basis of 'cosmopolitanism' (as an alternative to top-down 'globalised localisms') and for 'common heritage of humanity' (as an alternative to 'localised globalisms'), also goes in this direction (1995a). Finally, Giorgio Agamben's (1993) concept of a 'relation of reciprocal extraterritoriality' suggests the need to conceive European construction not as an 'impossible Europe of Nations', but as a European space that, rather than coinciding with national homogeneous territories, or with their topographical sum, points to the 'rediscovery of the ancient vocation of European cities' (1993, pp. 24-25).

'Difference is Us'

In fact, there no longer exists an institutional place sufficiently legitimated that can enunciate what differences exist and what their limits are. New forms of citizenship thus arise as differences by themselves whose legitimacy resides in themselves ('as different, we have the right to be equal'). The question lies in knowing what the limit of this coincidence of citizenship with difference is. For example, to what extent can one justify that the state demand observance of compulsory education by female gypsy children at the same time that it claims to recognise the cultural practices of an ethnic group? Or to what extent is it socially legitimate that what has been recognised as a handicap (for example, deafness) is reconfigured as difference and, therefore, as identity (a woman, deaf and lesbian, determined to have a deaf son by way of artificial insemination, states: 'for me, deafness is an identity and not a handicap' *Público*, 14 April 2002)?

The modern social contract legitimated itself – it is worth stressing once again – on the basis of community belonging and on the imagination of that which commonly united individuals and groups at the national level. In a first phase, the national saga not only gave centrality to the state as provider and regulator, it also attributed to the nation and nationals a legitimate ethnocentrism: citizens of the nation state, on the basis of their undeniable ontology, would determine who were to be the 'other' – both the external 'other' and the internal 'other'. For example, the external 'other' for the Portuguese were the Spanish, the French and the English, both as original enemies and as inevitable allies. The internal 'other' was, for example, the gypsy, who, since the sixteenth century, has punctuated national territory, and the peoples 'discovered' by Portuguese explorers, to mention only these. The discourse of economic modernisation has found, perhaps, even other 'others' (such as so-called 'traditional man') whose cultural difference made them an obstacle to the internal 'civilisation' process. Still, it is always by way of the nation state, or on the basis of its motives, that the 'other', 'them', are delimited.

The metanarrative of modernity, in turn, based on Reason, Humanity and History, founded, as we mentioned above, the national narrative itself. As a consequence, the 'other' was also delimited by the dominant forms of rationality, of social organisation and of representation of the past and future, as far as these were developed by western societies. This grand narrative of modernity legitimated, on the one hand, the action of nation states in all their centrality, and, on the other, the designation and classification of the 'other'. Presently, even the discourses and practices most concerned with the recognition of difference, with the 'other', are frequently victims of the modern matrix from which they part. These discourses continue to be the *locus* for determining difference, for deciding what difference is acceptable (tolerated) and which difference is real difference and who may express it. With whom should one talk? Is Le Pen as a partner in dialogue less valid than

Malcolm X? Is it possible to distinguish between the cultural practice of female circumcision and the decision to have a deaf child?

With the emergence of a form of 'demanded', or 'claimed', citizenship, and given this form has its origins, in the last analysis, in the incomplete character of the nation-state citizenship attributed through the modern social contract, the *locus* of determination of who is different has pluralised itself in such a way that there is apparently no longer any way of resolving this question at the nation-state level. The incompleteness of attributed citizenship derives from the fact that it is intrinsically incapable of translating recognition into participative citizenship. Gypsies, for example, although recognised as citizens in a universal sense, see their participation in society limited by ignorance of their difference as gypsies. In becoming pluralised, the voices of individuals and groups oblige difference to be seen and heard in the first person, both singular and plural: 'difference is me'; 'difference is us'.

New Forms of Citizenship and the Challenge of the Political Management of Education Systems

The recomposition of the modern social contract and the new emergent forms of citizenship result in subtle dilemmas for all those involved, at diverse levels, in the political management of education, above all of public education. This is especially true for those who see in education a privileged form of emancipation, that is, for those who see in education systems means for contributing, more or less, to the autonomy of individuals and groups. The dilemma consists in the fact that the very project of public education implies a proposal of 'Us' for 'Them', and all projects start off, in one way or another, from the optimistic assumption that their premises are just and their aims desirable. When 'They' start to resist participation in the project, not because of pedagogical difficulties, but due to option ('we don't want "your" education'), politicians and educators – especially the most generous – feel increasingly crushed by the weight of this resistance which is, at heart, a refusal.

Look, for example, at the relationship between gypsy communities and the school in Portugal. As is known, there has been an increase in recent years in the number of gypsy children going to school. Many analysts refer to this increment as related to the contract at the basis of the Minimum Income Programme, that is, this income is only given to families that assure that their children go to school. The aim (and the benevolence) of this policy is that, in this way, it is possible to integrate, via schooling, gypsy children into modern society, making them, in turn, potentially more employable on the labour market. Integration into the labour market by way of schooling constitutes, as Lenhardt & Offe have emphasised (1984), the first step in the transition from 'passive proletarianisation' (made up of undermining previous conditions of the use of labour power) to 'active proletarianisation' (made up of a first phase of contractualisation which includes central components such as motivation for waged work and the acquisition of the competencies necessary for carrying out such work). However, what happens is that some voices from the gypsy community are heard declaring that the exchange 'schooling for Minimum Wage' is not only a form of cultural bribery but that it is also the imposition of a form (and ethic) of work that clearly challenges the gypsy community's right to educate its children according to its way of life and to the norms, values and precepts (including prohibiting girls from attending school with the start of menstruation) which make it up. The experience of 'home schooling' in the United States (see Apple, 2000) shows that there exists an important number of individuals and groups, in the USA, that prefer to educate their children at home rather than risk the eventually negative effects that schooling may have on their beliefs, values and local ways of living. It is also true that this home-schooling movement is at times related to, and in many ways symbolises, frustration not with that which exists in the school, but, rather, with that which (they would say) does not exist: such as discipline, hard work, selective assessment, promotion of competition, and so on.

All takes place, then, as if the 'other' no longer is able to tolerate even the tolerance and generosity of which he or she is the object, precisely because the 'other' refuses to be an object and aims at claiming its own voice as subject of itself. There is in this attitude an evident link with the revolt of social groups which in the past brought into question the development of the capitalist economy and which demanded redistribution policies based upon, above all (as mentioned earlier in this text), the principle of equality of opportunity. And, as we have seen, the response (even today not only incomplete but newly threatened by an individualist and unpredictable casino capitalism) was developed through the attribution, by the nation state, of a citizenship that was above all social. But what we wish to underline here is the increasing demand for a policy based on the recognition of difference, on the claim for a form of justice that is not only socio-economic but also cultural. This demand, elaborated on the basis of identity(ies), places once again on the agenda a local demand that, in refusing to be identified with the territory of the nation state, sees itself as identifiable with multiple locales which extend across the world.

Caught up between the generous and apparently de-centred concern with regard to the 'other' and the refusal of the 'other' to be the object of this preoccupation, politicians and educators appear to be disarmed and disoriented. Disarmed, because the system of ideas that gave substance to their intentions and their practices appears to crumble under its own weight; disoriented, because, at ground level, they are confronted by an education system full of 'others' apparently deaf and indifferent to the generosity of the aims of education.

The possible solutions for this situation appear to be related to the following three considerations. In the first place, the new forms of 'demanded', or 'claimed', citizenship can only be sustained with the consolidation of modern, or attributed, citizenship, particularly true in semi-peripheral countries like Portugal. That is, the conditions of realisation of the claims of sovereignty inherent to 'demanded' citizenship are dependent upon, and simultaneous with, redistribution policies (for the reason that there is no quality without the question of quantity being minimally resolved). In the second place, the 'other', itself, has to recognise 'our' difference: in this conflict (dialogue), *difference is also us*. We all go to the bazaar (a place that is simultaneously public and private, made up of commercial transactions, activities of leisure and pleasure, filled with colours, smells and unsubmissive noises [Stoer & Magalhães, 2005]), for the most varied of reasons, as different persons, and it is as such that we meet each other there. 'Attributed citizenship' cannot hide this fact, which it tends to do when the question of quantity is not minimally resolved, that is, when there are no effective redistribution policies. In the third place, schooling has to be placed on the trajectories of social and cultural actors, and not the contrary. This means that the school itself also has to become a 'demand', a 'claim', and cease to be simply 'attributed'. In other words, the school as meritocracy constitutes perhaps the most important redistribution policy of democratic societies. But, as a redistribution policy, it appears to have, already for some time, become entangled in its own mesh and run out of steam. Its renovation depends upon its capacity to de-centre, to take on development logics that are not restricted to the nation-state level. To assume these other logics is, to all intents and purposes, the re-foundation of the school, and it is here that the appeal for new forms of citizenship can constitute one of its main axes.

It is paradoxical that at a time when so much emphasis is placed on inclusion, inclusive schooling and the so-called 'inclusive society', social exclusion appears to be more the norm than social inclusion. Unless one takes as a starting point the idea that the market is that which defines inclusion, having replaced in this function the nation state and its paradigm of social protection under the banner of the welfare state or *Etat Providence*. In this sense, inclusion can be seen as one of the discourses that enable the market to deterritorialise social relations at the nation-state level and then reterritorialise them at the supranational level. Thus, instead of regulating practices of exclusion, a global space is created where all persons, regardless of their differences, are *in*cluded as consumers. The paradox here, of course, is that inclusion is promoted on the basis of the eradication of differences rather than being defined on the basis of difference itself. This process is, once again, similar to the one carried out by the nation state as it developed over the eighteenth, nineteenth and twentieth centuries, for, here too, it was that which peoples shared in common (territory, language, religion, ethnic group, history) that became the determining factor for the definition of those included in the nation space and thus apt for citizenship.

Of course, the definition of inclusion based on the exclusion – or attempted eradication – of difference means almost inevitably new forms of exclusion, economic, social, political, cultural. Thus the starting point for an alternative conception of inclusion is reflection upon difference(s) and, on the basis of the way those differences are present in (European) societies, on social exclusion itself.

Notes

[1] It was perhaps Nietzsche who, for the first time and in a radical way, questioned modernity through a critique of Reason based on values (Nietzsche, 1976), that is, on the basis of a process (moral) external to reason. This made it possible to de-centre Reason and to unveil it as a non-universal discourse, masked by abstraction and universality.

[2] We recognise that not all 'communities' are of the same type. Morris (1994) distinguishes, for example, between 'communities of assent' (a kind of voluntary association) and 'communities of descent' (based on, for example, matrilineal descent).

[3] Robert Castel (1997) has referred to this phenomenon as the 'new social question' in which the excluded are no longer those exploited but indispensable; they are, rather, simply in excess. In this sense, being exploited becomes almost a privilege.

Bibliography

Agamben, Giorgio (1993) Beyond Human Rights, in Giorgio Agamben, *Means without End: notes on politics*. Minneapolis: University of Minnesota Press.

Anderson, Benedict (1983) *Imagined Communities*. London: Verso.

Apple, Michael (1998) Educating the 'Right' Way: schools and the conservative alliance. Paper delivered at the University of Minho, February.

Apple, Michael (2000) Away with All Teachers: the cultural politics of home schooling, *International Studies in Sociology of Education*, 10(1), 61-80. http://dx.doi.org/10.1080/09620210000200049

Ball, Stephen J. (1990) *Politics and Policy Making in Education*. London: Routledge.

Barnett, Ronald (1997) *Higher Education: a critical business*. London: Open University Press.

Bauman, Zygmunt (1992) *Intimations of Postmodernity*. London: Routledge.

Beck, Ulrich (1992) *Risk Society*. London: Sage.

Beck, Ulrich, Giddens, Anthony & Lash, Scott (1994) *Reflexive Modernization. Politics, Tradition and Aesthetics in the Modern Social Order*. Oxford: Blackwell.

Bernstein, Basil (1978) *Class, Codes and Control*, vol. 3. London: Routledge & Kegan Paul.

Bernstein, Basil (1990) *The Structuring of Pedagogical Discourse*. London: Routledge. *critique*. London:Taylor & Francis.

Bernstein, Basil (2000) Das pedagogias aos conhecimentos, *Educação, Sociedade & Culturas*, 15, 9-17.

Bourdieu, Pierre (1986) *Distinction: a social critique of the judgement of taste.* London: Routledge & Kegan Paul.

Braverman, Harry (1974) *Labor and Monopoly Capital.* New York: Monthly Review Press.

Castel, Robert (1997) *As Metamorfoses da Questão Social.* Rio de Janeiro: Editorial Vozes.

Castells, Manuel (1998) *End of Millennium (The Information Age: economy, society and culture, Volume III).* Oxford: Blackwell.

Castells, Manuel (2001) Growing Identity Organically, in Johan Muller, Nico Cloete & Shireen Badat, *Challenges of Globalisation.* Cape Town: Maskew Miller Longman.

Castoriadis, Cornelius (1998) De l'Autonomie en Politique: l'individu privatisé, *Le Monde Diplomatique*, February, p. 23.
http://www.monde-diplomatique.fr/md/1998/02/Castoriadis/10046.html

Cortesão, Luiza, Magalhães, António M. & Stoer, Stephen R. (2001) Mapeando decisões no campo da educação no âmbito do processo da realização das políticas educativas, *Educação, Sociedade & Culturas*, 15, 45-58.

Cresson, Edith (1996) *Livro Branco: Ensinar e aprender. Rumo à sociedade cognitiva.* Luxemburg: Serviço das Publicações Oficiais das Comunidades Europeias.

Dale, Roger (1989) The Thatcherite Project in Education, *Critical Social Policy*, 9(3), 4-19. http://dx.doi.org/10.1177/026101838900902701

Dale, Roger (2001) The Work of International Organisations: making national education systems part of the solution rather than part of the problem, paper presented to international seminar of teacher trade unionism, Nicosia, October.

Dale, Roger (2002) Globalização e Educação: Demonstrando a Existência de uma 'Cultura Educacional Mundial Comum' ou Localizando uma 'Agenda Globalmente Estruturada para a Educação'? *Educação, Sociedade & Culturas*, 16, 133-169.

Durkheim, Émile (1978) *Educação e Sociedade.* Oporto: Rés Editora.

Fernandes, José Manuel (2001) O mérito, a escola e a exclusão social: A minha réplica, *Público*, 6 January.

Fukuyama, Francis (1992) *O Fim da História e o Último Homem.* Lisbon: Gradiva.

Gellner, E. (1983) *Nations and Nationalism.* Oxford: Blackwell.

Giddens, Anthony (1990) *The Consequences of Modernity.* Cambridge: Polity Press.

Giddens, Anthony (1992) *As Consequências da Modernidade.* Oeiras: Celta Editores.

Giddens, Anthony (1994) *Beyond Left and Right: the future of radical politics.* Oxford: Blackwell.

Habermas, Jurgen (1999) The European Nation-state and Pressures of Globalization, *New Left Review*, 235, 46-59.

Habermas, Jurgen (2001) Why Europe Needs a Constitution, *New Left Review* (Second Series), 11, 5-26.

Hegel, G.W.F. (1965) *Introduction aux Leçons sur la Philosophie de l'Histoire.* Paris: NRF.

Kaldor, Mary (1995) European Institutions, Nation-states and Nationalism, in Daniele Archibugi & David Held, *Cosmopolitan Democracy*, 68-95. Cambridge: Polity Press.

Lenhardt, Gero & Offe, Claus (1984) Teoria do Estado e Política Social, in Claus Offe (Ed.) *Problemas Estruturais do Estado Capitalista*, 10-53. Rio de Janeiro: Tempo Brazileiro.

Lyotard, Jean François (1986) *A Condição Pós-Moderna*. Lisbon: Gradiva.

Magalhães, António M. & Stoer, Stephen R. (2002) *A Escola para Todos e a Excelência Académica*. Porto: Profedições.

Marshall, T.H. (1950) *Citizenship and Social Class and Other Essays*. Cambridge: Cambridge University Press.

McPherson, C.B. (1973) *Democratic Theory*. London: Oxford University Press.

Mónica, M. Filomena (1997) *Os Filhos de Rousseau*. Lisbon: Relógio D'Água Editores.

Morris, Paul (1994) Community Beyond Tradition, in Paul Heelas, Scott Lash & Paul Morris (Eds) *Detraditionalization. Critical Reflections on Authority and Identity*, 223-249. Oxford: Blackwell

Nietzsche, Friedrich (1976) *A Genealogia da Moral*. Lisboa: Guimarães Editores.

Rousseau, Jean-Jacques (1993) *The Social Contract and Discourses*. London: Everyman.

Santos, Boaventura Sousa (1995a) *Toward a New Common Sense. Law, Science and Politics in the Paradigmatic Transition*. New York: Routledge.

Santos, Boaventura Sousa (1995b) A construção multicultural da igualdade e da diferença, paper delivered at the VII Congresso Brasileiro de Sociologia, Instituto de Filosofia e Ciências Sociais of the Universidade Federal do Rio de Janeiro, 4-6 September.

Santos, Boaventura Sousa (2001) A territorialização/desterritorialização da exclusão/inclusão social no processo de construção de uma cultura emancipatória, paper delivered at the Seminar 'Estudos Territoriais de Desigualdades Sociais', 16-17 May, Pontifícia Universidade Católica, São Paulo.

Stoer, Stephen R. & Araújo, Helena Costa (2000) *Escola e Aprendizagem para o Trabalho num País da (Semi)periferia Europeia*, 2nd edn. Lisbon: Instituto de Inovação Educacional.

Stoer, Stephen R. & Magalhães, António M. (2001) A Incomensurabilidade da Diferença e o Anti-anti-etnocentrismo, in David Rodrigues (Ed.) *Educação e Diferença*. Oporto: Porto Editora.

Stoer, Stephen R. & Magalhães, António M. (2005) *A Diferença Somos Nós: a Gestão da Mudança Social e as Políticas Educativas e Sociais*. Porto: Edições Afrontamento.

Thompson, Paul (1989) *The Nature of Work: an introduction to debates on the labour process*. London: Macmillan.

Touraine, Alain (1997) *Pourrons-Nous Vivre Ensemble? Egaux et différents*. Paris: Fayard.

Notes on Contributors

Xavier Bonal is Associate Professor in Sociology at the Autonomous University of Barcelona, Spain, and co-director of the Social Policy Research Group (*Seminari d'Anàlisi de Polítiques Socials*, SAPS) at the Department of Sociology of the same institution. He has widely published in national and international journals and is author of several books on sociology of education, education policy and globalisation, education and development. He has worked as consultant for international organisations like UNESCO, UNICEF the European Commmission, and the Council of Europe. Since 2006 he has been Deputy Ombudsman for Children's Rights in the Office of the Catalan Ombudsman. *Contact*: xavier.bonal@sindic.cat

Pepka Boyadjieva is Professor at the Institute of Sociology at the Bulgarian Academy of Sciences, and part of the Fulbright New Century Scholars program. She is Chair of the Scientific Council of the Institute of Sociology and Secretary of the Central Certification Committee in Sociology, Anthropology and Cultural Studies, and also Academic Associate at the Centre for Advanced Studies in Sofia, member of the Editorial Board of the journal *Sociological Problems* and Vice-President of the Bulgarian Sociological Association. *Contact*: pepka@sociology.bas.bg

Jacky Brine is Professor of EU Education Policy at the University of the West of England, Bristol, United Kingdom. Her research interests are in the area of lifelong learning, particularly the policies of the European Union in which the European Commission has a legal competency to act: lifelong learning, vocational training, youth transitions (14-19), adult education and training, and higher education. Her analyses focus on constructions and trajectories of policies, on aspects of inter/national governance and on the classed, gendered and 'racialised' effects on learners and practitioners. *Contact*: jacky.brine@uwe.ac.uk

Roger Dale is Professor in the Centre for Globalisation, Education and Societies at the University of Bristol, United Kingdom. Prior to that, he was Professor of Education at the University of Auckland, New Zealand. He is currently Scientific Coordinator of the EU's Network of Experts in Social Science and Education (NESSE). He was the Academic Coordinator of GENIE in 2002, and is co-editor and co-founder (with Susan Robertson) of the journal *Globalisation, Societies and Education*. *Contact*: r.dale@bristol.ac.uk

Janet Enever is a Senior Lecturer at London Metropolitan University where she is Project Director of a three year European Commission-funded research study, Early Language Learning in Europe (ELLiE). She is also course leader for the MA Primary ELT: Policy & Practice. Her main research and consultancy interests are primary language policy and practice and the impact of globalisation on language provision.
Contact: j.enever@londonmet.ac.uk

Kathleen Lynch is Professor of Equality Studies at University College, Dublin, Ireland, where she holds a Senior Lectureship in Education. She was founder of the UCD Equality Studies Centre (established in 1990) and of the UCD School of Social Justice (2005). She is lead scientist for the Egalitarian World Initiative Marie Curie Transfer of Knowledge Award (2006-2010) for a project entitled Creating and Egalitarian and Socially Inclusive Europe (ESIE). Her book *Affective Equality: Who cares? Studies in Gender, Care and Justice* will be published by Palgrave in 2009. *Contact*: kathleen.lynch@ucd.ie

António M. Magalhães is Associate Professor at the University of Porto, Portugal, and a senior researcher at CIPES (Centre for Research in Higher Education Policies). He has published articles in *Higher Education Policy*, *European Journal of Education*, and *Globalisation, Societies & Education*, *Educação Sociedade & Culturas* among other journals. He has also published some books and chapters with Peter Lang, Routledge/Taylor&Francis, *Fundação Calouste Gulbenkian* and *Edições Afrontamento*, among others publishing houses. *Contact*: antonio@fpce.up.pt

Michael A. Peters has been Professor in Educational Policy Studies at theUniversity of Illinois at Urbana-Champaign, USA, since 2005, having previously held professorial positions at the Universities of Auckland and Glasgow. His main research interests are in educational philosophy, theory and policy studies with a focus on the significance of both contemporary philosophers (Nietzsche, Wittgenstein, Heidegger) and the movements of poststructralism, critical theory and analytic philosophy to the framing of educational theory and practice. He is also interested in philosophical and political economy questions of knowledge production and consumption and constructions of the 'knowledge economy'. His major current projects include work on distributed knowledge, learning and publishing systems, and 'open education'. *Contact*: mpet001@illinois.edu

Xavier Rambla has been Associate Professor in the Department of Sociology, Universitat Autònoma de Barcelona, Spain, since 2001, having been a lecturer at Universitat de Vic, Spain, from 1995 until then. Sociology of education and the analysis of social inequalities are his main research specialties, which he has developed by means of several projects funded by the Institute of Women (Gov. Spain), the Ministry of Science (Gov. Spain), the DG Education (European Commission) and other institutions. For the last years he has co-ordinated the Seminar for the Analysis of Social Policies (UAB: sapsuab.wordpress.com), and is a member of the Interdisciplinary Group on Education Policy (UAB-UB: www.ub.edu/gipe). *Contact*: xavier.rambla@uab.cat

Palle Rasmussen is Professor of Education and Learning Research, Department of Education, Learning and Philosophy, Aalborg University, Denmark. His research interests include educational policy (in national as well as international contexts), sociological theories of education and learning, vocational and professional education, adult education. He recently completed a major research project on adult education in the Danish peripheries. He is a member of the EU expert network in the social sciences of education, NESSE. *Contact*: palleras@learning.aau.dk

Susan Robertson is Professor of Sociology of Education, Graduate School of Education, University of Bristol, United Kingdom. Susan's recent areas of research and writing is on globalisation, regionalisation, state policy and the politics of knowledge and development. She coordinated the GENIE network 2002-2004, and is founding co-editor of the journal *Globalisation, Societies and Education*. *Contact*: s.l.robertson@bristol.ac.uk

M'hammed Sabour is a Professor of Sociology (Knowledge and Culture) at the University of Joensuu, Finland. He has authored and edited many books and articles. His main fields of research are higher education, intellectuals, cultural globalisation, brain mobility and European multiculturalism. He is the managing editor of the *International Journal of Contemporary Sociology*. mhammed. *Contact*: sabour@joensuu.fi

Stephen R. Stoer, who died in 2005, was Professor of Education at the University of Porto, Portugal, and senior researcher at CIIE (Centre for Research and Intervention in Education). He was a leading figure in the field of sociology of education and education policy analysis in Portugal and one of the founders of the CIIE (he was its first director). He co-ordinated numerous research projects in education and he was widely published in Portugal, Spain, Italy, United Kingdom, Ireland, Finland, Canada, France, Brazil, New Zealand, and United States.

Kirk P. H. Sullivan is a Reader in Phonetics and Educational Work at Umeå University, Sweden. He has studied or worked in England, Wales, Germany, New Zealand and Sweden. He is currently director of postgraduate studies in the Department of Language Studies and his research interests include higher education, language teaching and learning, and literacy. *Contact*: kirk.sullivan@ling.umu.se

Heinz Sünker is Professor of Social Pedagogics and Social Policy in the Department of Educational Sciences at the University of Wuppertal, Germany. His research interests include critical theory, sociology and politics of education, theory and history of social work, philosophy of education and childhood studies. He has published widely in areas such as democracy and political socialisation, and his most recent publication is *Politics, Bildung and Social Justice: perspectives for a democratic society* (Sense Publications). *Contact*: suenker@uni-wuppertal.de